REGNUM EDINBURGH 2010 SERIES

Mission Continues

Global Impulses for the 21st Century

Series Preface

The Centenary of the World Missionary Conference, held in Edinburgh 1910, is a suggestive moment for many people seeking direction for Christian mission in the 21st century. Several different constituencies within world Christianity are holding significant events around 2010. Since 2005 an international group has worked collaboratively to develop an intercontinental and multi-denominational project, now known as Edinburgh 2010, and based at New College, University of Edinburgh. This initiative brings together representatives of twenty different global Christian bodies, representing all major Christian denominations and confessions and many different strands of mission and church life, to prepare for the Centenary.

Essential to the work of the Edinburgh 1910 Conference, and of abiding value, were the findings of the eight think-tanks or 'commissions'. These inspired the idea of a new round of collaborative reflection on Christian mission – but now focused on nine themes identified as being key to mission in the 21st century. The study process is polycentric, open-ended, and as inclusive as possible of the different genders, regions of the world, and theological and confessional perspectives in today's church.

The titles of the Edinburgh 2010 Series are divided into two categories: (1) the three official titles of Edinburgh 2010, and (2) publications of various study groups, including the Edinburgh 2010 main study groups, transversal, regional and different confessional study groups.

These publications reflect the ethos of Edinburgh 2010 and will make a significant contribution to its study process. It should be clear that material published in this series will inevitably reflect a diverse range of views and positions. These will not necessarily represent those of the series' editors or of the Edinburgh 2010 General Council, but in publishing them the leadership of Edinburgh 2010 hope to encourage conversation between Christians and collaboration in mission. All the series volumes are commended for study and reflection in both churches and academies.

Series Editors

A full listing of titles in this series appears at the end of this book

REGNUM EDINBURGH 2010 SERIES

Mission Continues

Global Impulses for the 21st Century

Edited by Claudia Währisch-Oblau
and Fidon Mwombeki

First published 2010 by Regnum Books International

Regnum is an imprint of the Oxford Centre for Mission Studies
St. Philip and St. James Church
Woodstock Road
Oxford, OX2 6HR, UK
www.ocms.ac.uk/regnum

09 08 07 06 05 04 03 8 7 6 5 4 3 2 1

British Library Cataloguing in Publication Data
A catalogue record for this book is available from the British Library

ISBN 978-1-506476-10-0

Typeset by Words by Design Ltd

Distributed by 1517 Media in the US and Canada

Contents

INTRODUCTION

Claudia Währisch-Oblau and Fidon Mwombeki

In May 2009, 35 theologians from Asia, Africa and Europe met in Wuppertal, Germany, for a consultation on mission theology organized by the United Evangelical Mission: Communion of 35 Churches in Three Continents (www.vemission.org/en.) The aim was to participate in the 100th anniversary of the Edinburgh conference through a study process, and therefore reflect on the challenges for mission in the 21st century.

We decided not to invite renowned experts, but to have an open invitation through a call for papers, so that even practicing mission experts not yet well-known would have an opportunity to share their expertise. From the 60 paper proposals received 25 were invited for the consultation, together with a small number of mission practitioners who did not present papers. Invitations were also sent to theologians from the member churches of the Council for World Mission (CWM) and the Communauté Evangélique d'Action Apostolique (Cevaa), partner organizations of UEM that are also communities of churches in mission. We decided not to predetermine a theme or motto for the consultation but to allow various themes on mission to emerge from the papers themselves and thus to allow wide-ranging discussions. Indeed the papers were varied; each drew strong reactions, lively and even controversial debates. We were able to discover common concerns transcending very different contexts.

The collection of papers in this book has been taken from the papers delivered at the Wuppertal consultation. In some cases, short responses by one or two of the consultation participants were added to highlight the discussions that followed.

The papers are grouped into six major chapters. "Foundations of Mission" brings together five papers from African, Asian and European perspectives. Jerry Pillay reviews the major biblical-theological topics and stresses the importance of the image of the kingdom of God as the aim of mission. Mangisi Simorangkir looks at dialogue, contextualization, participation in justice and holistic development as the praxis of mission in an Asian context. Faustin Mahali reads the Great Commission in Mark 16 under the perspective of the empowerment of those who receive the message. Wilhelm Richebächer evaluates the model of the UEM as an ecumenical missionary communion (the model shared also by Cevaa and Council for World Mission), and Fidon Mwombeki challenges both a theology of the cross and a theology of glory and proposes a theology of blessing as a key to harmony.

"Mission Spirituality" is opened by Priscille Djomhoué who reconsiders the missionary narrative in Acts and draws conclusions for a new understanding of the Holy Spirit in relation to her Camerounian context. Roberta Rominger stresses that only a spirituality that is missionary can be called Christian. Ferdinand Anno looks at the missionary potential of liturgical renewal from the perspective of Filipino folk liturgies.

"The charismatic challenge" to the mission practices of Reformation Protestant churches was discussed time and again during the consultation. Abednego Keshomshahara describes it concretely from the perspective of a Tanzanian Lutheran, while Kingsley Weerasinghe, a Methodist from Sri Lanka, describes his charismatic practice of divine healing in a Buddhist environment.

The chapter on "Mission and Justice, Peace and Integrity of Creation" makes clear that mission can no longer be thought about or practiced without regarding social and political realities. Jochen Motte reflects on human rights and the rule of law, while Victor Aguilan describes the peace making activities which are part of the mission of the United Church of Christ in the Philippines. In addition, Yak-hwee Tan looks at the missionary witness in relation to ecological questions.

"Mission and Culture," particularly with regards to questions of globalisation and locality, was another issue that kept coming up during discussions, and a large number of papers and case studies dealt with this. The European context was discussed in a number of ways: Sören Asmus analyzes the German situation of religious plurality and burgeoning esotericism, while Reiner Knieling suggests contextual re-formulations of Christian doctrines like "Jesus is the Truth," sin and salvation, the cross and resurrection. Jutta Beldermann describes in detail a process of congregational development as missionary practice. Jean-Gottfried Mutombo reflects on his experiences as an African missionary to Germany, and Claudia Währisch-Oblau analyzes the challenge migrant churches in Germany pose to the established 'mainline' Protestantism. The Asian context becomes concretely visible in Anwar Tjen's case study of his own journey from traditional Chinese religion to Christianity through the study of the Bible. Two case studies from an African context round off this chapter: Christel Kiel illustrates both continuity and discontinuity between traditional African religion and Christianity in her study of a Maasai healing prophet, while Reinhard Veller describes the development of a Christian ritual to deal with the phenomenon of "avenging spirits."

Christian mission in a religiously pluralistic world encounters other religions, and this encounter is reflected in the final chapter of this book. Andreas Heuser describes the missionary theology and practice of a Ghanaian charismatic who is a convert from Islam. Chediel Sendoro analyzes the largely unsuccessful mission efforts on the Muslim island of Zanzibar, while Erick Johnson Barus details how the Communion of Churches in Indonesia defines its mission in terms of dialogue, cooperation and striving for a civil society.

The very varied voices collected in this anthology nevertheless have much in common: even where they are most theoretical it is obvious that all contributors come from missionary practice and bring in their contextual experiences.

Wuppertal, May 2010
Fidon Mwombeki
Claudia Währisch-Oblau

PART ONE
FOUNDATIONS OF MISSION

THEOLOGICAL FOUNDATIONS OF MISSION

Jerry Pillay

In attempting to establish the biblical foundations for mission the tendency has been to develop exegetical findings into a systematic 'theory' or 'theology' of mission. In this paper I follow the trend of recent scholars who proceed to examine the missionary character of the ministry of Jesus.[1] A variety of imaginary foundations for mission has been built over the years but what will really stand the test of time is what is based on the living God, the risen Lord and the Bible.[2] I shall briefly trace the significance of the Old Testament for a biblical understanding of mission and then proceed to look at the New Testament[3], paying particular attention to the ministry of Jesus[4] which, I believe, should shape the aim of Christian mission in the world today. I will then attempt to answer the question: "What is mission?"

Mission in the Old Testament

Scholars have argued that the Old Testament hardly provides a basis for Christian mission.[5] There is, in the OT, no indication of the believers of the old covenant being sent by God to cross geographical, religious, and social frontiers in order to win others to faith in Yahweh. The primary focus is on

---

[1] For example see David Bosch, Transforming Mission: Paradigm Shifts in Theology of Mission, Maryknoll, New York, 1999.

[2] Verkuyl considers some motives for mission which he classifies as "impure": The imperialist motive, the cultural motive, the commercial motive, and the motive of ecclesiastical colonialism. See J. Verkuyl, Contemporary Missiology: An Introduction, Grand Rapids (Michigan): Eerdmanns 1978.

[3] Although the entire Bible lays the foundations for mission it is in the New Testament that we see it at its best. The reason for this is that in the Old Testament there was an expectation that the nations were to be drawn to Israel and join Israel in its worship of God, the New Testament church actively goes and seeks out converts to the Christian faith.

[4] We look at the ministry of Jesus with the view that it covers the essential message of the New Testament. Bultmann contends that the message of Jesus is a presupposition for the theology of the New Testament rather than a part of that theology. See Rudolf Bultmann, Theology of the New Testament, New York: Scribner 1951, p 3

[5] Whilst Israel was not called to go and evangelize the nations in the Old Testament, this does not take away from the fact that the OT as a document, provides in the Abrahamic blessing the foundational paradigm of mission that is realized in the history of salvation through Abraham's seed.

God's relationship with the people of Israel who are considered as those elected by God. However, we see also that God is as concerned with the nations as with Israel. But this is not Israel's concern. If there is a missionary in the Old Testament, it is God himself who will bring the nations to Jerusalem to worship him there together with his covenant people. So essentially it is God who is on a mission to bring the world unto God. The concept of *Missio Dei*, or "God's mission," is an important principle surrounding our understanding of mission. This theological concept points us to the Triune God as the one who owns and orchestrates all mission work. A theology of God's sovereignty thus provides a key impetus for mission.

In the Old Testament mission is seen in the many themes that are found in the actions of God which form the indispensable basis for the New Testament call to the church to engage in worldwide mission work. Verkuyl[6] refers to these as: (1) the *universal motif* which points to the fact that in choosing Israel God never took his eyes off the other nations; Israel was the *pars pro toto*, a minority called to serve the majority, (2) the *motif of rescue and liberation* which is the soteriological theme of the Bible, that is, God's work of rescuing and saving both Israel and the other nations, (3) the *missionary motif* in which the prophets constantly remind Israel that her election is a call to service. Israel must be a sign to the other nations that Yahweh is both Creator and Liberator (Is 49:6), and (4) the *motif of antagonism*. The entire Old Testament is filled with descriptions of how Yahweh-Adonai, the covenant God of Israel, is powerfully wrestling against powers and forces which oppose his liberating and gracious authority. This motif is closely linked to the doxological theme: the glory of Yahweh-Adonai shall be revealed among all peoples. Then they all will come to know him as "the gracious and merciful God, slow to get angry, full of kindness, and always willing to turn back from meting out disaster" (Jon 4:1-2). The book of Jonah is also significant for a biblical mandate for mission because it sheds light on God's leading to the Gentiles.

Mission in the New Testament

It is in the New Testament that the worldwide call to mission becomes really alive. In fact it is fundamental to the Christian faith. There is no participation in Christ without participation in his mission and Jesus makes this perfectly clear to his disciples. His ministry, teachings and example all provide the basis for Christian mission in the world today. We now turn to examine this claim.[7]

---

6 See J. Verkuyl, Contemporary Missiology: An Introduction, Grand Rapids (Michigan): Eerdmanns 1978.

7 In this section I will attempt to do only a very brief look at the ministry of Jesus, therefore I will not divide them into separate headings. Also, it is not within the scope of this paper to do an examination of the entire NT, I shall therefore restrict my discussion to the Gospels and mention Paul's letters.

The ministry of Jesus

Jesus' life and ministry stands in the tradition of the prophets. Like them and John the Baptist his concern is repentance and salvation of Israel. In him salvation has arrived, and therefore the good news which Jesus proclaims describes a kingdom which had both already come and is yet coming. It is apparent in the ministry of Jesus that the proclamation of the kingdom of God becomes a priority. Jesus' miracles and parables provide help in understanding how the kingdom is revealed in this world. John's Gospel calls the miracles signs which point to the approaching kingdom and the majestic character of the Messiah. These miracles address every human need: poverty, sickness, hunger, sin, demonic temptation, and the threat of death. If we are to share in God's mission in the world today then we have to do it the Jesus way pointing to the kingdom of God. Bultmann claims that the dominant concept of Jesus' message, in keeping with Jewish apocalyptic expectations, is the reign of God.[8] This message concerning the kingdom of God is central to Jesus' call to decision.

God's mission is motivated by his loving will for the entire world, grounded in the atoning work of Jesus Christ and carried out by the Holy Spirit through the means of grace. This is clearly illustrated in the fact that Jesus opened his ministry on earth to Gentiles as well. Although Matthew 10 records Jesus' instruction to his disciples (to) "Go nowhere among the Gentiles and enter no town of the Samaritans, but go rather to the lost sheep of Israel," scholars generally do not see this as contradictory to the Great Commission to go to all peoples recorded in the 28th chapter of the very same book. The event which opened the way to the Gentiles was the resurrection. The Resurrected and Exalted Lord is the one who issues the mandate for the disciples and the church today to go and make disciples of all nations. Three terms in the Great Commission summarize the essence of mission for Matthew: *make disciples, baptize and teach.* The ultimate purpose of all these is to submit to the will of God as revealed in Jesus' ministry and teaching.

Similarly, Mark's Gospel carries a missionary mandate inviting human beings over to Jesus and his kingdom.[9] There is an explicit command to mission in verses 15 and 16 of Chapter 16: "Go into all the world and preach the gospel to the whole creation. He who believes and is baptized shall be saved; but he who does not believe will be condemned."[10] This missionary mandate is no less different in John's Gospel: to bring people to faith in Jesus Christ (Jn 20:31). John goes a step further to orient the call of mission not only around the person

---

[8] Rudolf Bultmann, Theology of the New Testament, New York: Scribner 1951.

[9] Even though Mark's Gospel should lack an explicit missionary mandate, its whole tone is missionary. By interpreting the facts about Jesus' life, death, and resurrection, he wished to call people to a faith decision for Jesus Christ.

[10] Although scholars generally view the concluding section as an addition to Mark's Gospel it does not take from the rest of the writing the missionary intent.

of Jesus Christ and his work, but around God himself.[11] Jesus sent out his disciples with the actual command to engage in mission with these words in John 20:21-22: "As the Father has sent me, so I send you."[12]

Now it would have been far less complicated if the worldwide mission mandate was left at making converts and disciples. However, that is not the case since the books of the New Testament seem to emphasize other aspects of mission as well. For example, in Luke the disciples are mandated to go with a specific message; they are to proclaim the events of Jesus' suffering, death, and resurrection as decisive for every person. The aim and significance of mission for Luke is established on Isaiah 61 which Luke mentions in chapter 4: 16-21. Applying the words of Isaiah 61 to himself, Jesus says the Spirit of the Lord is on him. He takes it further with this daring claim: "He has sent me to bring good news to the afflicted, to proclaim liberty to the captives, and recovery of sight to the blind, to set at liberty the oppressed, to proclaim the acceptable year of the Lord." For all practical purposes this text has replaced Matthew's Great Commission as the key text not only for understanding Christ's own mission but also that of the church.[13] It also indicates how mission must be done in the world today. To follow the way of Jesus is to choose 'suffering love' which attempts to identify with the pain and suffering of others.

As Luke retells the story of Jesus and the early church there are certain themes to which he returns again and again: the ministry of the Holy Spirit, the centrality of repentance and forgiveness, of prayer, of love and acceptance of enemies, of justice and fairness in human relationships. Luke also pays particular attention to the poor, women, tax-collectors, and Samaritans, and of Jesus' ministry to them. The entire ministry of Jesus and his relationships with all these marginalized people witness, in Luke's writings, to Jesus' practice of boundary-breaking compassion. It is therefore appropriate that David Bosch refers to the significance of Luke-Acts as "Practicing Forgiveness and Solidarity with the Poor" and sees in this another theological foundation for mission, which the church is called to emulate. This also continues to impact on the definition of mission with which the Christian church wrestles: Is it the

---

[11] Is God or Jesus the central figure in John's mission theology? Generally, it is not the message of God's existence or of God's love that is offensive, but whether God's love has found its decisive and ultimate expression *in Jesus.* Any ecumenism that is achieved at the expense of lessening the centrality of Jesus' work, claims, and requirements is not only of little value but is actually misleading and deceptive. The church's (missionary) proclamation must be *theocentric* by being *Christocentric,* since according to scripture, God's revelation and redemption were ultimately and finally accomplished in Jesus.

[12] It is perhaps worth mentioning that this text is today sometimes used to advocate for an "incarnational model" (to emulate Jesus' example and become like those we seek to serve) for the church's mission. However, there are others who dispute this stating that Jesus' love for his disciples is presented by John as a model for relationships of believers with one another, not as a model for their mission to the world.

[13] See David Bosch, *op cit,* p.84.

'saving of souls' or the 'transforming of society'? I shall return to this question later.

Turning to Paul's letters we note that the aim of mission seems to focus on the invitation to join the eschatological community. Paul sees the church as an interim eschatological community, the 'world in obedience to God'. Its primary mission in the world is to *be* this new creation. The church is missionary by its very nature, through its unity, mutual love, exemplary conduct, and radiant joy.

The church is not other-worldly. It is involved with the world, which means that it is missionary. The church is the church in the world and for the world which means that it is involved in creating new relationships among itself and in society at large and, in doing this, bearing witness to the lordship of Christ who is both Lord of the church and of the world.[14] The church is *now* the eschatological people of God and a living witness of the ratification of God's promises to his people Israel, precisely in its having a membership wider than the people of the old covenant. In spite of its theological importance, however, the church is always and only a preliminary community, en route to its self-surrender unto the kingdom of God.

Having made these brief insights into the biblical foundation for mission, we shall now attempt to draw these together to focus on the aim of Christian mission.

What is mission?

Attempts to define Christian mission have resulted in prolonged and relentless debates, and this is not surprising given the different biblical aims of mission as shown above. If we attempt a more specifically theological synopsis of 'mission' as the concept has traditionally been used, we note that it has been paraphrased as (a) propagation of the faith, (b) expansion of the reign of God, (c) conversion of the heathen, and (d) the founding of new churches.[15] Lesslie Newbigin has narrowed these into two terms described as "Mission" and "Missions". He states that:

> The Mission of the church is everything that the church is sent into the world to do: preaching the gospel, healing the sick, caring for the poor, teaching the children, improving international and interracial relations, attacking injustice. The Missions of the church is the concern that in places where there are no Christians there should be Christians. In other words, Missions means to plant churches through evangelism.[16]

---

[14] David Bosch, *ibid*, p.169.

[15] *Ibid.*

[16] Lesslie Newbigin, Mission and Missions, in: *Christianity Today*, August 1, 1960, p.23.

Lesslie Newbigin further adds that the aim of missions should be the establishment of a new Christian community that is as broad as society and is as true to the national situation. He has in mind here the idea of Christianization that is highly questionable today in a world that is characterized by religious pluralism and democracy.[17] The encouragement of inter-faith dialogue and cooperation today also draws the goal of mission as Christianization into question.

Lesslie Newbigin, however, is not unaware of such criticism. His immediate focus with regards to mission seems to be ecclesiocentric but he points out that this is not the only goal of mission. He states that in the past we have largely limited the goal of missions to the conversion of unbelievers and the planting of churches. This, he asserts, must remain the first objective. The trouble comes when this becomes the sum and substance of our missionary endeavour. He thus indicates that fighting against injustices in the world should also be the task of mission.

Our view of mission is not limited to the 'mere saving of souls' or the 'planting of churches'. Hoekendijk criticized the 'church-centric' view of mission pointing out that it does not fully correspond with the biblical view of mission.[18] Such a view of mission, though still prevalent, has lost its relevance in the present century.[19] In the emerging ecclesiology, the church is seen as essentially missionary in its nature. The church is not the sender but the one sent (1 Pet 2: 9). Its mission ("being sent") is not secondary to its being; the church exists in being sent and in building up itself for the sake of its mission. Missionary work is not so much the work of the church as simply the church at work.[20] This missionary dimension evokes intentional, that is, direct involvement, in society; it actually moves beyond the walls of the church and engages in missionary work such as evangelism[21] and work for justice and peace. The understanding of the church as sacrament, sign, and instrument has led to a new perception of the relationship between the church and the world.[22]

---

17 In the course of this century the missionary enterprise and the missionary idea have undergone some profound modifications. These came about partly as a response to the recognition of the fact that the church is indeed not only the recipient of God's merciful grace but sometimes also of his wrath. We have seen this in the apartheid church in South Africa.

18 J.C. Hoekendijk, The Church in Missionary Thinking, in: *International Review of Mission*, Vol. XLI, number 163, 1952, p.332.

19 Even the Pentecostal and charismatic churches in South Africa are showing a greater interest in community work, e.g. soup kitchens, skills training, etc.

20 T.F. Stransky, Evangelization, Missions, and Social Action: A Roman Catholic Perspective, *Review and Expositor*, vol. 79, pp.343-351.

21 Even the concept of "evangelism" has a plethora of definitions. See Bosch, *op.cit.*, pp.409-420, Our understanding of evangelism involves a broader definition than 'merely saving souls' (conversion).

22 This is contained in the emerging ecumenical paradigm of mission.

Mission is viewed as 'God's turning to the world.' This represents a fundamentally new approach to theology.

In the light of all this, a new comprehensive approach to mission is called for which has a message for both the whole world and the whole person.[23] Kritzinger points out that mission involves the whole person in her or his total situation in response to the whole Gospel.[24] The terms *kerygma* (preaching), *koinonia* (fellowship) and *diakonia* (service) in combination describe the main aspects of the witness (*marturia*) of the 'kingdom'.[25]

What then is mission today? Emilio Castro states that God's mission and ours is to bring in the 'kingdom'.[26] And the goal of the 'kingdom' is life in its fullness. Hence the 'kingdom' has to do with the welfare of the whole person, not excluding the social, political and economical aspects of life. Since God is interested in the life of the whole person, so must we if we are to take our responsibilities of mission seriously. Verkuyl states that the ultimate goal of the *Missio Dei* is the 'kingdom of God'.[27] From the countless biblical images and symbols which describe God's intentions, he selects this one as the clearest expression of God and his purpose.[28]

We therefore select the 'kingdom of God' as the central theme around which to understand mission. It would be difficult to find a more inspiring biblical theme when we face the challenges of the contemporary situation. This, however, does not mean that our choice is a matter of convenience. The Bangkok Assembly of the WCC of 1973 supports our view in the following statement:

> The selection of the symbol of the kingdom of God is not an arbitrary one: Firstly, because it is the central concern of Jesus Christ himself. Secondly, because we believe that it responds to the inspiration of the Holy Spirit that is calling our attention once again to that ongoing memory of the kingdom, to provide the

---

[23] J.C.Hoekendijk, The Call to Evangelism, *International Review of Mission,* Vol. XXXIX, number 154, 1950, p.170.

[24] J. J. Kritzinger, The South African Context for Mission, Cape Town: Lux Verbi 1988, p, 34.

[25] *Ibid.* A fourth one is also added to this list by others which *is leiturgia (worship)*

[26] Emilio Castro, Freedom in Mission, *Op. cit.*, pp.56-60. The author acknowledges that the use of the word "kingdom" is problematic particularly from a gender sensitive perspective. However, we shall still use it since it is commonly used by Christians and by the church in general. In order to maintain our sensitivity to gender issues we shall place it in inverted commas where possible.

[27] J. Verkuyl, *op.cit.*, p.203.

[28] *Ibid.*, p.200.

> intellectual and inspirational categories that will help the church in its missionary obedience today.[29]

Kritzinger also selects the theme of the 'kingdom of God' in his definition of Christian mission:

> We understand Christian mission to be a wide and inclusive complex of activities aimed at the realisation of the reign of God in history. It includes evangelism but is at the same time much wider than that. Perhaps one could say that mission is the 'cutting edge' of the Christian movement - that activist streak in the church's life that refuses to accept the world as it is and keeps on trying to change it, prodding it on towards God's final reign of justice and peace.[30]

We should now offer more clarity on what we hold the 'kingdom of God' to be, since this is an often misunderstood term. Biblically speaking, what is the "kingdom of God"? It has been the tendency to frequently narrow its borders to include only the inner life of the individual.[31] Verkuyl points out that such an interpretation is not wrong; it is, however, inadequate as the preaching of Jesus so obviously treats issues which extend beyond the individual soul.[32]

Moreover, some interpretations restrict the 'kingdom' exclusively to the church.[33] For instance, the old Roman Catholic view maintained that "*extra ecclesiam nulla salus*" (only in the church is there salvation).[34] The old Roman Catholic view obviously mistook the church for the 'kingdom'. But many scholars are quick to point out that the terms *basileia* and *ecclesia*, though related, are anything but synonymous.[35] The church is only a pointer to the 'kingdom of God.'[36] A further emphasis on this point can be observed in the words of Wilhelm Anderson in his contribution to the missionary conference at Willingen (1952):

---

29 WCC: Bangkok Assembly 1973. Minutes and Report of the Assembly of the Commission on World Mission and Evangelism of the World Council of Churches, Geneva: WCC, 1973.

30 Nico Botha, K.K. Kritzinger and Tinyiko Maluleke, Crucial issues for Christian mission – A missiological analysis of contemporary South Africa. In: *International Review of Mission* 83, January, 1986.

31 We have already shown how the ecumenical church has challenged this view.

32 J. Verkuyl, *Op. cit.*, p.197.

33 *Ibid.*, p.198.

34 See R.N. Flew, Jesus and His Church, London: Epworth Press for the Fernley-Hartley Trust, 1938, p.13; H.Roberts, Jesus and the Kingdom of God, London: Epworth Press 1955, pp.84, 107.

35 G.E. Ladd, A Theology of the New Testament, Grand Rapids, Michigan: Eerdmans 1975, p.111.

36 *Ibid.*, p.113.

> The church cannot be the starting point for a theology of mission: the origin of mission is found in the triune God, from whose nature and purpose the church receives the commission, impulse and power to engage in mission.[37]

Still, others claim that the 'kingdom' has come when the spiritual needs of humankind are satisfied; 'kingdom' involves the forgiveness of sins.[38] Castro, however, states that nowhere does the New Testament spiritualize the 'kingdom of God' or limit it to the spiritual side of nature.[39] Verkuyl points out that the 'kingdom' to which the Bible testifies involves a proclamation and realization of total salvation, one which covers the whole range of human needs and destroys every pocket of evil and grief affecting humankind. He adds that 'kingdom' in the New Testament has a breadth and scope which is unsurpassed; it embraces heaven as well as earth, world history as well as the whole cosmos.[40] Verkuyl further states that:

> The Kingdom of God is that new order of affairs begun in Christ which, when finally completed by him, will involve a proper restoration not only of man's (*sic*) relationship to God but also of those between sexes, generations, races, and even between man (*sic*) and nature.[41]

Judging from this, what may we say is the 'kingdom of God'? In 1Cor 15:24 Paul speaks of Jesus Christ "handing over the kingdom to the Father, after he has destroyed every ruler and authority and power." Here the 'kingdom' is understood as life free from the reign of all those forces which enslave humanity. These powers are understood as enemies which act against human life here and now – the final enemy being death (1Cor 15:42). By contrast, the 'kingdom' is where human beings are no longer subjected to destructive forces. In this sense, the 'kingdom' is related to helping people to become more human. This view of mission is captured most significantly in the North American report at the Uppsala Assembly in 1967:

> We have lifted up humanization as the goal of mission because we believe that more than others it communicates in our period of history the meaning of the messianic goal. In another time the goal of God's redemptive work might best have been described in terms of man (*sic*) turning towards God ... The fundamental question was that of the true God, and the church responded to that question by pointing to him. It was assuming that the purpose of mission was

---

37 Wilhelm Andersen, Towards A Theology of Mission: A Study of The Encounter Between the Missionary Enterprise and the Church and its Theology, M. C. Research Pamphlet Number 2, London: S.C.M. 1955, p.10.

38 J. Verkuyl, *op.cit.*, p.200.

39 Emilio Castro, *op.cit.*, p.48f.

40 J. Verkuyl, *op.cit.*, p.198

41 Ibid., pp.198-199

> Christianization, bringing man (*sic*) to God through Christ and his church. Today the fundamental question is much more that of true man, and the dominant concern of the missionary congregation must therefore be to point to *humanity in Christ as the goal of Mission.*[42] (Italics added)

By defining mission as the establishing of the 'kingdom of God' we are attempting to give a broad definition to mission. We are categorically stating that God's concern is with the whole world and with all humanity. We state that all history is God's history and whatever happens in the world today is also of special concern to God.[43] Tambaram (1938) pointed out that "the kingdom of God is within history and yet beyond history."[44] While we accept the latter, we must reinforce the fact that the 'kingdom' is to be understood in present reality as we work towards the liberation and humanization of the poor and the oppressed.

Unlike Lesslie Newbigin, we do not see a dichotomy between mission and missions. The one singular mission is the 'kingdom of God' which rules in justice and righteousness. Such a view of mission closes the gap between the 'saving of souls' and the 'transformation of society' as the aim of mission. It recognizes that in the ministry of Jesus there was a direct link between word and deed. Hence relevant mission today must emphasize both proclamation and praxis: it is not enough to speak about God, it is also necessary to show and hold him out to those who are blinded to his presence. Jesus did not only touch people spiritually but he also responded to their physical needs. This then must be the path for effective mission today. There is no purpose in preaching salvation and deliverance to those who are hungry and poor, whose concentration is in the groans of their stomach. It is therefore necessary to first feed them in order to obtain their attention. But even then this is in itself proclamation. It is a non-verbal communication of the love and grace of God which speaks for itself. Our words (*kerygma*) must give birth to concrete action (*praxis*). And our historical deeds must reflect the gospel message of the already coming kingdom. The word must become a living reality rooted in our daily experiences, and from within our experiences the word must find its meaning.

Proclamation and praxis are inextricably linked to each other. To proclaim is to act and to act is to proclaim. Thus it appears inappropriate to dichotomize between verbal Gospel proclamation on the one hand and a broader notion of Christian service on the other. The question is rather one of primary focus in a given context as expressed by the World Council of Churches:

---

[42] World Council of Churches, The Church for Others and The Church for the World, Geneva: WCC 1967, p.78.

[43] Wolfhart Pannenberg, Revelation as History, London: Sheed and Ward 1969, pp.125-130.

[44] See *International Review of Mission,* Vol. LXXII, Number 288, October 1983, p.525.

> There is no singular way to witness to Jesus Christ...There are occasions when dynamic action in society is called for; there are others when a word must be spoken; others when the behavior of Christians one to another is the telling witness. On still other occasions the simple presence of a worshipping community or man (*sic*) is the witness. These different dimensions of witness to the one Lord are always a matter of concrete obedience. To take them in isolation from one another is to distort the gospel. They are inextricably bound together, and together give the true dimension of evangelism. The important thing is that God's redeeming Word be proclaimed and heard.[45]

Conclusion

It is absolutely essential for the Christian church to have this holistic concept of mission as it ministers in and to the world today. The church must do so because it is found in the setting of a world of human suffering, pain and oppression and Christians, too, even though their citizenship is in heaven cannot deny their experiences in this world. All their experiences then in this life are also a concern for the church. The church cannot go on with blinkers ignoring the concerns of its people for justice, peace and a better life. The church must, as an agent of hope, participate in the establishment of a new transformed society. More than this it must attempt to be that *New Society*. This is the challenge that confronts the church in the world today.

---

[45] From an unpublished report.

THEOLOGICAL FOUNDATION OF MISSION: AN ASIAN PERSPECTIVE

Mangisi Simorangkir

Introduction

My purpose here is to discuss some of the theological foundations of mission from an Asian perspective. I do not profess to have the answer to all the issues, but I do try to make some suggestions. If we are to serve a continent like Asia, we have to know that Asia is a very pluralistic continent. There are many cultures there, many languages, many religions, many poor people, many skin colours, many countries, etc.

We have to add one thing, namely that Christianity in Asia had an alliance with colonial powers, westernization and capitalism, which continues to have an impact on missions. Rienzie Perera, a Sri Lankan theologian, is right to say:

> The introduction of westernized Christianity to Asia has created an identity crisis for the church and thereby the church is often identified as an arm of western imperialism. The fact that the theology, art, symbols and architecture of the church still are replicas of the west and the inability of the church to enter into a process of inculturation all confirm and acknowledge the critiques of the church.[1]

In the light of these external and internal challenges which the Asian church faces there is an urgent need to re-examine our missionary methods. There is also an urgent need to re-think existing methods. This does not imply that all past policies must be scrapped.

What is mission?

All Christians are missionaries who must 'go' into the world. As the famous Japanese theologian Kosuke Koyama, said, "so the missionary is sandwiched between Christ's saving reality and his neighbor's 'other-than-myself' reality ... He is 'in motion.' He has a definite direction to go 'into the world.'"[2]

Fridolin Ukur, the former general secretary of Communion of Churches in Indonesia, sees the word "into the world" as "bringing renewal ... This has

---

[1] Perera, Rienzie, Christian Identity in a Multi-Religious Context, in: *CTC Bulletin*, Vol. XXIV, No. 1-2 (April-August 2008), p.51.

[2] Koyama, Kosuke, Waterbuffalo Theology, Orbis Book: Maryknoll 1974, p.91.

many implications for development."[3] Development means 'change.' We know that it is not easy to break away from traditional ties; therefore some Christians are often opposed to change. Our basic motivation for constructive change is the belief that humanness is a gift from God and that we must have a positive appreciation of all humanity.

We can say also that mission is about being sent with the good news of God's love to all people in the world. What is the good news? "Cure the sick, raise the dead, cleanse the lepers, cast out demons." (Mt 10:7-8). Jesus says to John's disciples: "Go and tell John what you have seen and heard: the blind receive their sight, the lame walk, the lepers are cleansed, the deaf hear, the dead are raised, the poor have good news brought to them." (Lk 7:22).

Mission is manifesting the love of God

Donald McGavran points to the reality of life as the addressee of mission. "Mission to the world is simply this: to proclaim the whole gospel, to all people, in all their needs, wherever they live, whatever they do. The Gospel must be addressed to all people, to the geographical, political and economic ends of the earth."[4]

To bring the good news is to offer genuine loving service so that people will be drawn to salvation. This is the goal of mission. "Manifesting the love of Jesus is a goal that leads the missionary enterprise into an unlimited variety of service."[5] This "unlimited variety of service" includes such things as education, medical work, training, etc. which are elements of the community development ministry of the church.

We can see many examples of that "manifesting the love of God" in various mission fields of Indonesia. A Dutch missiologist, Hendrik Kraemer, in "From Mission Field to Independent Church," made observations in the mission fields of Indonesia. He observed the role of "manifesting the love of God" in non-Christian areas and how the missionaries worked hard for mission. He highly praised the devoted mission work in the Batak areas, North Sumatra, by German missionaries. He writes, "it belongs to the finest results of missionary activity in modern times."[6] This success was built on the sacrifices made by the missionaries, their perseverance, self-denial, patience, devotion and truly

---

[3] Ukur, Fridolin, Development and Mission, in: Douglas J Elwood (ed.), *What Asian Christians Are Thinking,* Quezon City: New Day Publisher 1975, p.91.

[4] McGavran, Donald, Wrong Strategy - The Real Crisis in Mission, in: Donald McGavran (ed.), The *Conciliar-Evangelical Debate: The Crucial Documents 1964-1976*, Pasadena: William Carey Library 1977, p.98.

[5] Coggins, Wade T., So that's What Missions Is All About, Chicago: Moody Press 1975, p.13.

[6] Kraemer, Hendrik, *From Mission Field to Independent Church*, London: SCM 1958, p.43.

burning desire to carry the Gospel. "The main spring of their labours was their simple-hearted and unshakeable piety."[7]

Mission is a proclamation of love. "The love that is needed goes out and seeks men wherever they are."[8] Mission in this sense is the bridge between the church and the world. We can point to an indispensable aspect of genuine missionary communication: "The true evangelistic movement is not that I take Jesus Christ into somebody else's life, but that Jesus Christ takes me into somebody else's life," as D.T. Niles, the Sri Lankan theologian said.[9] In other words, mission is Christian solidarity in all aspects of people's lives into which we permit ourselves to be brought by Jesus.

Here we see "manifesting the love of God" as mission and mission in it. A. von Denffer, a Moslem writer, estimated that in Indonesia "from 1971-1977, Christianity continued to grow by 44 percent, while the total population's growth rate for that period was only 19 per cent."[10] Von Denffer lists the good works of churches (manifesting the love of God) as a reason for this growth.

Mission is dialogue with others

Partnership in the struggle with non-Christians is the essential context of mission, especially in Asia as a pluralistic continent. A Christian community does not exist for itself.[11] Therefore, M.M. Thomas, a famous theologian from India, "is very much horizontally oriented in his contextualisation of the doctrine of salvation at the expense of the vertical relationship to God."[12] Thomas developed his thought in "The Struggle for Human Dignity as a Preparation for the Gospel" with reference to the document of the EACC (East Asia Christian Conference now CCA = Christian Conference of Asia) Assembly in Bangkok, 1964, "The Christian Community within the Human Community." The document states:

> Christian people must go into every part of the life of our people, into politics, into social and national service, into the world of art and culture, *to work with non-Christians* (my emphasis), and to be witness of Christ in all these realms. It means also that each congregation must know that it is put in the world by the

---

[7] Kraemer, *op.cit.* p.44.

[8] Gensichen, Hans-Werner, Living Mission - The Test of Faith, Philadelphia: Fortress 1996, p.84.

[9] Quoted in Gensichen, *ibid.*

[10] Denffer, A. von, Indonesia: A Survey of Christian Churches and Missions Among Muslim, London: The Islamic Foundation 1981, p.5.

[11] Poole, Garry, Don't All Religions Lead to God?, Grand Rapids: Zondervan 2003, p.58.

[12] Ro, Bong Rin, Contextualization: Asian Theology, in: Douglas J Elwood (ed.), *What Asian Christians are Thinking,* Quezon City: New Day Publisher 1976, p.51.

> Lord as his representatives and that it must therefore be chiefly concerned not with itself but with the world.[13]

The dialogue that took place between the church and others occured in three forms, in practical life, in organisational forma like in Indonesia with its Department for Religious Affairs,[14] and in seminars. Here below are examples of how Christians in Indonesia tried to have dialogues with others in praxis.

Our church, GKPI, has tried to have a dialogue in praxis through a water pump project for rice fields in Sei Rampah, in a religiously pluralistic and agricultural area in North Sumatra. The farmers there must use a big pump to raise water from the creek to water rice fields because the surface of the rice fields is about two metres higher than the creek. The farmers who use the pump are both Christians and Muslims. Some congregation members did not agree to have Muslims become members of that project. However, the project went ahead. But after three harvests the project was discontinued when the government built a water canal for the rice fields.

Another example of a dialogue in praxis is a community development ministry among the Hindu on Bali island by Rus Alit from World Vision Indonesia[15] Christian and Hindu built together a biogas unit using pig manure and trained people who wanted to know about biogas. These skills would be the tools for the people to help themselves.

Those examples created an open atmosphere for mutual sharing. But I must also report an incident in Medan, North Sumatra, on 3rd February 2009, to show the fragility of harmony and how the harmony between Christians and non-Christians in a pluralistic country like Indonesia can easily be disturbed. The incident began when a mass of people, about 2,000 protesters, were holding a rally to demand that the House of Representative approve the establishment of a new administrative province in Tapanuli. Aziz Angkat, the Speaker, who suffered from heart disease, died after the crowd forced him to hold a plenary session for the approval of the province. Doctors and police announced that Aziz died of a heart attack and not from injuries inflicted during that rally.

Some people said the demands for the creation of that new province had been masked by religious and ethnic tensions. The proposed Tapanuli province is mapped according to the current domain of the predominately Christian Batak Toba ethnic group. The North Sumatra Police detained the initiators of the proposed new province of Tapanuli (all Batak Christians). Moslem students and youth organizations rallied to condemn the brutal attacks. It is not impossible that this fatal incident would trigger sectarian conflicts in the

---

13 Thomas, M. M., The Struggle for Human Dignity as a Preparation for the Gospel, in: Douglas J Elwood, *op. cit.*, p.274.

14 Simorangkir, Mangisi, *Ajuran Dua Kerajaan Luther dan Relevansinya di Indonesia*, Kolportase Pusat GKPI, Pematangsiantar, 2008, pp.231-234.

15 WVI, 1986:April.

province, because of the relatively equal numbers of Christians and Muslims there as compared to other provinces. But until now (when I finished this paper), the people of North Sumatra can still be proud of the unity and cohesion of their society. Hopefully the sectarian conflicts that claimed thousands of lives like in Maluku will never happen in North Sumatra.

Dialogue between Christians and Muslims is needed in a pluralistic country and in the globalized world today. Aritonang is right to say, "the need to build a dialogue occurred not only in Indonesia but also in many other countries"[16] Although there have been so many interfaith dialogue forums initiated by various institutions and there were even many interfaith institutions founded, religious conflicts were rising. Therefore, dialogue in praxis is so important.

Mission is contextualisation

'Contextual' means "connected with, or depending on the context" (Webster's Dictionary). Thus, we can say that the contextualisation of theology is bringing the Gospel to the local culture and connecting it with the lives of the local people. Emphasis on contextualisation in theology insists that no text exists in a vacuum. We can understand text only in context. James H. Burtness, Professor of Systematic Theology at Luther Seminary, St. Paul, Minnesota, says, "contextualisation is a passionate cry for the recognition of the significance of this time and this place … without which the Word is dead word and the Christ a non-living lord."[17] To be non-contextual means to neglect the here and the now of the text. Asian Christianity should be bound by the Asian context. Indonesian theology should be based on Indonesian foundations.

In "The Christian Message in a Non-Christian World," Kraemer writes that the church needs a renewed consciousness of the purpose of its mission because "unconsciously people live on the deep-rooted assumption that missionary work is a kind of colonizing activity."[18] He wrote this book for use at the world missionary conference held at Tambaram, India, in 1938. In 1921, he had gone to Indonesia as a representative of the Netherlands Bible Society, and in almost two decades as a working missionary and translator there, he gained first hand background knowledge for the writing of this book. Although Kraemer's book was written 71 years ago, it is still relevant for understanding the challenges to mission in a non-Christian country. The foreignness of Christianity to the non-Christian world requires that it be contextualised and indigenised. Kraemer

---

16 Aritonang, Jan S. and Karel Steenbrink, A History of Christianity in Indonesia, Leiden-Boston: Brill 2008, p.853.

17 Burtness, James H., Innovation as the Search for Probabilities: To Re-Contextualize the Text, in: The Theological Education Fund (ed.), *Learning in Context*, London: New Life Press, 1973, p.13.

18 Kraemer, Hendrik, The Christian Message in a Non-Christian World, Grand Rapids: Kregel, 1961, p.37.

contended that it is possible to "interpret the Christian truth in Chinese to Chinese and in Tamil to Tamils."[19] Although he strongly supported the concept of indigenisation, he carefully added, "the way towards becoming an *indigenous* church goes through becoming first a real church."[20] The church in its social involvement is the salt and the light for and in the world.

Before Kraemer's time, Roland Allen, a former missionary to North China from England, showed how contextualisation in the missionary methods of the 19th and 20th centuries contrast with St. Paul's missionary methods.[21] According to him, in addition to using the Hellenistic way of thinking, St. Paul stressed the role of training local people for mission work. The secret of success in St. Paul's work "lies in the beginning at the very beginning. It is the training of the first converts which sets the type for the future."[22] In his conclusions he said that a sense of mutual responsibility of all the Christians for each other should be carefully inculcated and practised.[23] In other words, St. Paul stressed contextualisation in his missionary method and showed that contextualisation in mission must begin with the local people (as Nommensen in Sumatra). Christians are a ministering community rather than a community gathered around a minister or missionary.

Mission needs contextualisation, especially in Asia, because here the Gospel is often seen as "an expression of Western imperialism under the guise of religion, as being something which is quite unrelated to the felt needs of Asia."[24] We can see this urgent need in Asia's rejection of the church (e.g. persecution in many areas). To understand the mood of Asia today is to "take seriously the feeling of resentment against Christianity as having been in effect an agent of imperialism."[25] Therefore, we are facing the important task of defining the contextualisation process of churches in Asia.

Nicholls sees contextualisation in theology as a dynamic process "in obedience to Christ and his mission in the world, on the interaction of the text as the word of God and the context as a specific human situation."[26] He points to Jesus himself as "the supreme model of contextualization. His every command was *de facto* a command to contextualization."[27] Recently, some scholars, especially liberation theologians, have made extensive use of the

---

19 *Op. cit*, p.303.

20 *Op. cit.*, p.411.

21 Allen, Roland, Missionary Methods: St. Paul's or Ours?, London: World Dominion Press 1956. (First edition 1912).

22 *Op. cit.*, p.105.

23 *Op. cit.*, p.195.

24 Warren, Max, Challenge and Response, London: SPCK 1960, p.7.

25 *Op. cit.*, p.9.

26 Nicholls, B J, Contextualization, in: Sinclair B. Ferguson and David F. Wright (eds.), *New Dictionary of Theology*, Leicester: Inter-Varsity Press 1988, p.164.

27 *Ibid.*

concept of contextualisation as part of a wider theological debate. They argue that since Scripture is culturally and historically conditioned, its message is situational. "Theological knowledge comes only from participation in action and reflection on praxis."[28]

Mission is participation in justice

After World War II, churches believed that Christians should do something for justice. Here, "mission was direct action to achieve more justice in human relationships."[29] This new concept does not narrow the understanding of the need for the verbal announcement of the Gospel. "The time has come to replace the 'church centred' approach in missions with a 'world centred' approach."[30]

The fourth General Assembly of the WCC in Uppsala, Sweden, July 4-20, 1968, under the theme "Behold, I Make All Things New," marked a milestone in the development of ecumenical missionary theology and strategy, with humanity as its theological keyword. The stress on humanity was continued at the eighth Conference on World Mission of WCC, in Bangkok 1973, with its theme "Salvation Today". At this conference, "the emphasis at Uppsala on integrating the vertical and horizontal dimensions … was fully incorporated into the key statement of Section II."[31] Peter Beyerhaus reported that the third part of Section II of the Bangkok conference spoke of "Salvation in Four Dimensions." They are: (1) the struggle for economic justice, (2) human dignity, (3) solidarity and (4) hope.[32]

In 1964, the churches in Indonesia, at the 5th General Assembly of DGI, (Council of Churches in Indonesia, since 1985: PGI, Communion of Churches in Indonesia), developed a new concept of mission to confront their very challenging and dynamic situation. "The churches seemed to rediscover their calling and see new patterns and forms for carrying out their mission amid the second phase of national revolution."[33] This General Assembly of DGI affirmed that service and spiritual care must become a unity (1Cor 12). The word 'service' here means 'ministry,' which must be understood as more than simply charitable work. It is participation in justice and solidarity which embraces the spiritual and the physical, church and society, charity and social concerns. It is

---

[28] *Op. cit.*,p. 165.

[29] Glasser, Arthur F. and Donald A. McGavran, Contemporary Theologies of Mission, Grand Rapids: Baker Books 1983, p.17.

[30] Gensichen, Hans-Werner, Living Mission - The Test of Faith, Philadelphia: Fortress 1996, p.17.

[31] *Op. cit.*, p.93.

[32] Beyerhaus, Peter, Bangkok '73: The Beginning or the End of World Mission?, Grand Rapids: Zondervan 1974.

[33] Cooley, Frank L, The Growing Seed, Jakarta: BPK1981, p.295.

a creative and constructive participation of churches in Indonesia in the process of nation building aimed at a "just society".

In 1971, at the 7th General Assembly of DGI (now PGI) in my home town of Pematangsiantar, North Sumatra, the unity of witness, fellowship, service and development was further deepened to achieve justice in all spheres of life. According to the report of that Assembly:

> The church is sent into the world to proclaim the Gospel of Jesus Christ. The Gospel is the good news of repentance and renewal available to mankind (Mk 1:15), together with the freedom, justice, truth and peace (*shalom*) which the Lord intends for the world (Lk 4:18-21). We are called to participate responsibly in efforts to liberate people from their suffering, caused by backwardness, poverty, sickness, fear and the lack of legal guarantees. We are called to participate fully to achieve justice in all spheres of life.[34]

The churches in Indonesia are strongly motivated by this statement to understand the missionary calling for justice in a comprehensive manner. The first part of justice is liberation from oppressive power and its structures. Jesus teaches us that all power is to be used in service to others. He proposes liberation in the political field at a deeper level. He says, "Whoever wishes to become great among you must be your servant." (Mk 10:43). He washes the feet of his disciples and asks them to wash one another's feet (Jn 13:14). He asks his disciples to love their enemies (Mt 5:44; Lk 6:27,35). He wanted to say that "power and authority had to be genuine service, limpid and uncorrupted, not self seeking and not wanting to perpetuate itself for power."[35]

Mission is community development ministry, a holistic mission

My grandmother told me that in order to attract children of her time to come to Sunday school, the missionary would distribute to them lollies, or small mirrors, or pencils. It is a mission strategy. However, mission strategy may be changed, "one can not change in mission," says Kraemer, "it is witnessing in words and acts to Christian truth and life and the building up of Christian communities."[36] Of course, the only motive for mission is to call people to God. Social action, like community development ministry (CDM), is not the main missionary goal.

CDM is not intended to run economic businesses. Mission history notes that churches could be trapped by such a concept. The best example is A.H.

---

[34] *Op cit*, p.296.

[35] Balasuriya, Tissa, Jesus Christ and Human Liberation, Colombo: Centre for Society & Rel. Publication 1976, p.57.

[36] Kraemer, Hendrik, The Christian Message in a Non-Christian World, Grand Rapids: Kregel 1961, p.287.

Francke, a Lutheran Pietist from Halle, Germany,[37] who sought a reformation of the world through business. His main goal was the transformation of social life in the economic realm. An impressive variety of economic enterprises found a more or less permanent place in his mission activities, including a publishing house, a pharmacy, a drug wholesale business, and a newspaper. He was also involved in international wholesaling in spices, drugs, sugar, wine, tea, coffee, furs, and jewellery. Thus, Francke's enterprise could be characterized as "kingdom of God capitalism."

CDM is not a ministry to make people rich in terms of the developed Western countries. It is not a ministry with its focus on having modern luxurious electronic gadgets such as TVs, telephones, stereo sets, houses with swimming pools, seats on a jet plane for a holiday on Bali, etc. The CDM of the church is intended to guide people to a healthy development, in order that Jesus Christ may become the foundation of their development, life, meaning, values and purposes. "For in him all things in heaven and on earth were created." (Col 1:16).

The core purpose of CDM is to enable people to give an answer to their own problems. In other words, it aims to give them a fishhook, not fish, to enable them to help themselves. It is an activity of the church to help individuals learn ways of dealing with and adjusting to life situations. The CDM of the church is a process in which all people achieve their full human potential to become free from all social evils, so that they become responsible persons who take initiatives in solving the problems existing in family, society, and the nation. CDM is, therefore, a liberation process because this ministry "liberates people from the ravages of nature, disease, fear, myths, prejudice, the abuse of power, the rejection by peer groups and society at large."[38]

If we agree with Warren who says that the Asia of today is the product of the Western impact on the Asia of yesterday and of all the yesterdays of four hundred years, we need creativity in mission to Asia. We need a "change of mind, a *metanoia*, a willingness to turn over a new leaf … that the place of reconciliation, of redeemed relationships, is to be found."[39]

Conclusion

Therefore, churches in Asia which suffered much but still accepted the Gospel with joy (1Thess 1:6), in their mission should initiate a serious analysis of their contexts and practices of their theology through:

---

37 Yeide, Harry, Jr., Studies in Classical Pietism-The Flowering of Ecclesiola, New York: Peter Lang 1997, pp.39-41.

38 Balasuriya, *op. cit.,* p.30.

39 Warren, Max, Challenge and Response, London: SPCK 1960, p.7.

1. Programmes of a humble approach to inter-faith dialogues.
2. Programmes of contextualisation and indigenisation of theology, music, architecture etc.
3. Programmes to eradicate poverty through holistic ministry.
4. Programmes to enhance advocacy for justice, peace and the integrity of creation.

A Biblical Perspective on Mission amidst Unsustainable Livelihoods in Africa

Faustin Mahali

The mission of the church in Africa[1] has always been identified with the provision of social and diaconal services such as education and health care. This role of the church was coincidentally played when Africa had already been colonized, whereby mission in this case was translated as galvanizing imperialistic exploitative ideas of the northern countries.[2] Africa was considered merely a materialistically needy continent, and the church was seen as a provider of aid.[3] Such an asymmetrical representation of the church has undermined the mobilisation of human and material resources for the development of the church and its people in Africa. This asymmetrical representation has also created a dependency-syndrome.[4]

Africa South of the Sahara includes countries which are categorized as the least developed countries in the world.[5] Livelihoods in this region are indicated by the UNDP as follows: the average life expectancy of individuals is 48.3 years. Literacy is 51.4%. Enrolment in primary, secondary and tertiary institutions of the people who should be studying is 46%. The GDP per capita is US$ 1,070.[6] The data from the UNDP gives a general picture of the unsustainable economic planning, and hence the untapped rich natural resources which could ensure sustainable development. When one compares the GDP to the values of health and education which Africa subscribes to, it

---

1 "Africa" will always refer to Africa South of the Sahara.

2 *Cf.* David J. Bosch, Transforming mission: Paradigm Shifts in Theology of Mission, Maryknoll, New York: Orbis Books 1991, p.2.

3 Faustin Mahali, "Becoming the Church in Tanzania," accepted for publication in the *Lutheran Forum* for Spring, 2009.

4 M. T. Speckman, The Bible and Human Development in Africa, Nairobi, Kenya: Acton Publishers 2001, p.29. See also, Faustin Mahali, The Contribution of the Church to Poverty Reduction Policies: A New Theological Agenda," in: Benjamin Simon (ed.), *Society and Church in African Christianity*, Usa River, Arusha: Makumira Publication, 2008, p.71.

5 The UNDP report on Human Development Index (HDI) value for 2006 approximates that all least developed countries south of the Sahara have the least 0.381 HDI value compared to the first value which is 0.968, http://hdr.undp.org/en/statistics (accessed on 9 February, 2009).

6 *Ibid.*

implies that the majority of people in Sub-Saharan Africa are leading a very desolate life.

Missionary outreach approaches have recently been redefined to meet the challenges of estrangement and dehumanisation caused by the oppressive global economic systems.[7] The good news of God's salvation is preached amidst vicious global free-market economic infrastructures.[8] This precarious situation calls for the church to go back to its roots where the first Christians "showed the [liberating / healing] power of the risen Christ in their midst,"[9] by sharing their faith and by (re)distributing property depending on the needs of individuals and institutions at large. This is because the region is so terrified by the plagues of abject poverty, hopelessness, and powerlessness that it needs a strong theological framework to bring back to life the lost hope. This paper discusses historical-critical approaches in the light of socio-anthropological and socio-cultural methods for a sound contextual exegesis of the biblical theology of the Synoptic and Johannine evangelists (Mt 2:16-20, Mk 6:14-18, and Jn 10:10) with the hypothesis that if mission theology needs to move towards a holistic paradigm, it should adopt a Markan tradition in order to have a shift from God's empowerment of not only the carrier of the gospel, but also the receiver.

Methods of biblical interpretation in postcolonial Africa

From purely[10] and moderate[11] hermeneutical approaches of biblical theology with their biases in discussing the role of Africans in development to classical historical critical approaches which do not really incorporate the African world view, the emphasis of contextual exegesis to arrive at the meaning of the original text in its given context would appropriately interpret the message of the Bible into the reader's context of the mission field.[12] In this case, a

---

[7] *Cf.* J. Andrew Kirk, What is Mission? Theological Explorations, Darton, Longman & Todd Ltd. 1999, pp.215-217.

[8] M. T. Speckman, The Bible and Human Development in Africa, Nairobi: Acton Publishers 2001, 17-18.

[9] Gerald O. West, The Academy of the Poor: Towards a Dialogical Reading of the Bible, Sheffield: Sheffield Academic Press 1999, p.10.

[10] See J. N. Mugambi, Christian Theology and Social Reconstruction, Nairobi: Acton Publishers 2003, pp.28-31. *Cf.* Ukachukwu Chris Manus, Intercultural Hermeneutics in Africa: Methods and Approaches, Nairobi: Acton Publishers 2003, pp.2-6.

[11] Speckman, *op. cit.*, p.63. Lamin Sanneh, Translating the Message: The Missionary Impact on Culture, Maryknoll, New York: Orbis Books 1991, pp.18 & 161.

[12] Gerald West, Biblical Hermeneutics of Liberation: Modes of Reading the Bible in the South African Context, Pietermaritzburg: Cluster Publications 1991, p.pp.179-180. *Cf.* René Padilla, "Hermeneutics and Culture – A Theological Perspective," in: *Down to Earth Studies in Christianity and Culture*, Grand Rapids, Michigan: Eerdmans Publishing Company 1980, pp.67-68.

contextual reading strategy should not only provide a critique of the inadequacy of historical-critical exegesis, but also complement it with contextual perspectives. I hypothesize that the sharp partition of exegesis and life experiences in Western theologies has its origin in the Bible itself, namely, in the "capitalistic" paradigms of institutionalized slavery which compromised the radical emancipating message of Jesus Christ into the virtue of charity.[13]

The need to recapture a holistic paradigm which is intertwined with exegesis and daily life situations is not only African, but also significant in Western biblical scholarship, especially in the circles of feminist theology, and in the circles of those who advocate the understanding of the Bible in its own context.[14] Feminist theologians advocate the incorporation of life experiences of women into historical critical methods, and add social scientific interpretations to unmask patriarchal and exploitative paradigms of the methods to allow a true contextual understanding of the gospel. Fiorenza, for example, criticizes historical-critical methods and social scientific interpretational models of the Bible that are dominated by patriarchal and oppressive structures. She states that exegesis also need not disqualify other models of exegesis which include life experiences of the readers of the Bible.[15] Just this idea of Fiorenza indicates that even in the Western world's biblical interpretations there is a new trend trying to engage life experiences with the dynamics of the process of interpretation, together with an awareness of maintaining the integrity of the text.

Moreover, the introduction of social anthropological methodologies[16] into the interpretative discourse on the Bible leads to a better dialogue with the worldview of antiquity in the field of the understanding of healing and miracles as manifested by God's breaking through into the corrupt world. The works of Strecker[17] and Guijarro[18] on the exorcism of Jesus provide a wider spectrum of social understanding of healing in the context of the early church. It is from this perspective that Strecker indicates that events in the NT (in this case exorcism / healing) can only be understood as social constructs and not as introspective

---

13 *Cf.* Mahali, The Concept of Poverty in Luke*, op. cit.*, pp.44-49.

14 Wolfgang Stegemann & Bruce J. Malina (eds.), Jesus in neuen Kontexten, Stuttgart: Verlag W. Kohlhammer 2002, pp.7-9.

15 Elisabeth Schuessler Fiorenza, "Der wirkliche Jesus," in: Wolfgang Stegemann & Bruce J. Malina (eds.), *Jesus in neuen Kontexten*, Stuttgart: Verlag W. Kohlhammer 2002, p.31.

16 Against Mugambi's proposal of a shift 'from theological anthropology to [only] theological introspection,' *Christian Theology and Social Reconstruction*, pp.23-24

17 Christian Strecker, Jesus und die Besessenen: Zum Umgang mit Alterität im Neuen Testament am Beispiel der Exorzismen Jesu, in: *Jesus in neuen Kontexten*, pp.53-63.

18 Santiago Guijarro, "Die politische Wirkung der Exorzismen Jesu," in: *Jesús in neuen Kontexten*, pp.64-74.

psychological aspects through complete rationalisation.[19] It is my understanding that this criticism of Western interpretative models is not only directed at specific, chosen texts, but also it can be replicated in other texts. It is from this background that the chosen biblical texts for mission theology will be read and interpreted, with the hypothesis that the texts of Mk 16:14-18 and John 10:10 provide better prospects of holistic mission theology for sustainable livelihoods in Africa than that of Matthew, because in former texts, it is the sent agent who is not only the subject of the life-giving message, but also the receiver.

Biblical theology of mission: great commission as equivocal?

Many scholars base their mission theology on the "great commission" (Mt 28:16-20). The preference of the Matthean text over that of Mark is because from the text-critical point of view Mk 16:9-20 is believed to have been added by later readers of Mk 16:1-8, and has no valuable manuscripts as witnesses of the text.[20] However, there might be another reason for the Matthean priority: the Markan text insists much more on the empowerment of the receiver of the gospel, than on the empowerment of the carrier of the message. That is why it is important to discuss the Matthean ritual of commissioning Christians in relation to the texts of Mk 16:14-18 and also John 10:10. The aim here is to see how the sent agent relates to the receiver of the message.

According to the Bible, Jesus told the eleven disciples to "go and make disciples of all the gentiles, baptizing them in[to] the name of the [my] Father, and of [me] the Son, and of the Holy Spirit, teaching them to keep all that I commanded you. . ." (Mt 28:16-20). The emphasis here is in making disciples and teaching Jesus' gospel, while going and baptizing becomes a continuous responsibility of the agent for the expansion of the church. This is an order to the disciples to maintain the Christological relevance of the [historical] Jesus who spent much of the time with them healing and preaching the love of God.[21] While this is a report to the church of what happened, what happened cannot be attributed to the teaching of the law alone. What is commanded here is the manifestation of Jesus' power which has broken through the corrupt and sick world. In fact, disciples are commissioned to go and empower the world with God's life giving message (John 17: 8, 18-19).

The synoptic texts (Mk 16:14-18 par.), therefore, have the aim of telling something in common. Christians are obliged to go and empower the world

---

[19] Strecker, Jesus und die Besessenen, *op. cit.*, pp.62-63. *Cf.* Speckmann, *op. cit.*, pp.175-207.

[20] Joachim Gnilka, Das Evangelium nach Markus, 2. Teilband: Mk 8:27-16,20, 5. Auflage, Neukirchen-Vluyn: Neukirchener Verlag 1999, p.350.

[21] Mt 4:23; 8:1-4; 8:5-13; 9:6-8; 9:20-22; 9:18-19, 23-26; 9:27-32;12:22; report of healing sick people in the region 14:34-36; 15:21-28; healing many sick people 15:29-31; 17:14-21; 20:29-34.

with the Word of life of God which is not only manifested in Jesus Christ through the teaching of the love of God and the neighbour, but also through the power of restoration of life.[22]

Bultmann, the popular representative of biblical dialectical theology, argues that for the early church, "... Jesus' person and work appear to them [early Christians] in the light of Easter faith..."[23] That means, all that is reported about the historical Jesus, the teaching, the healing, and probably the resurrection should be rationalized, and the outcome of his project was the demythologization of the healing miracles of Jesus.[24] Bultmann proposes discontinuity, and not continuity (fulfilment), especially when he announces that "the dawning of the old eon as the advent of abolishment of old law and advent of new law implicitly determined the course of the new eschatology in the church."[25] But extreme objective historical critical methods resulted in the exclusion of the Markan text as a core part of the great commission.

Käsemann tries to limit the mission of the historical Jesus to Israel, and the mission of the resurrected one to the Gentiles.[26] He believes that the inclusion of the Gentiles in the promise of salvation is a continuation of the Old Testament tradition which is God's mission and should not be owned by any human endeavours.[27] The paradigm here is still the resurrected Jesus as a motive to the mission, and not the historical Jesus, because the historical Jesus restores Israel – while the resurrected transforms the Gentiles. In this case, the God of the promise to Israel and to the Gentiles becomes the God of 'Western Christians,' who live in a different world than that of the Jews and other Gentiles. However, Mark's gospel should be considered holistically as aiming at preaching "the powerful breaking in of the kingdom of God" combined in the manifestation of God's healing power on earth in the historical Jesus and glorification after the empty tomb.[28]

---

22 Mk 3:2 (healing); 1:39; 3:15; 3:22; 3:23; 7:4; 7:26; 9:18; 9:28; 16:9 16:17 (related to casting out demons)

23 Rudolf Bultmann, Theology of the New Testament, New York: Charles Scribner's Sons, 1951, p.43. Gerhard Barth, Matthew's understanding of the Law, in: Guenther Bornkamm, Gerhard Barth, & Heinz Joachim Held (eds.), *Tradition and Interpretation in Matthew,* London: SCM Press Ltd. 1960, 134.

24 Rudolf Bultmann, "New Testament and mythology: The mythological element in the message of the New Testament and the problem of its re-interpretation," in: Hans Werner Bartsch & Reginald H. Fuller (eds.), *Kerygma and Myth: A Theological Debate*, London: S.P.C.K 1960, pp.4-5.

25 Bultmann, *Theology of the New Testament*, *op. cit.*, 43. Barth, Matthew's understanding of the law, p.135.

26 Ernst Käsemann, New Testament Questions of Today, London: SCM Press Ltd. 1969, p.89

27 *Ibid.*, p.88.

28 Udo Schnelle, The History and Theology of the New Testament, London: SCM Press Ltd. 1998, p.216-217.

According to Jürgen Roloff, for Mark, the miracles belong to the historical Jesus, while for Matthew, miracles should only be understood as auxiliaries for the better understanding of the resurrected Jesus and his eschatological teaching authority.[29] Miracles indicate the fulfilment of the promise of the healing power of the merciful servant of God.[30] Healing, exorcism and miracle activities are carefully included to inflate the function of the teaching, and they are actually not a component of the mission discourse. This is not holistic empowerment of the receiver, because a hungry or sick receiver cannot understand the teaching well.[31]

The contribution of biblical theology to holistic mission in Africa

The African trend in the theology of mission for sustainable development owes much to the classical 'African theology' and 'liberation theology' from the 60s to the end of the 80s. These two liberative models have paved the way for a comprehensive model of contextual exegesis which in the long run will not only deal with socio-economic liberation in Africa for sustainable livelihoods, but also contribute to the missionary debate of Christianity and dialogue among nations.

It was indefensible to regard the "great commission" as only being primarily concerned with going to plant the gospel while the content of the teaching of Jesus referred to engaging in the liberation processes of the oppressed and in solidarity with the poor (Mt 22:37-40).[32]

It is evident in Africa that the main cause of low life expectancy, increasing illiteracy, and low income is not only the unjust global economic infrastructures, but also African social patterns which maintain the status quo through tyrannical political systems. These systems have created mega-families (nations) which did not make use of clan systems to forge responsible cooperatives but reduced them to pieces. As a result, the mega-families produced corruptive factions based on ethnicity in an attempt to win back micro-entities lost in the process of nationalism. Therefore, attributing the African plight only to outside forces of injustice is a fallacy when it comes to formulating a workable theological paradigm for development in Africa.

A creative project of Speckmann proposed a link of contextual exegesis to sustainable development in Africa by emphasizing mobilisation of what he calls "micro-potentiality" needs greater attention here.[33] He infers that for Africa to do away with the syndrome of dependency on developed nations for

29 Jürgen Roloff, Neues Testament, 7., vollständig überarbeitete Auflage, Neukirchen-Vluyn: Neukirchener Verlag, 1999, 121.

30 *Ibid.*, p.121-122.

31 *Cf.* Jesus feeding the multitude, Mk 6:30-44 par.

32 David Bosch, *op. cit.*, p.81.

33 M.T. Speckman, *op. cit.*

economic plans, aid, and relief, it needs to mobilise human resources for a better start in sustainable development. He proposed a theology of development which sources its efforts from contextual exegesis and alternative development theory. He argued that Africa needs a different development theory as the existing classic development theory is foreign and its goals create a dependence syndrome that allows developed countries to easily tap resources from Africa. Africa needs a vision based on biblical emancipating paradigms through contextual exegetical approaches to discover the God who not only provides food, shelter, and medicine, but also empowers a person to be able to work for his or her living and to sustain his or her development. However, his compromising of historical critical methods with the biased notions of attributing the dependency syndrome to global imbalanced economic infrastructures can still sabotage the self-examination of the African discriminatory social pattern.

Contextual biblical theology interprets the incarnation of the Word of God in a deeper way. From this new perspective, God did not come to put a demarcation between two worlds, but to reconcile, and restore the whole world (Jn 1:14; 16:3; 10:10). If the understanding of the continuity of God's saving act in Jesus Christ is maintained, therefore, God reveals himself equally to every creature in this world, and equally transforms every creature. This demands that the mission of the worldwide church needs to see Africa not as an object of the mission, but as a participant in mission. Africa is God's creation, the creation of God who became incarnate in Africa as elsewhere.

It is from this perspective that the Markan theology of mission, which puts more emphasis on the receiver of the gospel of life, should be emphasized more. In the Markan texts, the empowerment of the disciples is all-encompassing, as the disciples, upon reception of baptism and teaching, receive healing and life and 'resist even all effects of poisonous fluids from snakes (Mk 16:18).' The empowered disciples are not allowed to privatize this power for themselves, but are obliged to extend this power to others by miraculous deeds and the driving away of evil spirits. This is a big problem for a rational and legalistic world to understand the implication of this Markan "mystical" statement of mission.

The mechanical understanding of the Markan mission theology through textual criticism is misleading. The text should be understood from the Markan "religious" worldview as comprehensive and self-explanatory. In the Markan perspective of mission, we see not only a résumé of God's purposive liberation incarnated in time and place, but also the holistic inclusion and empowerment of the receiver as the ultimate core of the teaching. On one hand, a serpent designated destruction and corruption (Gen 3:14), but on the other hand, the "serpent made of God" provided liberative power from the yoke of oppression and restored lives of Israelites in the desert (Num 21:8). Thus, believing in Jesus as the sole life giver (John 10:10b) liberates one from oppressive institutions, while at the same time one gains eternal life. This life is shared through commission, that is, through carrying this message of the promise of life to others. In fact, it is participating in the mission of God that takes place when the agent and the receiver come together and become responsible to God and for their coexistence. It would probably be important to maintain this, and talk about commission, and not mission, for even terms like partnership are doing injustice to what we have been commissioned to and for. A shift of paradigm to actively engage the recipient in the process of mission will shift the thinking to a critical analysis of the local needs of the church (de-globalization), and because the local is part of the universe, it will also contribute to the solutions of global challenges. Today, a lesson is given to us that doing development irrespective of empowering local communities can lead not only to the loss of many lives of God's creation in Africa and elsewhere, but also to the degradation of the environment.

When Africans understand that they are equally the receivers of the life-giving message of Jesus Christ, they will no longer look at the agent as the colonizer, but as a co-worker and carrier of the commandment of God who teaches and brings the message of God's empowerment to the whole world. This is important because all (carrier and receiver alike) according to John 10:10 are challenged by the fact that if they both do not abide by the orders of Him, who is the life-giver, they all have fallen into the traps of cheating and stealing. It is important to go back to the biblical paradigms of holistic mission because many civil service organisations, including faith-based organisations in Africa, have politicized empowerment, and some have turned to robbing the rights and privileges of those who have been called the most vulnerable.

The challenge of the outcome of our mission theology is that it has always been quantitative and counted the number of Christians being baptized. It is time now to think of ways, as it is indicated in the Markan "great commission", to empower many Christians and non-Christians in Africa after baptism so that they confess, teach, and live their faith, and above all participate in the agenda to restore God's creation.

Prospect of contextual theology for the well-being of Africa

This paper indicated that livelihoods in Africa are threatened by increasing forceful local and global economic infrastructures which estrange, dehumanise, and destroy God's creation. It was found that the church in Africa has contributed a great deal to the upheavals because of consciously or unconsciously being misused by imperialistic paradigms and ending up compromising its fundamental teaching of holistic mission for the liberation of humankind and creation from structural and individual sin. The church in Africa, as agent and receiver of the life-giving biblical tidings, is required to thoroughly understand the will of God mediated to it through the biblical message.

The historical-critical method developed as an exegesis of the experiences of God's humanity in history needs be acknowledged and complemented with the life experiences of the reader. In order to develop a relevant context for the Bible to interact with the church in Africa, the church needs to establish a well-equipped research institution with contextual, quantitative, and qualitative approaches to discover and uncover socio-political, socio-economic, socio-cultural, and socio-anthropological dynamics in order to determine the axes of evil within Africa, and to transcend these experiences by the comprehensive interpretation of global oppressive social patterns in order to demolish the existing hegemonic infrastructures which devastate existence in the Sub-Saharan region.

The paradigms which maintain the interrelatedness of the context and the context of the biblical message are in line with the purpose of the incarnate God, whose transforming power has been displayed in the life and death and resurrection of Jesus Christ. Christians as receivers and agents of God's mission should co-exist, co-participate, and be co-missionaries to fulfil God's will of restoring humanity and creation. It is in this sense that a true sharing of reflections on the positive opportunities of globalization provides the prospect of protection against the vulnerability to dehumanization and threats posed by the negative aspects of globalisation for the well-being of God's creation. Therefore, the church in Africa needs to prophesy and live a quality life physically, mentally, and spiritually to curb the challenges of dehumanisation and the challenges of spreading Pentecostalism that proclaims the mostly individualistic and futuristic eschatological tendencies of prosperity that mystify the realities of life on the planet.

Response by Roberta Rominger

I read this paper with great interest and I am in complete sympathy with the project Mahali identifies, of enabling a reading of scripture that will challenge the dependency culture created by colonization and open the door to a reading that emphasizes the empowerment of the gospel-hearer. I agree absolutely that such empowerment is what the gospel is about and that the dependency culture is an offence against the fullness of life that is God's will for people in Tanzania and everywhere.

I think he could do better, however, than to base his new mission theology on such a dubious text as Mark 16:15ff. Much of the Christian world now recognises the limitations of the historical-critical method. But how can this text be sufficiently authoritative to bear the weight of Mahali's argument when it is so clearly derivative? It is not there in the best manuscripts. That matters. I don't buy the suggestion that this version of the Great Commission was sidelined because it suggests empowerment of the hearer rather than the evangelist. It has been sidelined because it reads like somebody's attempt to "fix" a flawed gospel ending by drawing on bits of this and that from the rest of the New Testament.

Could not Mahali's argument be better supported by following a different strand of New Testament writing? In preparing my paper, I was struck by the New Testament's inescapable message that we are called, not to admire Christ, but to follow him; that his first disciples were "empowered" from the start by being included in work that was way beyond what they understood or thought they could do; that being "in Christ" makes us new creations; that the mind that was in Christ should be in us too; that it is no longer I who live but Christ who lives in me; that we are to be transformed by the renewing of our minds; that we are to do the things Christ did, and greater things besides. This message comes at us from all directions in the New Testament. Surely it provides a firm basis for a missionary discipleship that rejects the after-effects of colonial oppression. I agree with Mahali that the words of scripture need to be read in the context of the life experiences of the reader. The Bible challenges us to claim our liberation – it gives us nowhere to hide!

UEM – For the Growth of the Church and the Transformation of the World: On the Dynamics in Theology and Organization of UEM as an Ecumenical Missionary Communion

Wilhelm Richebächer

Church and mission related at a new level of quality (Historical and theological evaluation)

When in the summer of 1996, the United Evangelical Mission was transformed from a regional German missionary society into an international church communion in the service of mission, this was assessed in different ways. There was confidence at finally having stepped onto the path of a tangible partnership, but there were also doubts. In the light of intercultural decision finding processes, practical questions arose concerning the future strain for management and administration. But there were also basic inquiries such as the question whether an obsolete mission institution was perhaps struggling to survive by changing into a multinational mission corporation with "western structures" and a head office in Wuppertal. If this were the case, ran the criticism, the former "mission churches" in the South would be incorporated in a new style as "business partners", but still not in a less "colonial" way.[1]

Whatever the judgment on the UEM may be after these 13 years, the historical documents show quite clearly: it was not founded in the first place for reasons of organization but for the pursuit of a common vision and mutual respect. Here, after decades of theological ripening, a consensus on the basis and method of mission as well as intensive negotiations about a common strategy had sought and found their appropriate organizational structure.[2]

a. The consensus of mission theology states that mission does not work from North to South or vice versa, but engages the entire church of Jesus Christ all over the world in conveying the message of reconciliation to all mankind.
b. The strategy leading to the reform of the UEM was: a legal and financial frame set by European churches or associations can no longer dictate what is possible

---

[1] Concerning the latter compare above all: H. Luther, Arbeitsstrukturen (*Working Structures*) ZMiss 4/1996, p.249 ff.

[2] *Cf.* P. Sandner, Der Weg zur Internationalisierung der UEM. Erinnerungen (*The path towards the internationalization of UEM. Memories.*), Wuppertal: UEM 2007. The historical comparison of CEVAA, WMM, and UEM by K. Funkschmidt titled "Earthing the vision", Frankfurt: Peter Lang 2000, very valuable due to its profound investigation, emphasizes this aspect in accordance with its title.

for a common understanding on the Gospel and its effects (donor-recipient structure). On the contrary, this frame must be shaped by listening to each other and giving mutual advice.
c. In terms of structure, this led to the transformation of a mission agency of German Protestant churches into an international communion of churches and institutions dedicated to mission.

Many people were impressed that the association had a structure characterized by a Christian spirit, grounded on a time-tested theological basis (constitution) and capable of reacting in a flexible way to questions of international ethics (human rights). These qualities prove that it was not mere pragmatism that made the members join, but that they felt the obligation to act in common because of their common destination (*cf.* Acts 4:20) and common history.[3] This process[4] has added an interesting chapter to the history of the relationship between church and mission. Since the beginning of Protestant 'overseas mission' by the missionaries from Halle and Denmark in South India some 300 years ago, Protestant churches and organized world mission sometimes criticized and sometimes ignored each other, and sometimes they had phases of mutual attraction. Already in 1938, at the World Missionary Conference at Tambaram / India, the delegates had on principle agreed upon a stronger allocation of world missionary responsibility to the churches (instead of private or other public communities as before). This programmatic change took some time to be implemented;[5] the first step was a cooperation of regional church-related missionary societies in Europe, based on geographical considerations.

At Bangkok in 1973, the unilateral north-south directed missionary work was radically questioned, giving rise to the emergence of a growing number of direct church partnerships. It became obvious that the institution of 'regional missionary societies' could only be an interim solution. Therefore, it was only consistent for the churches and institutions united in the Vereinigte

---

[3] This common history has aspects of shame and grief that have to be commemorated and emphasized over and over again in the present atmosphere of reconciliation (such as five years ago on the occasion of the 100th anniversary of the war of extermination which the German colonial power waged against the Herero and other peoples in Namibia). The common history, however, also recalls early occurrences of reconciliation in theology and cooperation in partnership; *cf.* p.Sandner, *op.cit.*, p.4, or in the history of Bethel Mission: E. Johanssen, Bilder aus einer entstehenden evangelischen Christenheit in Ostafrika (*Images of an emerging Protestant Christianity in East Africa*), Evangelisches Missionsmagazin 1927, H. 1, 18 – 22.

[4] By now, we may speak of an established process and not only of a project, as it was called in Funkschmidt, *op. cit.*, pp.300-346 because of its coincidence with the official foundation.

[5] This is valid despite the integration of International Missionary Council as a union of missionary societies with the WCC in New Delhi in 1961; *cf.* O. Schumann, Die Seite der Schriftleitung (*Editor's page*), ZMiss, 4/1996, p.202.

Evangelische Mission to entrust the mandate of missionary work to a network of responsibility within a communion of churches – after a process of consultation that lasted for 18 years (from 1978, Bethel consultation, until 1996, Bethel UEM General Assembly).

The partners in charge of the reform process fulfilled their tasks with very careful reflection[6], taking their time to discuss experiences, new concepts and new structures, yet without coming to a standstill:

a) They allowed as many levels as possible within the partner institutions to take part in the consultations (synods, but also leading clergy were often involved[7]).
b) They sought advice and evaluation from competent advisors with expertise and experience in the field of cooperation (assessments by EMW 1993 and by WCC).
c) And they realized at an early stage that regional structures had to be allowed sufficient importance within the future communion.[8]

So who is the UEM today?

The UEM is a growing communion of churches and institutions united by a joint history of mission, dedicated to give mutual help in dealing with the present-day missionary challenges. In this communion, the associated churches and institutions share their understanding and responsibility for passing on the Gospel in word and deed. Such sharing of responsibility signifies for those who are in some way dominant, e.g. by material superiority, the willingness to forego the exercise of power, clearly demonstrating the new quality of ecumenical coexistence. The mandate to manage this communion has been transferred to a supra-church level, while safeguarded by the competence of the General Assembly, consisting mainly of church representatives, to determine its constitution and guidelines.

Careful documentary examination of the development leading to the new UEM reveals the urgent concern not to destroy the churches' consciousness of their own responsibility for mission that had only just begun to grow, by forming an independent, international hyper-structure comparable to former

---

6 Reckoning from 1996, some three decades of searching for an adequate partnership structure preceded this process. However, from 1973 onwards, first suggestions were to be heard from responsible reformers (Menzel 1973; deVries 1975; G. Jasper jun. 1976) which led in the direction of the UEM process, which gained distinct contours from 1988 on; *cf.* Gerhard Jasper, Zum notwendigen Hören auf Lausanne – auch nach Nairobi, Evangelische Mission Jahrbuch 1976, ed. by Verband Evangelischer Missionskonferenzen, Hamburg 1976, pp.46 – 65; as well as Funkschmidt, *op. cit.,* pp.30 ff. Likewise remarked by p.Sandner, *op.cit.,* p 11 and others, and K. Funkschmidt, Structures and Theology, IRM XCI, 2002, p.397.

7 From my church alone Bishop Dr. Jung in Mühlheim, 1988; Bishop Prof. Dr. Zippert in Ramatea, 1993.

8 Thus already recorded by V. Jung in an observation as an asset in the development of the UEM in comparison to CEVAA. Jung, V., CEVAA: Um einen Tisch versammelt (*CEVAA: Gathered around one table*), Jahrbuch Mission 1996, p.218

associations or societies outside the churches.[9] At the same time, given the tendency to regard mission as a special or cross-sectional function of ecclesial expression or simply a process of mutual self-help between churches, it had to be borne in mind that church and mission are never completely identical.[10] Mission is not owned by the churches, even though, or rather precisely because, the church represents the indispensable historical fellowship of faith through the power of the mission of reconciliation of God in Christ and through the one Christian baptism.

It is, among other things, the basic Protestant understanding of the church which ensures that the new UEM communion pays attention to both those basic insights. The churches and institutions associated in UEM share this basic understanding as expressed in the constitution. According to this basic understanding, the church is in itself created by the reconciling word of God addressed to the sinner. Thus the church herself *is* already mission, as she struggles to give shape to the Word by listening and answering as well as in the mutual sharing of her members. That takes place even before and during the exercise of her responsibility for her activity in the world, namely for the mission she *has*. For whenever the members of the church of Jesus Christ as well as the different historical churches in the fellowship of the worldwide body of Christ share their gifts, they never share just themselves. As a Eucharistic communion they share the grace of reconciliation and peace with God, a grace reaching beyond this communion towards all mankind.[11]

In terms of theology, 'mission' can, therefore, be defined as a communication process in which the fellowship of reconciliation between God and humans, and between human and human, is created and renewed. As such it serves the Word by which the church is born and which she translates for all mankind. This dialogue between God and human is mediated by the Holy Scripture, conducted in brotherly and sisterly consultation, and serves to create and renew the church.[12]

---

[9] *Cf.* an analogous undertaking, though in a completely different process with different results, in Basel Mission. Wolfgang Schmidt, Die Basler Mission im Gesamtprozess der Erneuerung ihres Auftrages, ihrer Verfassung, ihrer Struktur und ihrer Beziehungen, ZMIss 4/1996, pp.217 ff.

[10] *Cf.* in this connection the discussion of Bishop J. Kibara's suggestion (1978) to integrate such a dedicated missionary communion into the structures of confessional world alliances in Funkschmidt, *op. cit.*, p.275 f.

[11] Learning to honour the sharing of gifts, thus sharing one another with all the joys and worries of life, is an essential learning process within missionary existence of churches; *cf.* H. W. Huppenbauer , Mission heißt, das Evangelium teilen (*Mission means sharing the* Gospel), ZMiss 4/1996, pp.214- 216; *cf.* K. Funkschmidt, *op. cit.*, pp.7, 56, 59, 60f.

[12] In this process the church is no more – and no less – than offspring and steward of mission. This is reflected in the UEM constitution in § 2(1) by the statement that this community relies on its being "(founded) on the Holy Scriptures of the Old and New Testament" and on this basis shall "serve the purpose of joint action in mission."

Great ideals! Flexible strategies? Adequate resources? (Present-day concerns)

The UEM partners make great demands on themselves: they want to take seriously both the world-wide dimension of the Christian church including her mutual responsibilities as well as the fact that in the end Christian mission can always only take place regionally or locally.

However, these great demands might quickly put too great a strain on the personal and economical resources which are nowadays rather being reduced than expanded.[13] Up to now, it 'turned out all right' because the churches which are multilaterally connected in the association also gave indirect and exemplary vitality to the UEM process by taking care of their bilateral relations. Nonetheless, during the first decade in which the new structure was put into practice many questions came up, some of which have not been thoroughly discussed, let alone resolved. Yet they have already allowed small steps in the process of organizational reform.[14] The crucial questions shall be dealt with in the following sections:

- Have the essential goals of church communion in mission been consistently pursued, adequately discussed and jointly modified?
- Have the concepts, strategies, and the new overall structure proved successful? Has it been possible to preserve acceptance and active cooperation in all churches and institutions involved? Which modifications have already been made?
- What are the future challenges within the entire ecumenical network and how are they to be met?

A growing church and a fairer society! (Clarification of goals)

Referring to the insights of recent research in mission theology, we should first clarify the goals of Christian mission. Therefore, within the overall mission theological situation named above, it is necessary first of all to distinguish between the eschatological horizon of the *missio Dei* as a whole, which is part of the gift granted by God within His act of salvation through Jesus Christ, and the objectives defined for the *missio ecclesiae* within this horizon. Whoever does not make this distinction will always run the risk of confusing the basic

---

13 Especially by German members! The UEM-specific nature of ecumenical partnership in comparison to other ecumenical unions (CEVAA and CWM) that have existed for some 150 years (p. 175 – 179), is presented in a plausible manner by J. Wietzke, Suchbewegungen zu mehr Partnerschaft (*On the search for more partnership*), Jahrbuch Mission 1993, pp.172-181, but also critically assessed with regard to potential strains for the various planes of ecumenical work in the churches involved (pp.179 – 181).

14 So at the General Assembly in Borkum / Germany June 2008.

theological and eschatological conditions of church and mission with the diverse forms of missionary activities of the church.

The eschatological horizon of the *missio Dei* encompasses the kingdom of God proclaimed by Christ (Lk 4:18 f; Jn 20:21) and the present eternal salvation by the assurance of justification for the sinner (Jn 3:16), and it represents as a whole the condition enabling ecclesiastical mission, indeed the entire existence of the church. This horizon together with its related effects enables the church and all her members to fulfil the task of missionary action in this world, the *missio ecclesiae*. Due to the eschatological horizon, this mission has two goals which should not be played off against each other as may be seen in the current debate about the competition between "missionary" and "development" agencies in the EKD[15]:

> Goal 1: Growth and renewal of the church, by winning people for the communion of believers and to a fellowship in accordance with the word that is preached, listening to God and to each other and helping one another accordingly, and
>
> Goal 2: The development of social life in the service of humankind, as the church – for example with diaconal services – sets the signs for more equitable politics and economics, in the sense of the reign of peace in the Kingdom of God introduced by Christ.

It has to be emphasized: neither of these two goals is beyond the eschatological horizon of *missio Dei.* That is the origin, justification, and motivation of the call to "repentance and new life", as it says in paragraph 2 of the UEM Constitution, whether referring to the renewed life given to justified sinners in the communion of Christ or to the renewal of stewardship of God's creation resulting from it. But something else applies: neither of these two goals is independent of the other, since in both cases the healing action of the Triune

---

15 However, it may be proved here how helpful it is to distinguish between the two goals, besides the a. m. distinction between an eschatological horizon of mission and its goals of activity. The two goals of mission, namely 'church growth' and 'social development', are necessarily distinct, yet closely connected, so that it is clear: both goals and tasks have to be understood, from a theological point of view, as constituent parts of church mission, even though they fulfil the mission of Christ in different ways and with different cooperation partners. A certain confusion regarding the determination as well as separation of goals for both expressions of mission had come up during the last decades, mainly because Western mission theology was still suffering from its mission history, which was perceived as compromising, and therefore hesitated to define mission as church activity. They preferred to withdraw behind the formula of the *missio Dei*, as it were behind an impenetrable eschatological reservation against all further determinations of mission, instead of preserving both differentiation and connection between *missio Dei* and *missio ecclesiae* and defining for the latter the most urgent necessities. More is to be said in this connection at a different place, since that would go beyond the scope of the UEM topic in this article.

God is transported with and through the church, either by preaching or – by her very existence – demonstrating freedom. When the Gospel is directed to what the church from her perspective regards as 'outsiders', offering them an impulse to transform their lives, this process is usually designated as 'mission' and often clothed in phrases such as 'church is always church for others.' Nonetheless it is very important to make sure that a further goal is not neglected, namely the invitation to join up in the body of Christ in the form of a specific and binding membership in a church.

It is certainly easier to stipulate the goals of Christian mission than to make them compatible with one's own existence or even to achieve them methodically and then to check them off as 'accomplished'.[16] We would be happy if we could always radiate the great joy effected by the Gospel simply by using our specific characters as individuals and institutions – for the benefit of the church and society as a whole. But a mission of continuous 'radiation' for which people occasionally enthuse in glowing terms is just not at our disposition. We cannot construct 'credible speech and life;' we can only expose ourselves to God's endearing love by our daily study of the letter and spirit of reconciliation – in spite of, indeed in view of our limitations and failures.[17]

There is no mission without a specific echo within the body of Christ in the form of a temporal church. What good to us – and to all those who are waiting for the best news of all – is a private and personal confession of faith, or one which can only be communicated at all within an elite international group, but not put into specific practice in a local church?[18] This goal of inviting people to

---

16 People believed in this possibility at the very beginning of the world mission movement; *cf.* J. Mott in Edinburgh 1910, as well as later on when development was regarded optimistically. In the course of the past century, however, all the world's churches had to learn that this mission could not be fulfilled in a historical period of time; *cf.* the title (transl.) 'Mission accomplished?' of the *Jahrbuch Mission 2009* that will come out these days.

17 Within the framework of our limitations we should have confidence in this love granted to us in the power of the kingdom of God. We know that our human and organizational resources are limited, also as a missionary community. So we can only cope if we share our and other people's talents, accepting them as God's gifts for us all. Therefore we may boldly define the specific cooperation in a temporal church as the place designated for the mission invitation.

18 Especially in the year 2009, when Calvin's 500th birthday anniversary coincides with the 75th anniversary of the Barmen Theological Declaration, the UEM would be well advised to make conscious use of a Reformed tradition which is strongly represented in some of its partners' history, according to which the church's order is part of her nature and therefore has to be shaped in line with the Gospel. – On the subject of exaggeration of outward orientation (centrifugal trend) within mission *cf.* Funkschmidt, *op. cit.*, p.187.

come to our churches should be more strongly emphasized in a missionary church communion such as the UEM.[19]

More room for action, without loss of participation (The process will continue)

Three factors mentioned above have to be coordinated continuously[20] in a recurring cycle of checks: (a) common concepts of content, (b) common strategies and (c) common structures.

The latest example of this adaptation process can be named here. In the first 8-10 years the UEM management and advisory bodies concentrated their attention on the strengthening of parliamentary structures of participation. The objective was to create a system allowing all partners the most equitable representation through their delegates, respecting the various regions, ages, occupations and genders, and this aim has been steadily followed with growing success. On the other hand the questions concerning the concept and content of missionary and ecumenical work or modern and effective working strategies were pushed into the background.[21]

Soon, however, it became necessary to correct this tendency to emphasize structural reforms.[22] Thus the responsible bodies had to focus on the review of

---

19 In more general comments, regard for local 'missionary situations' in the different churches among the members was named as *desideratum* or chance for the process from the very beginning of the UEM process; *cf.* U. Beyer, In einem Boot. Ökumene – Mission – Weltverantwortung (*In one boat. Ecumenism – Mission – Responsibility for the World)*, Jahrbuch Mission 1993, p.184 and U. Beyer, Ökumenische Partnerschaft: Das UiM-Experiment geht weiter (*Ecumenical partnership: The UiM experiment continues*), Jahrbuch Mission 1994, p.202, as well as Wietzke, *op. cit.*, pp.178, 180. Yet the members' mutual support as well as necessary mutual help in finding methods of adequate contextual evangelisation has hardly been specifically worked on anywhere. In the past years, it seemed as if the task of congregational development had nothing to do with the missionary concept of the UEM communion, namely its worldwide missionary orientation. This can be illustrated by the reaction of Indonesian UEM members to proposals by the Executive Secretary Evangelism, Rev. Währisch-Oblau in the year 2008: "We never knew that UEM is engaged in such kind of work ..." (Personal communication, 20 February, 2009). First signs of a change in direction are recognizable in the strategy paper of the Region Germany within the UEM dated 2007.

20 This can also be gathered from the continuing further inquiries about the adequacy of structures on the occasion of consultations, as early as the development phase between 1978 and 1996.

21 That this might be a potential problem is already hinted at in Funkschmidt's impressions (1998) of the first two years of UEM work, *cf.* p.269.

22 In times of careful resource sharing fundamental questions could not be overlooked, such as the following (at least since the GA in Manila in 2004): "What actually comprises the common understanding of mission which binds us together in a special

concepts and strategies. This investigation revealed that, in addition to intensifying specific areas of cooperation such as the social services, more attention should be paid to the common task of missionary congregational development in the interests of the growth of church life in every region. The new UEM programmes had to meet this priority without abandoning the indispensable claim of a holistic, practical witness to the Gospel. This may be made easier in that UEM is not a communion of churches in every respect.[23]

Contextual mission in ecumenical responsibility (Focal points for future cooperation)

Even in the early stages of growing together the UEM communion was spoken of as "exemplary ecumenism".[24] Today we must take a new look to see in which way the UEM might be considered exemplary.

Presupposing that this is the case, in this final chapter I would like to propose two special areas of work corresponding to the two goals of the church's mission mentioned above to be emphasized.

Before that, I would like to outline once again the points which make the UEM particularly interesting and relevant for ecumenical theology.

UEM as 'exemplary' in terms of new criteria of quality for ecumenical fellowship

The *proprium* of UEM lies primarily in the mature partnership in mission which is vital for the church, specifically in the fields of church growth and world responsibility. It is by no means self-evident that this cooperation takes place irrespective of general cultural borders and inner-Protestant denominational boundaries. Growing together in this ecumenical communion can only work if both these cross-border dimensions are consciously tackled.

For this purpose it is ideal that this communion which is exemplary for the entire church only comprises a limited number of partners who know each other well from their bilateral partnerships.[25] For here it is impossible to neglect within the relevant context the latent cultural and economic differences existing

---

fellowship such as ours?" Or: "Do we need our mission societies as a second type of development agency alongside others?"

23 This claim – which is not achievable – is still suggested by the UEM subtitle "Communion of Churches in Three Continents" (see constitution, § 1), quite apart from the fact that not all its members are churches.

24 Ulrich Beyer, *op. cit.*, Jahrbuch Mission 1993, pp.182 – 186.

25 From the beginning of the UEM process there was a call for improved quality of partnerships in a manageable but multilateral framework; *cf.* Beckmann, Die unvollendete Integration (*Unfinished integration*), Ökumenische Rundschau 31, 1982, pp.68 – 75.

between the partners. And wherever there are concrete religious encounters there is no way of avoiding the doctrinal theological differences which still exist, for example baptismal theology or the ordinances of church life (e.g. ordination and issues of ministry). They have to be treated in such a way that they do not, as so often in the history of the church, act as a hindrance to the interaction in church fellowships which are existentially necessary.

Admittedly, issues repeatedly arise which pose questions to the traditional ecumenical thinking which has developed notably in the churches of the Northern hemisphere, such as the following: is it actually possible to build a strong network of church fellowship – albeit for a specific purpose – cutting across theological doctrinal differences?

Of course, at this point the UEM communion as a whole could say: is it not so that our communion nowadays is much more involved in questions of inter-cultural and ethical differences and means of overcoming them than dealing with doctrinal differences? Going deeper into that issue they will discover: only when both, ethical and doctrinal, criteria for authentic ecumenism have been considered in their intrinsic connection can one investigate the specific depth of theology which is possible in the UEM communion and ask: in what modern form do our traditional doctrinal differences appear within the family of Protestant churches today? To take a particular example, this question might be posed like this: how do the members of this communion manage to do justice to the equal dignity and capability of receiving the vocation to preach the Gospel for all who have been baptized (whether they are "men or women, Jews or Greeks, slaves or free"; *cf.* Gal 3:28)?

Two special areas of work in the future

'Church growth' – missionary congregational formation after inter-contextual consultation

The aim designated above as 'church growth' has already been emphasized as one central focus of the UEM cooperation. With their sharing *koinonia*-structure the UEM partners should not only act as witnesses for the society around them in an increasingly globalized world.[26] This structure should also act as an invitation to the classical theological fellowship in word and sacrament (*Confessio Augustana VII*).

All the partners need a renewal of real church life in their own area. The partners in the Northern hemisphere are particularly suffering from the loss of members due to demographic and socio-cultural developments. For the partners

---

[26] As the UEM has postulated since its internationalization (strengthened by the World Mission Conference in St. Antonio, 1989; *cf.* the remarks by p.Sandner regarding this process of mutual stimulation, experience, processes of UEM restructuring, *op.cit.,*, p.18).

in the South the limits of church growth are experienced not so much with regard to membership gain, but rather with regard to their being grounded and rooted in their own culture. For example, will there be enough candidates called to and qualified for full-time service in the event that international partners withhold their financial assistance?

Both religious contexts are still challenged by new mentalities of charismatic piety that are spreading all over the globe. They must demonstrate self-confidence and be prepared to learn.

The conditions for attractive preaching, for dialogue oriented towards the target group and also for the active participation of many members of the congregation in shaping church life can however only be assessed regionally.[27] The Gospel wants to help each individual human to find new impetus and enthusiasm in his specific life situation.[28] It is necessary both to 'regain' existing church members as well as to recruit new members among those who had hitherto been living outside the church.[29]

In planning appropriate strategies for congregational formation the UEM partners ought to look over one another's shoulders. In particular, representatives of partner churches with the same denomination, but differing cultural and social contexts, have an eye for the right mix of impartiality and sympathy for the concerns of the local church. Admittedly, for the German UEM partners it might also mean getting involved not just with representatives of the UEM partner churches, but also with members of a congregation with a foreign language and origin in their own neighbourhood. However, it appears questionable whether an advisory team should be solely composed of representatives of churches living in the same social context, who are thus potential competitors, since Protestant churches and foreign-language congregations are often wary of making contact because of their differing forms of piety.

One should also be skeptical about the suggestion that models of spiritual life and congregational growth can be directly transferred across cultural boundaries. At first the demonstration of the exotic but non-transferable model[30]

---

27 This factor of regional charisma has been recommended to the UEM communion in comments on the process from the very beginning; e. g. by V. Jung, *op. cit.*, JBM 1996, pp.217, 219.

28 This was called to mind by T. Sundermeier in his ceremonial lecture "Mission – Kraft der Erneuerung" (*Mission – Power of renewal*) on the occasion of the 175th anniversary of the Rhenish Missionary Society here in Wuppertal in 2003.

29 This is stated by my own regional church in a study on recruiting new members dated 2005, titled "Anderen begegnen. Mitglieder gewinnen" (*Encountering others. Winning members)..*

30 Thus, it wouldn't make much sense to directly continue the former models of evangelistic teams which had not proved successful in the 70s of the 20th century, neither in the shape of JafM teams at the UEM 1978 (*cf.* Funkschmidt, *op. cit.*, pp.276

may create a great mutual impression, but the advisory teams should give serious priority to the translation of concepts and methods into the other contexts. The goal must be mutual assistance in finding a context-oriented missionary model, for which the local church alone ultimately has to take responsibility, even if it was unmistakably inspired by the advice of 'third parties'.[31]

A recent experiment showed how helpful a multilateral consultative communion of partners can be for a German Protestant church, when church partners in Africa and Asia gave their advice on the missionary conditions in the North Elbian Church.[32] Similar consultations could be organized by the UEM.

'The development of social life' *Partnership projects in diaconia and development*

The principal implementation of that goal of Christian mission defined as 'church development service' can at present be found in the churches' efforts for a reconciled coexistence of the peoples in the Northern and Southern hemispheres, both politically and economically. Here the members of the UEM communion can make an exemplary contribution as a fellowship of partners who have been freed from past guilt and reconciled with one another. That starts with the way they treat one another, being able to freely advise and correct their co-workers as brothers and sisters, without having to worry that their objective, but possibly uncomfortable criticism would lead to veiled

f.) nor in the shape of the AACs in the CEVAA society which developed an analogous international structure.

[31] The French nun Francoise Sterlin is a good example of such intercontextual learning. One day, during her service in Congo, she asked herself: "What do I get from the Africans?" A strange, yet understandable question which she answered for herself emphatically in a way which I can well understand after having lived in Tanzania myself some ten years ago: "I discovered", she continued, "the liveliness of the church in Zaire which was just attempting to inculturate the Gospel in her country. I discovered a church sparkling with life, services that dealt with real every-day life, lay people leading local congretations, a bishop and a people who dared to adapt Christian life to the needs of their country. Until today, I have been influenced by witnesses like Cardinal Malula. Although my family and my education were unequivocally Christian, I owe to Africa the desire and the taste of building up church together with others. Only as a foreigner did I discover the significance of my baptism. Africa has converted me to the church." quoted according to H. Müller, Françoise Sterlin – Ordensfrau und Missionarin in Frankreich (*FS – Nun and missionary in France*), in Jahrbuch Mission 2003, p.148 (also recorded in Sundermeier, Mission, ceremonial lecture 2003).

[32] See Nordelbische Evangelisch-Lutherische Kirche, Dokumentation: Internationale Visitation und Konsultation zum Reformprozess der Nordelbischen Evangelisch-Lutherischen Kirche (NEK), Hamburg 2005 (*Church office of the North Elbian Church,Documentation of an international visitation and consultation in relation with a reform process of the church)*, esp. p.15 ff.

allegations of 'colonialism' or, in the other direction, 'under-development'.[33] At the same time this fellowship as believers reconciled in Christ has an effect on the conscious handling of the partners' commonly shared history – a history of mission and church development, but also of violence. This effect may have taken place in an exemplary fashion in commemorative years such as 2004 or 2006, when a living testimony was required in a world "torn" by revenge and violence (UEM Constitution § 2).

Finally, however, this reconciled cooperation has to take on tangible shape in present-day development projects. In the face of the global financial crisis of a hypertrophic economy, there is a growing political recognition that ethical responsibility for business processes can only be achieved by means of a renewed connection between economic, mostly monetary transactions and the material values of supply and trading. But this re-linking can never work without the involvement of each region concerned. In this situation, regional projects carried out by a partnership of churches, businesses and educational institutions such as universities can provide new impulses for self-development of a local society. Issues such as 'youth unemployment' or 'decentralized energy supply' are certainly equally topical in the North and the South, so that joint advisory teams with a high degree of intercultural and inter-regional knowledge and expertise would be just as useful in this field as in the case of congregational formation outlined above.[34]

With specific cooperation in these two fields of church mission the UEM communion can do excellent ecumenical work.

---

33 *Cf.* W. Richebächer, Partnerschaftliche Mission (*Mission in partnership*), Mitarbeiterbrief UEM 1999, pp.14 – 21.

34 *Cf.* a cooperation project between the Evangelical Church of Hesse-Waldeck, the University of Kassel, and business enterprises in the region with the aim of supporting regional structures in Hessen in connection with development projects of partner churches in the South, entitled "Wirtschaften im Dienst der Menschen" (*Economies in the service of humans*), Kassel 2008.

The Theology of Blessing in Missionary Preaching

Fidon Mwombeki

Introduction

In this essay I would like to make three arguments. First, that the 'theology of glory' in so far as it is understood to propagate prosperity or success as a result of faith and faithfulness to God is wrong in missionary preaching. Second, that the 'theology of the cross,' when it explains suffering and poverty as signs of the presence of God in the believers' lives is also wrong in missionary preaching. Third, that instead of the two juxtaposed theologies, a 'theology of blessing' could provide a key to a balanced approach in missionary preaching.

The discussion about gospels of prosperity and of the cross is so ubiquitous that only a brief analysis of their appeal as 'good news' in missionary preaching is necessary. Then I will introduce what I call 'a theology of blessing' arguing that God's blessings are for and on all people regardless of their physical and material situation. And through this approach, the gospel empowers both the rich and the poor to overcome their handicap.

Theology of glory and theology of the cross

The terminologies 'theology of glory' and 'theology of the cross' were contextually coined by Luther in the famous Heidelberg disputation mainly to argue that human beings are totally incapable of fulfilling God's law; their salvation is totally dependent on the act of Jesus on the cross, which they receive only by faith. As it is summarized in Wikipedia:

> For the theologian of glory, we use reason and our own perceptions to increase our knowledge about God and the world. Thus, because an action appears to be good, it must be good. For the theologian of the cross, it is only from the self-revelation of God that we can learn about God and our relation to God – and the most perfect self-revelation of God is God's Word become flesh, Jesus the Christ. Thus even if an action appears good still Christ died on the cross for my sins and sinfulness, so it must not be as good as it appears [1]

However, these theologies have been taken further by theologians to express many different things apart from God's revelation. The theology of the cross

[1] http://en.wikipedia.org/wiki/Theology_of_the_Cross, accessed January 2009.

has been taken as "a key signature for all Christian theology."[2] Many Protestant theologians regard the theology of the cross as an approach and spirit of doing theology that underlies all genuine theology.[3] The theology of glory, however, has not been so much taken up in standard discussions of Luther's theology, except as an opposite of the theology of the cross.

As a Lutheran theologian myself, I agree totally with Luther's thesis at Heidelberg in this regard. God is indeed incomprehensible. Therefore, I have trouble to agree with Luther that God reveals himself *only* through suffering, precisely because just as we *cannot* comprehend the manifestation of God through good things, we cannot either through suffering. God remains God, paradoxical and refusing to be tamed by our theologizing. I have argued earlier that I find it difficult to apply the theology of the cross to understand or justify human suffering.[4]

Prosperity as theology of glory

I am convinced that indeed the triumphalistic prosperity gospel is a theology of glory and therefore unwanted and wrong in missionary preaching. However, its problem is not success or prosperity, but rather to link prosperity with proof of God's favour or revelation. The theology of glory or "prosperity theology"[5] links worldly success with faith, and calls people to repentance so that they shall be endowed with prosperity in its broadest sense as Faith Lugazia says in relation to Africa.[6] In prosperity preaching with its clever use of modern media, this gospel makes some disturbing claims.

---

[2] Jürgen Moltmann, The Crucified God, trans. R.A. Wilson and John Bowden, London: S.C.M. Press Ltd. 1973, p.72.

[3] See broader treatments of this subject in among others, Alister McGrath, Luther's Theology of the Cross, Blackwell Publishing, 1990; Walter von Loewenich, Luther's Theology of the Cross, trans. Herbert A.J. Bouman, Minneapolis: Augsburg 1976; Douglas John Hall, The Cross in our Context: Jesus and the Suffering World, Minneapolis: Fortress Press 2003; Gerhard Forde, On Being a Theologian of the Cross: Reflections on Luther's Heidelberg Disputation, 1518, Grand Rapids: Eerdmans 1997; Robert Kolb, Luther on the Theology of the Cross, in: *Lutheran Quarterly* XVI no. 4 (Winter 2002): pp.443-466.

[4] Fidon R. Mwombeki, The Theology of the Cross: Does it Make Sense to Africans? In: Niels Henrik Gregersen et. al. (eds.), *The Gift of Grace: The Future of Lutheran Theology,* Minneapolis: Fortress 2005, pp.101-116.

[5] Faith K. Lugazia, Empire's Export of Prosperity Theology: Its Impact on Africa, in: Karen L. Bloomquist (ed.), *Being Church in the Midst of Empire: Trinitarian Reflections*, Minneapolis: Lutheran University Press 2007, pp.181-191.

[6] I find some of her analysis anachronistic, and the links with political and economic developments in Africa a bit problematic. For example, it cannot be true that prosperity gospel came to Africa in the 1980s (p.183) but much earlier as she herself shows on p.184.

First, that being a Christian makes your life prosperous. Jesus brings to the believer financial security, physical well-being, professional progress, and a modern life style. Poverty, disease, and lack of progress are problems that people should believe God eliminates. All biblical promises which were promised to Israel as they moved into the holy land are ours as the new Israel. All land, all houses, all cars, all the money belong to God and God wants to give them to believers (Josh 14:9). Jesus has overcome the world (Jn 16:33) and became poor so that you become rich (2Cor 8:9).

Second, that we can know who is a true believer by seeing their physical prosperity: with rich, healthy, intelligent children, promotion at work, or a profitable business. Those who do not prosper do not have the right faith or enough faith. Third, that since success in life depends on the relationship between you and God you can do something about it. Avoid sinful behaviour, pray harder and longer (Mk 9:29), increase your faith (Lk 17:9) and avoid the mistake of Ananias and Sapphira (Acts 5:1-11) of not giving fully what you are prescribed to give (a tithe). In fact, your failure is only your fault.

Those of us contradicting this prosperity gospel sometimes go too far by claiming that those who preach this gospel do so only to defraud their members. Both in the OT and NT, prosperity is in its essence not evil and we should not be skeptical of people living 'good lives.' It is indeed good news to proclaim to people that God actually cares about their situations, about the things they lack in life, about their pain and concerns. We care for those suffering from disease, hunger, thirst, poverty, social stigma, etc. We pray for them so that God actually does something somehow to change their situation. Then if and when God actually does intervene and solves their problems, should we say that there is something wrong with them because they are wealthy or healthy? We cannot honestly think there is something godly about poverty and exclusion.

How should we explain the reality of success? We cannot explain why bad things happen to good people and good things to bad people. Throughout the Bible and in church history it has never been possible to fix God in some template. People like Moses, the judges, kings, the apostles, and later in life people like Martin Luther, Paul Gerhardt, John Calvin, and others in our time have gone through some form of hell in their lives. Despite faith and prayer, Christians still get sick, lack food and a good life; they die early, suffer, fail examinations, get demoted at work, see their houses collapse during earthquakes, have their money stolen, etc. Prosperity gospel is bad news for them since it makes them think that it is their fault, or that they do not believe enough, or that their salvation is not complete because they do not materially or physically prosper.

Suffering as theology of the cross

On the other hand, there are those who push the theology of the cross beyond the revelation of God in Christ as Luther intended, and apply it to address the question of suffering of the followers of Christ. That is questionable. Truly the connection between believers and suffering cannot always be simply wished away. Christians should carry their own crosses, or as Paul figuratively claims, participate in the suffering of Christ. During times of tribulation, this gospel becomes a consolation to those who can do nothing to change their situation.

However, the Bible talks about Christians suffering for the sake of (faith in) Christ. We can hardly say that most of the suffering going on in the world is because of faith. Starvation from drought, women raped by rebels in Congo, elderly mothers struggling to feed orphaned grandchildren because of AIDS, landless poor in Namibia because white farm owners refuse to pay them a legal minimum wage, or Tamil refugees chased out from their areas during the civil war in Sri Lanka – none of this suffering has to do with faith or with Christ.

I find Luther's claim that God chooses to reveal himself in suffering and shame, that we can identify the presence of God only in suffering somewhat dangerous.[7] We cannot limit God's revelation and action only to situations of suffering. If this were the case, the gospel would become a call to asceticism and self-justification. Nobody should be led to believe that because of suffering or want, he or she is in a right relationship with God.

The theology of blessing: a balance and a key?

Christians take blessing seriously. When a pastor visits a home (at least in Africa) people request that he or she does not leave without blessing the home. The pastor is invited to make an invocation at meetings and to pronounce a blessing at different occasions in Christian lives. It does not matter, whether poor or rich, very religious or not, people want to receive blessings from God.

This is because people know God is active in their lives. The rich or the poor come to thank and praise the Lord for blessings. Several bring an offering of thanks to God in the church, and ask the congregation to join in thanksgiving. Sometimes the congregation is not told what these blessings were but they join in thanksgiving. The blessing may be a promotion or pay raise at work, or surviving an accident, or a successful business contract, or a conclusion of a court case, or a child passing an examination, etc. Regardless of their economic or social status, people believe God is responsible for the success.

The concept of blessing can be a balance and a key. On the one hand, it brings good news to the prosperous because it prohibits a temptation to stigmatize prosperity and well-being. People living in prosperity should not be forced to feel guilty as if wealth necessarily came from injustice and evil. A

---

[7] Mwombeki, *op. cit.*, pp.109f.

proper understanding of blessing is good news to the wealthy; they are also under the love of God and God is happy when people are enjoying life. At the same time it rejects the notion that prosperity is a sign of obedience to God, or an approval of God which we earn because of our faith or good morals. We do not earn blessings, for blessings are simply provided by God, without any correlation with one's piety or 'righteousness.'

On the other hand, the theology of blessing pronounces also good news to those who are not that successful in worldly matters, or are suffering. Their lack of success and their suffering is not always due to their own failures, so they should not feel guilty. Neither is it always due to injustice, so they should not fall into the temptation to resent and hate the wealthy. Sometimes, they may find God's presence and blessing even in their suffering. The concept separates salvation from success. Neither the rich nor the poor are justified because of their social situation, but all are covered by the grace of our Lord.

Even though this theology does not answer the question of differences between people, it concludes that God blesses people differently. We cannot explain these differences. In the same family people are born with different capabilities and characters, which at the end make them very different in life. Some are born with a very high IQ and others with a very low IQ. Some are born with inherited, chronic diseases. Some are born in deserts and others in rain forests. Some are born in countries with developed infrastructures while others must spend hours walking to fetch water. Trying to look for reasons why God would allow such differences is falling into the trap of the theology of glory. Here I totally agree with Luther, that what God has not decided to reveal to us should be left just like that.

The meaning of blessing in the Bible

The word root "bless" appears not less than 400 times in the Bible (NRSV), with several meanings. First, it means a promise or assurance for success when it comes from God: at creation when God blessed the first couple (Gen 1), to Abram after election (Gen 12) in which nations through faith share (Gal 3:8-9).

Second, people bless others in which case a blessing is a form of prayer or wish so that God can bless e.g. Jacob to the tribes of Israel (Gen 49); Isaac to Esau and Jacob (Gen 27); David to people (1 Chron 16:2), Solomon (2 Chron 6:3); Simeon to Jesus (Lk 2:34).

Third, people bless things, though this is not common, e.g. blessing a day – making it holy (Gen 2:3, Mk 14:22), or food – making it increase (Mk 6:41).

Fourth, people bless God, a formulation very extensively used throughout the Bible especially in psalms and songs. The formulation "bless the Lord" is to be understood in the sense of "praise the Lord." The Lord does not benefit from people, only that people sing the Lord's praises.

Blessing is understood through how it is manifested in the life of the people. In any case, blessing means success, prosperity in a broad sense (Gen 17:20; 24:1; Deut 28:2-12). Sometimes, it is manifested in increase of wealth and population, e.g. Laban because of Jacob's presence (Gen 24:35); high productivity in the field for Isaac (Gen 26:12); good health (Ex 23:25); or strength as a nation and military victory (Deut 15:6).

As for the question of whether God's blessing is conditional on human behaviour, the Bible is contradictory. Deuteronomy clearly builds on this premise (Deut 11:26-27; 30:16-20), while the book of Job rejects it. But there clearly is no biblical basis to claim that all those who obeyed God became rich or healthy or lived longest. Even the most loyal and faithful believers faced problems, suffering, poverty and even an early and painful death.

Poverty, wealth and the gospel

I will now focus on the aspect of wealth and poverty in light of our understanding of blessings since this aspect is at the centre of the prosperity gospel as well as the gospel of suffering.

Poverty and the poor in the Bible

It is not possible to discuss extensively the issues of poverty and wealth here, but I will try to give a summary of their treatment in the Bible. J. David Pleins gives us a great biblical analysis of the terms "poor" and "poverty" in the Old Testament.[8] He surveys the six Hebrew words for "poor" or "poverty",[9] which denote basically two meanings: a lack of economic resources and material goods as well as political and legal powerlessness and oppression. The poor constituted a "diverse body of social actors: small farmers, day laborers, construction workers, beggars, debt slaves, village dwellers."[10] He makes an observation that not the etymology of the words but rather the context and their use provide a basis for understanding their meaning since even various authors of different biblical books utilize the words in different senses. After a lengthy analysis on the basis of different biblical textual traditions, he concludes that poverty is a decisive issue in the prophetic and legal traditions, which show the harsh living conditions of the poor: hunger and thirst, homelessness, exploitation, legal injustice, lack of land, etc.[11] Prophets protest against the oppression of the poor by the rulers. The legal texts seek to ensure social well-being of the poor through the redistribution of wealth and restrictions regarding slave labour, all intended to ease the burdens of the poor. The liturgical traditions (e.g. Psalms) offer prayers on their behalf and present a God who assists the poor in their distress. In the book of Proverbs, to the wise poverty is

---

[8] J. David Pleins, "Poor, Poverty" in *The Anchor Bible Dictionary*, vol. 5, ed. David Noel Freedman, New York: Doubleday, 1992: 402-414.

[9] They include: *'ebyoen, dal, mahsoer, misken, raesh, 'aeni and 'anawim; p.403.*

[10] *Ibid.*, p.402.

[11] *Ibid.*, p.413

either a result of laziness or a result of God's judgment. There is a notable scarcity of the language of poverty in the pentateuchal and historical books, even in the case of Exodus.

A NT analysis is provided by Thomas D. Hanks[12] on the basis of different authors of the NT books in relation to all the words *ptochos, hysterematos, endees, chreia* which generally connote "persons and groups lacking (totally or in some degree) the necessities of life: food, drink, clothing, shelter, health, land / employment, freedom, dignity and honour, etc."[13] He starts with James due to his close affinity to the OT, who prophetically denounces oppression and abuse of wealth. James does not, however, advocate a total abandonment of home, family possessions and trade.[14] Going through the so-called Q sources to the Hebrews, Hanks concludes that there is considerable diversity in the NT. Any attempts to harmonize the NT teaching and draw general conclusions are not fair. Whether defending the "Christian virtue of capitalism" or socialism / communism, one must be highly selective and use "control texts" often lacking in careful exegesis.[15] Hanks makes some cautious remarks on the "emerging theologies of liberation" as well as socio-economic and anthropological studies of the NT about the debate regarding the poor.

In general, poverty is an issue that is treated extensively in the Bible. Poverty is a reality in a society, whether Christian or not. It is undesired, but it has never gone away. There is unfortunately no call or programme to end it, but there is a lot of how to handle its endless presence. What we find is unfortunately the impression that the Bible speaks "about" the poor, and "for" the poor, meaning the subjects of the message are not poor themselves.

Wealth and the wealthy

There is not so much written about the wealthy. We have seen above how the 'prosperity gospel' is criticized in the mainline churches while it is propagated in some charismatic churches. The World Council of Churches together with its related (Europe based) development organizations sponsored a study process in the late 1990s to document 24 case studies mostly in the developing countries under the code-name: Project 21.[16] In the foreword to the report, Dr. Konrad Raiser, then General Secretary of WCC says: "Even though the biblical tradition is much more explicit about excessive wealth and the ways it can corrupt human community, the Christian churches have been reluctant to

[12] Thomas D. Hanks, „Poor, Poverty" in *The Anchor Bible Dictionary* vol. 5, ed. David Noel Freedman. New York: Doubleday, 1992: 414-424.

[13] *Ibid.*, p.415.

[14] *Ibid.*, p.416

[15] *Ibid.*, p.422

[16] Michael Taylor, Christianity, Poverty and Wealth: Findings of 'Project 21', WCC Publications, London: SPCK and Geneva: WCC 2003.

address the ethical and spiritual issues related to wealth."[17] The report explores both poverty and wealth, and goes as far as to recommend an "economy of enough" whereby there should be a socially and ethically acceptable limit of wealth beyond which accumulation becomes greed and is no longer ethically and socially acceptable.[18]

In the Bible, clearly wealth is in many instances a blessing since God makes people successful by increasing their possessions. Jesus makes no categorical condemnation of those who are wealthy. He loves them as well; he goes into their homes just as he goes into the homes of the modest ones. He answers their questions, and he responds to their requests. In the Acts and the epistles they are noted by name, especially those who supported the mission of the early church, e.g. by hosting the first house churches in their large homes.

At the same time, God is very explicitly rebuking, instructing, even judging the rich for irresponsible use of their wealth and for unjust means through which they became rich, e.g. corruption and fraud. He condemns their misuse of political and social power against the poor in society. He condemns their exploitation and oppression of the poor. It is in this sense that God pronounces judgment against the rich and stands for the poor. He instructs the rich never to misuse the political and social power that is associated with wealth. He calls them to share their wealth with the needy.

Gospel to the poor, gospel to the wealthy

'Project 21' makes the following observation concerning the teaching of the churches about poverty and wealth:

> The teaching of the churches is varied and confusing. It can be organized into four types: Spiritualizing' which tends to ignore social issues and accept poverty; 'prosperity' which regards riches as rewards for faith; 'liberation' which makes freedom from injustice the focus of the gospel; and 'holistic' which looks for right relations all round between God, 'man'[sic] and creation.[19]

Limiting blessing to spiritual aspects is wrong because God is interested also in our material and physical well-being, although not always as a result of our obedience to him, or our faith in Christ. Not all believers enjoy material prosperity or permanent well-being. In this sense liberation theology has great merits, stressing that material prosperity is supposed to be for all as a blessing from God. But the gospel cannot be limited to freedom from injustice only. God's blessings are spiritual as well. Not all who are free from social and economic injustice enjoy the blessings of God. Wealth does not guarantee

---

17 *Ibid.*, p.ix.

18 *Ibid.*

19 Ibid., p.25.

satisfaction and peace in Christ. The wealthy still need the gospel about their relationship with God. A holistic approach is definitely the right approach, whereby the gospel is proclaimed to all for holistic liberation.

Conclusion

We have argued that both a prosperity gospel and the sentimentalization of suffering are wrong. God has poured blessings for all. The blessings of God are supposed to be enjoyed by all in all aspects of life. The problem is that these blessings are not enjoyed equally by all God's people for different reasons.

Poverty robs people of their dignity, subjecting them to oppression and exploitation. God calls people to love the poor and to champion their fight for justice instead of taking advantage of them in any way, because they are entitled to share in the blessings of God to the world. The poor do not share in God's blessings mainly because of the human injustices that can be overcome. But God does not hate or condemn the wealthy simply because of their wealth. Wealth is part of God's blessings. And the poverty of individual people is not always a result of exploitation by the wealthy, as if the poor were always innocent. Many times the poor contribute to their own poverty as well through their habits and wrong choices (e.g. too large families, laziness, wasteful spending, etc.) In other cases, poverty is caused by environmental factors (e.g. in desert or flood-prone areas).

However, in order to enable all people to share God's blessings, we are called to dismantle unjust economic, social and political structures and systems that hinder some people to share the blessings of God fully. Because of our faith, we are called to support diaconic action – feed the hungry, clothe the naked, house the homeless wherever they are, to give them a chance to share in God's blessings to the world. Since diaconic interventions are unsustainable and sometimes dehumanizing, we are called to work on systemic transformation to ensure people's dignity and honour and remove obstacles for their own meaningful sharing in God's blessings.

The concept of blessings enables us to pronounce the gospel of empowerment to the poor. They should be able to see the world differently: not only as victims but also as those endowed by God in different ways. They should be empowered to see the world full of blessings that they should responsibly take part of – shunning laziness and ignorance, and feeling the power of God within them to work for themselves to change their situation. There are far too many people in the world who suffer because of laziness, excessive alcoholism, from men's exploitation of women and children through unjust cultural traditions, etc. Even though these people may be poor, within their own communities they are not doing enough, even though they are able to, to change their situation.

The wealthy as well need the gospel of Jesus Christ. They need to be saved from their self-centeredness and materialism. They need to be aware of the responsibility they have to help others also to share in God's blessings, knowing that whatever they have is part of God's blessings for all. They need to be reminded of God's condemnation of injustice, greed, and arrogance. But they should never be made to feel guilty about working hard, about making intelligent investment decisions that are profitable, about frugality and responsible stewardship of what God has entrusted them with. These people need to feel good and be thankful to God about their success, not to feel guilty about it. Therefore, the theology of blessing brings good news to all, just as God is God of all.

Response by Sören Asmus

The impulse of the Gospel as good news addressing both the poor and the rich and the need to take both social realities into consideration is strongly supported by the recent exegetical observations in the area of cultural history. For the Gospels and the New Testament as a whole it could be shown that there is a mutual exchange of upper and lower class values. While the members of the upper classes learn the value of co-operation and solidarity, the poor learn the value of virtues and thus are able to lead their lives with self-control.

This is to say that in the Mediterranean culture of the times around Jesus and the early church the Christian communities valued the aspect of *agape*, of love to the neighbour and the faithful very highly, expecting all Christians to share their possessions and possibilities according to the needs of the community. These values were rather practiced in the lower classes at that time, but now they were made obligatory for the upper class Christians too. On the other hand, no-one expected lower class people to stick to the classical virtues as honesty, control over emotions, and proper behaviour. However, as the Sermon on the Mount as well as the advice in the Letters for families and communities show, these rather upper class values were now also expected from all Christians.

In regard to a theology of blessing both are needed, too: the awareness that blessing is appreciated and a gift which should be shared as well as the understanding that regardless of one's own social status the gift of a faithful and thus virtuous life is in itself a blessing, even if it is not accompanied by external riches. Thus the blessing becomes a critical function while still being a sign of the love of God towards all of his creation. While a successful economic or private life, health and children, fulfillment in work etc. are truly blessings which should be received from a merciful God, they are still bound to the value of *agape* and solidarity. On the other hand the life in line with the ethos of the Christian life and its values is in itself a liberation from temptations and expectations of the society, and in receiving the reality of justification by faith a blessing from God is already at work in the life of each Christian, so that there is no need to question faith as such. Still no true Christian community is thinkable without solidarity and love, so that the blessing of the one will be shared in some way with the others.

Thus the churches need a balanced theology of blessing to encompass the whole of the Christian life in its teaching and spirituality.

PART TWO

MISSION SPIRITUALITY

The Holy Spirit and Mission in the Church Today: The Acts of the Apostles

Priscille Djomhoué

Acts of the Apostles: the Gospel of the Holy Spirit

Testimony is the essential element of missionary activity, and the book of Acts in the New Testament gives us many resources in this field. In the first chapter, the risen Christ says to the apostles:

> But you will receive power when the Holy Spirit has come upon you; and you will be my witnesses in Jerusalem, in all Judea and Samaria, and to the ends of the earth. (Acts1:8).

These words contain at the same time a promise and a mission: the promise of the reception of the Holy Spirit and the mission which is conferred on the disciples. This mission consists of being witness to the risen Christ in Jerusalem, in all Judaea and Samaria and to the ends of the earth. According to Luke, the reception of the Holy Spirit is first, and the mission conferred to the disciples is second. In fact, the disciples will be able to move only after having received the Holy Spirit who is the authority without which their mission does not have a direction. Their success depends at the same time on their obedience and on the impulse that the Spirit gives them.

In the New Testament we have 379 uses of the word *pneuma* (Spirit): 19 in the Gospel of Matthew, 23 in that of Mark, and 24 in John. Luke is the author who spoke the most about the *pneuma*: there are 106[1] occurrences in the diptych Luke-Acts, 36 in the Gospel and 70 in the Acts of the Apostles where he is mentioned in 20 chapters out of 28, and at least 7 times in certain chapters (8 and 19). Luke "gave him such a place that the Acts are to be considered as the Gospel of the Spirit."[2] The activity of the Holy Spirit is spread in a series of facts in which God intervenes to carry out his plan of salvation:[3]

---

[1] H. Bachmann. W. A, Claby *Computer Konkordanz zum Novum Testamentum Graece von Nestle- Aland 26. Auflage und zum Greek New Testament, 3rd ed.*, Berlin: Walter De Gruyter, 1980, p.1558-1559.

[2] Daniel Marguerat, *La première histoire du christianisme (Les Actes des apôtres)*, p.149.

[3] Joseph Doré, *Dictionnaire de théologie chrétienne: les grands thèmes de la foi*, Paris, Desclée, 1979, p.130.

> The keynote of the Acts of the Apostles is the expansion of the church through the power of the Holy Spirit. (...) Without this they would have been empty and powerless to communicate Christ.[4]

The role of the Holy Spirit in mission

Building the church

Jesus says: "John baptized with water, but you will be baptized with the Holy Spirit not many days from now." (Acts 1:5) This promised baptism will be realized in the event of Pentecost. Placing Pentecost at the beginning of the Acts of the Apostles, Luke wants to show that the Spirit is at the origin of the birth of the church, and that it is under his impulse that the witnesses have to work. At Pentecost (2:1-13), the Spirit is visible and audible: in the noise of a hurricane, in the flames of fire appearing on each of the twelve, in the din which assembles the multiple languages. The group of twelve loses its Galilean particularism and becomes the core of the universal church (v.6-11).

Guide of the mission

The Holy Spirit appears as the inspirer of the word, the organizer and leader of the internal life of the church, and the guide of the mission: the seven must be "full of the Spirit and of wisdom" (6:3) to manage the communal charity. But, actually, they will act as witnesses of the word. Stephen is a man " full of faith and the Holy Spirit" (6:5), but on this basis, the Holy Spirit seizes him when he acts to testify (6:10; 7:55), especially in front of the Sanhedrin. The Spirit is at the same time a latent presence in the people qualified for testimony, and an impulse related to the events. He gives assurance above all: 2:29 (Peter); 4:13 (apostles), 4:29.31 (community); 28:31 (Paul). The Spirit does not replace the witness, but he pushes him or her to engage by giving him "words and wisdom".

In the Acts of the Apostles, the Holy Spirit directs the steps in the mission of the church. He empowers the missionaries to preach the Gospel with audacity, unites the community, breaks cultural barriers and intolerance, works against tribal discrimination by encouraging openness, and reconciles divergent parties in the field of the mission: Peter preaches to Cornelius (chapter 10); a new church comes into being in Gentile Antioch (chapter 11); Barnabas and Saul are sent forth (chapter 13); the Jerusalem council (chapter 15); mission expands to Europe (16).

---

4 Son Yong Yo, Holy Spirit and Mission, http://cwmpcts.org/main/cwm-resources/study/mission-theology/01mission-theology/yjsong-e001.htm, accessed 10 January 2009.

Empowering the disciples to preach the Gospel with audacity

The Spirit gives the aptitude to speak with audacity. By doing this, he is at the heart of the miracles. He has always something to do with the proclamation of the word, he is the Spirit of prophecy; in the speech of Peter on Pentecost, the eruption of the Spirit is understood like an event of prophecy (2:17). The Spirit does not lead to glossolalia, but to the communication of the word. In the house of Cornelius, "they heard them speaking in tongues and extolling God": (10:46). In Ephesus, when Paul had laid his hands on the disciples, "they spoke in tongues and prophesied" (19:6). Preaching is dependent on the work of the Spirit: it "is filled of Spirit" that Peter speaks to the people of Jerusalem (4:8). The wisdom of the Spirit gives irresistible force to the word of Stephen (6:10), and similarly to Barnabas in Antioch (11:24). The witnesses are martyred, threatened and struck (21:30-33), they are imprisoned (12:3-4) and killed (12:1). As opposed to what one could have expected, it is in the suffering that some of them express the zeal to advertise the Gospel (22:6-13). Facing threats, the apostles answer: "We must obey God rather than any human authority" (5:29). The behaviour of the witnesses, their very fidelity, is related to the impulse of the Spirit.

Uniting the community

The growing first church community is united under the benevolence of the Spirit: "They devoted themselves to the apostles' teaching and fellowship, to the breaking of bread and the prayers. Awe came upon everyone, because many wonders and signs were being done by the apostles. All who believed were together and had all things in common" (2:42-45) and among them there was no poor (4:34).

The episode of Ananias and Saphira (5:1-12) is significant; it translates the benevolence of the Spirit into the unity of the community. The couple who sold a property for the profit of the community, but declared only part of the sum, are uncovered by Peter and fall dead at his feet. The punishment of death is justified by the attempt of the couple to break the harmony of the community (5:3).

Mobilising the missionary and breaking cultural and ethnic barriers

The demonstration of the Spirit at Pentecost has the character of a universal promulgation of the message. Luke wanted to represent all the people of the earth by enumerating them but the people listed in the story of the coming of the Holy Spirit are still, at this moment, faithful Jews and proselytes of the diaspora, then installed in Jerusalem. By leading Philip towards the Ethiopian eunuch, the Spirit spreads the Gospel further beyond (8:29, 39). It is the Spirit who brings Peter to Cornelius' house, to sympathisers of Judaism (10:19-20; 11:12). The Spirit is at the basis of the missionary activity of the church of Antioch towards the Gentiles and the missionary travels of Paul (13:2-4). He prevents Paul from working only in Asia Minor and through this pushes the mission towards Europe (16:6-10). This is the last change of course necessary for the Gospel to reach "the end of the earth". How did the Spirit work concretely to break the barriers and to increase the openness of the Jews?

What is the real problem in the story of Peter and Cornelius? The answer can be found both in these words of Peter to Cornelius and his relatives: "You yourselves know that it is unlawful for a Jew to associate with or to visit a Gentile" (10:28a); and in those of the Christians in Jerusalem to Peter on the other hand: "Why did you go to uncircumcised men and eat with them?"(11:3) The problem is not the conversion or the baptism of Cornelius, but the transgression of the Jewish laws which prohibit relationships with the Gentiles. By bringing together under one roof Peter and Cornelius, each of whom can be seen as a representative of his background, the Spirit overcomes this law. The account of Acts 10-11:18 is meant to break the separation which existed between Jews and Gentiles, therefore, the story is constructed not like an account of conversion,[5] but as a narrative of bringing together. In other words, the text itself can be understood as the work of the Holy Spirit who establishes cordial relations between those who do not belong to the same ethnic grouping.

In the visions of Peter, the Spirit is at the origin of the change of orientation, it is he who actually mobilises Peter towards Cornelius:

> While Peter was still thinking about the vision, the Spirit said to him, "Look, three men are searching for you. Now get up, go down, and go with them without hesitation; for I have sent them." (10:19b-20).

This order of the Spirit which mobilises Peter towards Cornelius and towards the Gentile world, is recounted by Peter in his report to the Christians in Jerusalem: "The Spirit told me to go with them and not to make a distinction between them and us (...) we entered the man's house" (11:12). This passage clearly tells us that the missionary is not always sent to a person or a community who share his or her religious convictions or cultural behaviour. Mission under these conditions is difficult, because it requires that the missionary personally is released from obstructions which would prevent him or her from functioning. In the case of Peter, religious culture is a true barrier which needs to be broken down in several steps: initially the voice which he resists, then the Holy Spirit who mobilizes him and leads him to cross the barriers of a culture and a religion in which he had grown up. The Spirit is the one who organises the mission and who mobilizes Gentile towards Jew, and vice versa. He is the agent of openness on both sides:

---

[5] I think that Acts 10-11:18 is not a story of conversion at all: Peter is a believer, Cornelius also, with the characterisation of the latter made clear in Acts 10:2. The vision of Cornelius is clearly defined as an answer to his faith (10:3-5).

> And as I began to speak, the Holy Spirit fell upon them just as it had upon us at the beginning. And I remembered the word of the Lord, how he had said, 'John baptised with water, but you will be baptised with the Holy Spirit.' If then God gave them the same gift that he gave us when we believed in the Lord Jesus Christ, who was I that I could hinder God? (11:15-17)

Conciliating divergent parties in the mission field

In the church in Africa and particularly in Cameroon, it is not easy for the pastors to work together in mission in the same environment. Due to the great number of Christians, some parishes are assigned two or more pastors. But in this situation, ethnic and cultural differences are often the cause of misunderstanding and division among the missionaries (pastors). Also, at the general level of the church, cultural diversities are at the root of some rivalries and the division of the church in tribal sections even in the cosmopolitan towns. The book of Acts also addressed such issues, and the conference at Jerusalem is one of the great examples where the author shows how the Spirit engineers the bringing together of divergent parties.

The conference at Jerusalem is all about the unity of the church as far as theology and doctrine are concerned. The first point of view is presented at the beginning of the story (15:1): the Jews require that Gentiles follow the Law of Moses. The second point of view is carried by Peter, Paul and Barnabas: Peter's language takes account of the experience that he had before with Cornelius (Acts 10-11): he recalls to the Christians of Jerusalem the event of Caesarea, stressing the fact that the Gentiles had received the Holy Spirit like the Jews. Clearly, God does not discriminate between Jews and Gentiles (15:9). Peter's argument is progressive: after having posited that God does not discriminate, Peter recalls salvation by faith and grace which means that nobody can be saved by obedience of the Law. In this way, imposing the yoke of circumcision on the Gentiles and expecting their total obedience of Moses' Law would be an attempt to try God. Peter thus opposes the circumcision of the Gentiles. His standpoint is supported by Paul and Barnabas when they testify to what God, through them, has done for the Gentiles. The solution of the problem raised in the conference at Jerusalem is thus to recall the role of the Holy Spirit which is to unite divergent poles (15:8-9).

The Holy Spirit as Agent of Renewal and Openness

The Acts of the Apostles paint the image of a Christian community in full, a community where the word of God is communicated effectively, and a community where the action of the Spirit is visible through miracles. One can see the importance of the Spirit in this early Christian church: He leads the missionaries to develop a new vision of the world, exceeding tribal, cultural and racial barriers to spread the Gospel in an unknown universe. The Spirit is the one who renews the missionaries and who also helps them to renew their working methods continuously by adapting them to each context:

> It is the Holy Spirit who empowers us for service in the Kingdom of God. The renewal of missionary zeal in our time will entail a rediscovery of the person and works of the Holy Spirit in the Christian mission[6].

The Holy Spirit and mission in the church

The world is experiencing remarkable changes today, and the problems of antiquity, while not totally overcome, do not arise any more in the same manner. This situation requires a change of paradigm for mission. But the churches in the world today, particularly the mainline churches, are decreasing: their parishes are getting emptier, and the Christians seem dissatisfied with the actions of the church in the society. Vis-à-vis this decline, how can the Acts of the Apostles inspire a re-launching of mission? Do the revival churches, to which many Christians from the mainline churches flock, have a solution to propose? In other words, how can we reconsider this third person of the Trinity who is now not much considered in the mainline churches; this third person who made the mission successful in the early church and who is the reason of the emergence of Pentecostal churches today?

The mainline churches and the Holy Spirit in Cameroon today: the situation

In Cameroon today, we face a situation in which many families are divided because some members have left the mainline churches for a Pentecostal one. A student at the Faculty of Protestant Theology in Yaoundé wrote a dissertation in which she analyzed the experiences of her family.[7] She is from a family of ten children, the youngest of which is 26 years old. This student is actually the only one in her family who has remained a mainline Protestant. Some of her brothers and sisters founded a community with Pentecostal tendencies, and the others simply registered with new churches. This situation is typical of many Cameroonian families today.

Even the Christians who remain in the mainline churches often attend meetings and prayers in the Pentecostal churches during the week, and only go to their church of origin on Sunday. It is striking that conservative mainline Protestants will call such people sectarianists.

Why do people leave the mainline churches? Several reasons explain this movement. First of all, there is the fraternal warmth lived out in the Pentecostal milieu: worship is alive, and people experience the fullness of the Holy Spirit.

---

6 Son Yong Yo, Holy Spirit and Mission, in http://cwmpcts.org/main/cwm-resources/study/mission-theology/01mission-theology/yjsong-e001.htm, accessed 10 January 2009.

7 Albertine Tchoulack, *Controverse sur le vécu du Saint esprit au sein de l'EEC*, Mémoire de licence, juin 2007, p.1.

The Holy Spirit is the agent of renewal who breaks monotony and makes everything always new and attractive. In these churches, the space is opened to every Christian to express and to testify to what the Holy Spirit has done in his or her life, and how this Holy Spirit is orienting the life in the church community. F. van der Mensbrugghe rightly observed that:

> Pentecostalism reaches the person on levels that other churches do not reach, those of the religious, the emotional, and the pre-conscious."[8]

One of the reasons that explain the success of Pentecostal churches in Cameroon is that the Holy Spirit about whom one speaks little in the mainline churches occupies a dominating place in theology and practice, to the detriment (unfortunately) of Christology: it is the Spirit who vivifies, who awakes and distributes extraordinary gifts. In this paragraph, I will not be analysing Pentecostal pneumatology from a critical point of view. What I would like to stress is the light which it brings to the mainline churches while reminding them that they grant an insufficient place to the third person of the Trinity whose role is to renew the church and mission. In other words, what will the instituted churches gain by reconsidering the Spirit as a very important factor or their mission? How can the churches reconsider the Spirit as this authority who will enable them to answer existential problems of mission? The mission must answer to the real and specific problems of the people to whom the missionary relates.

Empowering mission by reconsidering the place of the Holy Spirit as an agent of renewal in the church today

The mission to carry the witness of Jesus Christ to the ends of the earth is still valid today. But it is no longer possible to understand mission only as the displacement of an envoy from one country to another, from the North to the South and vice versa. The North and the South must collaborate, but the mission must start in the local community (Jerusalem symbolically taken as the starting point), in our own community and must address the actual problems of the people: mission must take up the multiform challenges, for example in Africa, of tribalism, health, poverty, climate change and so on. The Holy Spirit who is the catalyst of this mission will give in Africa and in Cameroon its dynamics and its orientation so that this mission will not be closed and monotonous. The Spirit will prevent the missionary from being confined to a particular tribe, from working for those coming from his own geographical and familial environment by enlightening him like Peter (Acts 10:34-35). This orientation of this mission, both in themes and content, must be contextual

[8] Françoise van der Mensbrugghe, *Le mouvement Charismatique,* Genève, Labor et Fides, 1981, p.6. Translation from French by the author.

today; it must meet or adapt to the needs of the local communities, those to whom the good news is addressed. This aspect, in my opinion, seems to be lacking alarmingly today in Cameroon, in Africa and in some parts of the world. However, the orientation of the mission towards crucial problems of the Christians is not possible without the illumination which comes from the Holy Spirit. Indeed, the perpetual renewal which gives the missionary and the church the ability to assume effectively their testimony is not possible without the action of the Spirit who regenerates. Finally, it is the success of the mission at the level of the local community which gives the necessary impulse to extend it outside.

MISSION SPIRITUALITY

Roberta Rominger

Introduction

The mission is God's. Its arena is the whole created universe. By virtue of their creation in the image of God, and by God's gracious choice, human beings have a role to play in God's enterprise. Directed by God-given visions of how the world would be if God's will were truly done, human mission engagement endeavours to incarnate God's love, justice, healing and hope in the world we know. Measured against the scale of God's intentions, human beings are small and weak, hampered by fear and inadequacy. Their lives are fragile and short. It is ludicrous to think that God's vision could ever be realised by human agency. But for reasons beyond our understanding, God seeks our partnership, includes us in the dreaming, and uses our efforts with results that change the world and give meaning to our lives.

For Christians, mission finds its perfect expression in the life, death and resurrection of Jesus Christ. He was divine and human, one with God in the vision that gives mission its substance but one with us in expressing his vocation through human action. Christians know themselves invited to embody Christ's ongoing ministry in their own witness and action through the guidance and power of the Holy Spirit. Mission is not the imitation of a great leader who lived long ago, nor the application of a set of values and teachings from one generation to another. It is the continuing incarnation of a Saviour who is alive in and through the people who, collectively, are his body.

This paper explores the dynamics of living the Christ-life in the experience of ordinary Christians. It is offered against the background of the urgency of God's mission in a world threatened by climate change, corrupt economic systems, drastic extremes of wealth and poverty, the ravages of HIV/Aids, and violent conflicts.

Spirituality

Spirituality "concerns the whole of human life, viewed in terms of a conscious relationship with God, in Jesus Christ, through the indwelling of the Holy Spirit and within a community of believers".[1]

Such a definition reclaims a word which, in popular usage, is subject to a host of distortions. In common usage, "spirituality" is seen as pertaining to the

---

[1] David Cornick, *Letting God be God*, London: Dartman, Longman & Todd, 2008, p.7.

inner life, as opposed to life in the world. It points to "being", as opposed to "doing". Since mission is clearly about doing, the juxtaposition of "mission" with "spirituality" immediately sets up the expectation of a long list of dualities: spirit vs. body; soul vs. flesh; spiritual vs. physical; abstract vs. concrete; imagination vs. reality; faith vs. politics. Behind these oppositions lies another set which is even more insidious: prayer vs. action; Mary vs. Martha; sacred vs. profane; pure vs. defiled; eternal vs. temporal; heaven vs. earth.

There is no place for such dualities in a physical world infused by a living God. Nevertheless, they do ring true to human experience. There is a brokenness in us that recognises a division between our inner and outer lives, our "being" vs. our "doing". Some of us are born with an in-built preference for activism and others for contemplation.

This brokenness is exacerbated in a church whose worship life focuses inward, only then urging people to engage in "mission" as an optional and often unpopular extra. The sickness pervades the world of mission as well, where too often the point is to get out and do something, whether or not that "something" is God-directed. Mission at its worst can even be an expression of an atheist mindset: there is no God, or at least no God that matters, so we'd better get on and do what needs to be done ourselves. Such mission, marked by drive and determination, lacks the grace that always characterises the work of God.

Contrast this with a story from a current British mission. Traditional churchgoing has been in decline for many years in Western Europe. In Liverpool, a large city struggling to make the transition to new forms of livelihood after the collapse of its industrial economy, the mighty Methodist Central Hall faced closure. In a previous generation it had drawn hundreds of worshippers to the city centre and hosted a wide range of midweek activities, but successive ministries had been unable to reverse the decline in worship attendance. In the late 1990's Central Hall closed. But rather than withdraw from the city centre, the Methodist Church appointed a minister, the Rev. Dr. Barbara Glasson, to plant something new. She was given free licence to try to discern what the shape of God's mission might be in a context where the traditional methods had failed.

What would any of us do with such an assignment? The temptation was to attempt high-energy evangelism or church planting according to one of the many models available from other people and places. That way, given enough hard work, there would hopefully be something to show for the denomination's resources and trust. But this would have been an expression of that functional atheism: there isn't any God to direct this, so I need to do something myself.

Instead, Dr. Glasson chose to trust God. She immersed herself both in God and in the city, and for the first year she simply walked the streets, met the people who live and work in the city centre, and reflected and prayed as she observed the changing seasons and moods of the city. In her wanderings God gave her a word, "bread". She didn't know what it meant, but in time she found herself led to invite some of her new friends to make bread with her. This simple action grew into a ministry that has now touched the lives of hundreds of people, from homeless people and asylum seekers to city bankers and university professors. They meet in a shop front "church", and they make bread together, and they talk of God. While the bread is rising they share in simple Bible study and worship. They exercise a presence in the city centre where the welcome is unconditional, human need is met with the compassion and wisdom of Christ, and a Christian community is formed out of a band of unlikely individuals.[2]

For human action to be true mission, it must be the expression of God's purpose and power and not mere human do-gooding. Prayer and action must unite in human lives offered to God. Prayer without action can be narcissistic in the mould of too much contemporary "spirituality". Action without prayer can be misguided in any one of hundreds of directions. The two belong together if Christian mission is to be authentic and effective in fulfilling God's intentions.

One author goes even farther:

> Any experience of Christ that does not lead us to share his passionate concern for others is misunderstood or simply imagined no matter how powerful or life-changing it may be. If, on the other hand, our experience of Christ leads us to a regard for others and a willingness to risk time and energy in the service of human need, then that experience has met the primary test of authenticity. Spiritual experience is the liberation of the self from preoccupation with itself. It is the beginning of freedom to care about others with abandon.[3]

Wisdom from the tradition

The Christian tradition offers time-honoured tools for the cultivation of the Christian life. The list will be familiar: personal and corporate worship, prayer, Bible reading, the sacraments, alms-giving or charity, fasting and feasting. These are called means of grace because they are channels for a personal encounter with God. Together they constitute a rule of life designed to form us in the image of Christ.

An international multicultural church will have many stories to share about how these traditional means of grace find expression in the churches of today. Worship finds new heights and depths through our different cultural expressions. Bible study is newly revelatory when someone from a different perspective shares what they see. Communion is electrifying when east and west, north and south gather around the table with Christ as their host, and their unity in him is a tangible reality. The challenge of the south has pressed the

---

[2] Barbara Glasson, *Mixed-Up Blessing: A new encounter with being church*, Peterborough: Inspire, 2006.

[3] Howard Rice, *Reformed Spirituality*, Louisville: Westminster John Knox Press, 1991, p.165.

north to reconsider the practice of charity, with justice as an essential expression of the love of God.

East or west, north or south, the tradition comes alive when people realise that they are not simply going through the motions in conforming to the practices they have inherited, but connecting with a power that will transform their lives and, through them, the life of the world.

Reuniting traditional spiritual formation with mission

Mission in the sense of sharing in God's purposes for the world is all but absent from the list of traditional spiritual disciplines. The church, therefore, must bear its share of responsibility for the mindset that sees "being" and "doing" as separate concerns. The tradition would seem to encourage people to attend to their Christian formation in a protected environment, free of distractions and anything that might derail them prematurely, following the prescribed path to its promised outcome. In this approach fledgling Christians take on challenges as and when they are capable of meeting them without being overwhelmed. They are insulated from anything that might threaten their steady, cautious progress.

Jesus took a very different approach with his disciples. He did not take them away into a church sanctuary for careful nurturing in the faith prior to exposing them to Christian living. On the contrary, he invited their presence and participation from the beginning of his ministry and taught them along the way. This was learning by doing. He threw them into situations they were not equipped to handle and confronted them with challenges that raised questions they could not answer and problems they could not solve. He led them to Jerusalem long before they understood why his death was necessary and what it would mean. He left them to work out the implications of the resurrection without the benefit of an instruction manual.

Following the example of Jesus with his disciples, the programme for Christian formation should be expanded to include friendship, love, laughter, proclamation, healing, exorcism, encounter, welcome, challenge, rejection, encouragement, reflection, correction, conflict, protest, defiance, and hard work. The result from the beginning is a unity of action and character. Faith in God is not theoretical but a lived experience. Community is not a vague ideal but a bonding forged in facing challenges side by side where brother and sister know that they can depend upon one another and that if necessary they would lay down their lives for each other[4].

A Christian life modelled after the ministry of Jesus keeps its focus in the moment and pays attention deeply to people and events. Since God can only be encountered and the Spirit's promptings can only be obeyed in the present

[4] John 15:13.

moment, this simple but challenging practice should be at the centre of a mission spirituality. We must listen, watch and receive, treating people with the respect we would pay to Christ himself were he standing before us. We must be attuned to the moment, constantly asking, Where is God? What is God doing here? What is God saying?

Such an approach breaks with tradition by giving explicit authority to the experience of ordinary human beings. Barbara Glasson speaks for many feminist theologians in defending this approach:

> Usually theologians talk of dialectic between tradition, experience, Scripture and reason and different strands of theology give different points of embarkation. I want to encourage you to begin with experience, because it is the place where everyone can get in on the conversation... Then there is the need to hold the Scriptures and tradition alongside the experiences, not to correct them or interpret them in a set way but rather so that they can shed light upon each other.[5]

Christianity was born when the disciples of Jesus began to tell their stories, the fruit of their personal experience, and others discovered the Holy Spirit as a reality in their experience too. Mission spirituality calls us to see ourselves as characters in the current chapter of the Acts of the Apostles, called into partnership by a living God who wants to act in and through us. We must stand tall with the courage of people who know that they know God – but with the humility of those who never forget that they know God only in part.

The traditional practices of the church take on deeper meaning against this background. Worship becomes a celebration of the community's life in God. Prayer becomes an honest searching before God of all the needs and gifts of the day. Bible study becomes companionship with previous generations of seekers whose experience can interpret and inform our own.[6] Calvin's vision that every Christian home should be a mini-monastery[7] comes alive.

Intentional practices also have a role to play because the transformation of our minds and hearts into the mind and heart of Christ is a matter of human dedication as well as divine action. "Spiritual journeying," says one writer, "blends utter determination with unrelenting effort, tapping deeply every ounce of stamina and the fullness of human *effort*, while, in a dance of delicate balance, is fully dependent on *grace*, surrender, letting go, and yielding to reliance on God."[8]

---

[5] Glasson, *op.cit.*, p.28.

[6] Howard E. Friend, Jr., *Gifts of an Uncommon Life*, Virginia: Alban Institute, 2008, p.7.

[7] Rice, *op.cit.*, p.60.

[8] Friend, *op. cit.*,p. 3.

The experience is a human one

The perception of a duality that separates spirit from body has too often separated people from appreciating the physical experiences through which God is known. If religion is about spiritual matters and if God is spirit, then the experience of the human body is irrelevant at best and a serious obstacle at worst. Much of traditional spiritual writing treated the body as an impediment to faith requiring rigorous discipline and submission.

But what would the Jesus story be without the journeying, the encounters with hungry, hurting people, the cold water of baptism, the fellowship around bread and wine, the risk of travelling without the assurance of necessities, the foot washing, the anointing with perfume, and all of the ordinary seeing, listening, tasting, and responding of disciples? What would it be if it were a spirit rather than a body that suffered the crucifixion? What is it if only a spirit participated in resurrection, with no promise for human bodies?

In an incarnational faith, our physicality is a doorway into practical holiness. Mission spirituality is about caring hands, obedient feet and gracious and prophetic voices, not pious spirits and disembodied contemplation. It is no mistake that in instituting the sacraments Jesus said, '*Do* this', not '*Think* this' in remembrance of me.[9] It is embodied humanity that God loves, and embodied humanity that Jesus lived. "I have the immense joy of being *man*," Thomas Merton wrote, "a member of a race in which God Himself became incarnate…And if only everybody could realise this! But it cannot be explained. There is no way of telling people that they are walking around shining like the sun."[10]

Living the Jesus life poses the challenge of re-orientation from our usual priorities. As embodied creatures, we are made with strong wills and a self-centred approach to life. I believe that the human will and selfishness are genetic, functioning at the level of instinct. They are what has enabled us as individuals and a species to survive in often hostile environments. Even in the easiest of surroundings we must look to our own needs and comforts if we are to provide for ourselves. The human capacity for survival is amazing, and a strong will is key to this. But it is only a short step from the will that enables survival to the will that lays greedy claim on more than its share. Clearly, human free will, greed and selfishness are the cause of much of the pain and evil in the world.

The fact of our selfishness does not detract from the wonder of who we are, created in the image of God and capable of embodying God's purposes for the world. But this self-directed will must be converted and sanctified by a

---

[9] Barbara Brown Taylor, "Our bodies, our faith", *Christian Century*, vol. 126 no. 2 (27 January 2009), p.24.

[10] Thomas Merton, *Conjectures of a Guilty Bystander*, New York: Doubleday, 1968, pp.157-8.

conscious desire to conform to the will of God. The traditional spiritual practices are designed to fix our attention on God in order that we might welcome and incorporate the transformation. Prayer is central, and courage with it. In order to embody a deeper, richer life, we must make ourselves vulnerable. We are not God, but we are called to offer the words and actions through which God's love and justice are embodied in our daily experience.

The role of the church

Belonging to a community of faith is vitally important, be it large or small. A worshipping community brings the Jesus story to life by immersing itself in it, reading and re-reading, proclaiming, pondering, discussing, and seeking to embody it. At Holy Communion the worshipping community meets around the table to participate in the obedience and passion of Jesus.

The church is what it is because of the Jesus story. Jesus was a revolutionary character who subverted the culture of his day by the stories he told and the people he consorted with. He taught that the last would be first and lived it by his association with tax collectors, prostitutes and sinners. His parables turned respectable expectations on their head to provide a window into a kingdom that would operate by rules quite different from those governing the society he knew. This subversiveness continues to challenge the church of today out of its complacency so that it becomes a missionary agency, seeking to live God's kingdom in the midst of the world's kingdoms. The story of the cross is central: Jesus died at the hands of the old regime in order to rise with the promise of the kingdom now made tangible in his risen life.

Alone, it is unlikely that any of us would respond to the Christ event with anything approaching the courage and passion it warrants. Certainly none of us is capable of discerning objectively between our desires and God's, nor can we be sure whether a voice that is calling us to mission in any particular form is the voice of God. The Christian community supports us, challenges us and holds us accountable. Undergirded with the wisdom of past generations through scripture and inherited tradition, the community has the tools for seeking and authenticating the will of God. For every time that a lone prophetic voice speaks the truth to a faith community headed in the wrong direction, there are many times that the community offers correction to an individual erroneously determined to go his or her own way. Seeking God's calling together we are more likely to overcome the self-deceptions engineered by our innate selfishness.

Churches can also be self-centred, of course:

> Looking at itself through the eyes of the world, the church realizes that it is disreputable and shabby, susceptible to all human frailties; looking at itself through the eyes of the believers, it perceives itself as a mystery, as the incorruptible Body of Christ on earth. We can be utterly disgusted, at times, with

> the earthliness of the church, yet we can also be transformed, at times, with the awareness of the divine in the church.[11]

The church has an important role to play in offering its members opportunities to fulfil their Christian calling which might not be available to them as individuals. The church's programmes and projects institutionalise mission, creating layers of administration and bureaucracy that try the patience of activists who simply want to get on with the work. However, those programmes and projects offer a framework for Christian discipleship in which every person has something to contribute to a combined effort through which much can be accomplished. They advertise the need for volunteers and funders and people who will give support in prayer. Together we embark on work that none of us would be brave enough to undertake alone. Together we can offer one another the support and encouragement that enables work to continue in the face of intractable problems, frustration and discouragement.

Building an effective, faithful Christian community is therefore in itself an important element in mission spirituality. The baptizing of new believers into the Christian community is a missionary activity not only because of the saving of their individual souls but because they then become part of the company of Jesus story, actively helping to discern God's mission and committing themselves as participants. The church (*ekklesia*) is the company of those who are called (*kaleo*). Each brings gifts which can be discovered and nourished for the good of the common enterprise.[12] This discernment is part of the adventure. Each of us needs the help of the others to identify our part in the living of the Jesus-story in our time and place.

Barbara Glasson of the Liverpool bread church received advice from a fellow minister at a time when she could not see what God wanted her to do. "Keep open to what is coming and all the crazy interconnectedness that will and won't make sense at the moment – or perhaps for quite awhile – and listen to your feelings of delight, surprise, confusion, anger, bewilderment – and where you come alive."[13]

Some of us will have large, public roles to play, as leaders with responsibility for sharing a vision with others or as architects of significant change. Others will play minor roles behind the scenes. One is not better than the other. God calls each of us and each contribution is valued. Sometimes it is the smallest gift that has the biggest sacrifice and the strongest faith behind it.[14] In God's economy the size of a contribution may look very different. Faithfulness consists in stepping out, doing what we can, contributing what we

---

11 Howard Snyder quoted in David J. Bosch, *Transforming Mission: Paradigm Shifts in Theology of Mission*, New York: Orbis Books, 1991, p.389.

12 Friend, *op. cit.*, p.4.

13 Glasson, *op. cit.*, p.34.

14 Mark 12:41-44.

have, and leaving the big picture to God. We may never know that our modest gift was what tipped the balance and enabled the miracle to happen.

As beginners in mission, we will make mistakes. Immaturity is glaringly evident in well-intentioned outreach that nevertheless is self-centred:

> Welcome me – I have come to fix you.
> I know what you need.
> I am what you need.
> I know the truth – I am going to bring God to you.
> Accept my charity and don't bother me with your talk of justice.
> I am sacrificing myself here – why aren't you grateful?

Whole churches can be guilty of these travesties of mission. We need one another as partner churches to challenge and teach each other. Mission in the shape of Christ is self-giving, centred on the other, and seeks no recognition or reward.

God is patient and long-suffering in the face of such mistakes. God's wisdom recognises our need to learn. Through the results of our actions and the response of other people God holds up a mirror to us to see our immaturity, not to shame us into inaction, but to encourage us to try again, older and wiser. God also uses our most blatant mistakes to bring about gracious ends, thus humbling us and affirming us at the same time. We learn and we grow.

Growing into the shape of Christ is a lifelong project.[15] It depends upon all that is learned through the adventures along the way. It depends both on individual effort and the nurture and challenge of the church community. It happens through time-honoured means of grace and new experiences. But ultimately it depends on God, whose desire underlies and suffuses the mission and whose power fulfils it. Mission spirituality is the fulfilment of life offered to God in response to the love of God not only for humankind but for the whole created order. It is the gift of seeing with God-inspired eyes, hearing with God-inspired ears, feeling with a God-inspired heart, and thinking with God-enabled intelligence. It is where human life finds its highest purpose, meaning and delight.

---

[15] Ephesians 4:13.

TOWARD A LITURGICAL APPROACH TO RE-ROUTING MISSIONS: RESISTANCE MISSIOLOGY AND LITURGICS IN THE PHILIPPINE SETTING

Ferdinand Anno

In this paper, I propose discussing mission through the liturgical approach i.e. the renewal of worship. Worship remains elemental in the praxis of mission – as a symbolic rehearsal and consecration of missionary work. Within the rubrics of liturgy and missions, the praxis of mission also shifts from its colonialist orientation toward a more liberating direction that proceeds from the people at the bottom. Being a theology in motion, a liturgy renewed can serve as a theological prologue to the re-routing and praxis of missions. Succinctly put, the praxis of worship is a preparation for a missiological self-understanding.

This discussion proceeds from a re-thinking of worship life vis-à-vis the theology and diaconal commitments of Christians as informed or framed by the Trinitarian affirmation of the church. The pastoral setting of this review is a people's struggle, i.e. the Filipinos' *pakikibaka* (struggle) for a fuller humanity, specifically as ritualized in protest mobilizations. What this essay attempts to contribute is a review of a central credo of the church as a frame of or resource for liturgical reflection on the Filipino life-rite (also popularly framed as the passion, death and resurrection of the Filipino people). Progressively, this builds up into a discussion of the church's credal affirmations and its implications for worship renewal in particular – and the liturgy and missions in general.

The worship of the Triune God

We believe

In One God: Creator, Redeemer and Sustainer, who provides order, purpose, meaning and fufillment to all creation.

That in Jesus Christ, who is born of Mary, God became human and is sovereign Lord of life and history.

> That in the Holy Spirit God is present in the world, empowering and guiding believers to understand and live out their faith in Jesus Christ.[1]

The formula of the Christian creed of the United Church of Christ in the Philippines, a member church of the United Evangelical Mission, opens with an affirmation of God as "Creator, Redeemer, and Sustainer." In the light of a people's struggle in a precariously idolatrous location, it is absolutely essential, first and foremost, to affirm God as both the subject and object of the liturgical act.[2] It needs reiteration that the renewal of worship is a public affirmation of a decision for God over and against submission to the reign of the mammon-god. Presently, the latter is inundating both the corporeal and ethereal realms, building for itself a domain that poses as a political competitor to the vision of God's reign. As a *cultus* of God's reign, worship is directly faced with this confrontational reality of mammon. The praise of God needs to take shape, as Brueggemann puts it, 'as a doxology against idolatry and ideology.'[3]

More than being the first of the six articles constituting the statement of faith of the United Church of Christ in the Philippines, the affirmation of God as the Trinity also establishes an interpretative principle for the faith. The Trinity remains the fundamental grammatical frame through which the Christian community interprets the reality of God.[4] The church views the work of God, and that of missions, from a narrative of relationship defined by the Trinity. But how to communicate an ancient and complex Hellenic doctrinal formulation as the Trinity remains a task essential to enhancing the dynamism and relevance of the Christian faith today. In an attempt to state more clearly this mystery of a three-in-one divinity, the Trinity Working Group of Presbyterian Church - USA states:

> We have come to believe that no name, no metaphor, no set of words or phrases – however thoughtful, poetic or profound – will ever be able to say everything that could be said about the mystery of God's love made known to us above all in Jesus Christ and sealed in our hearts by the Holy Spirit.[5]

---

[1] The United Church of Christ in the Philippines' Statement of Faith.

[2] Marva J. Dawn, Reaching Out Without Dumbing Down: A Theology of Worship for This Urgent Time. Cambridge: William B. Eerdmans Publishing Company 1995, p.75ff.

[3] The very title of Brueggeman's review of Sigmund Mowinkle's seminal work on the psalms. Brueggemann, Walter. Israel's Praise: Doxology Against Idolatry and Ideology. Philadelphia: Fortress Press 1988.

[4] Jürgen Moltmann, The Trinity and the Kingdom of God. London: SCM Press 1981, pp.61ff.

[5] See The Trinity working Group of the Presbyterian Church-USA, The Trinity. God's Love Overflowing: A Preliminary Report to the 216th General assembly of PC-USA, 2004, pp.3-4.

Nonetheless, the said body came up with a description that it says is profoundly scriptural and rooted in tradition – the Trinity is the 'God who is love overflowing':

> 'God's Love Overflowing' is our attempt to express the amazing riches that flow boundlessly from the triune God who in loving freedom seeks and saves us, reconciles and renews us, and draws us into loving relationships that reflect the eternal oneness of God.[6]

Furthermore, in Asian commentaries on the Trinity as God's love story with God's creation, another Presbyterian, a Taiwanese engaged in the reconstruction of theology with Asian resources, had been earlier meditating on the far more expansive 'non-Trinitarian' scenarios of God's love.[7] Using the lenses of the East Asian 'third eye', C.S. Song wrote of Asian stories as also theatres of God's redemptive love for beyond the geo-historical and *story*cal confines of classical Trinitarian confession, the love of God also gushes out, giving birth to other stories and faith communities. Whence the classical 'Father / Creator, Son / Redeemer and Holy Spirit / Sustainer' naming of God is not exhaustive of the YHWH reality. The Trinity is a redemptive, incarnational, and sanctifying force of life bounded only by God's creative power.

Moreover, the Trinitarian way of understanding God is a built-in corrective to Christian theological dogmatism, including pigeon-holed Trinitarianism. It is itself a theological argument against the 'friends of Job'-like complacency of theological establishments. God's freedom as expressed in God's creative love is what demolishes the limiting anthropocentric (meaning, centered on what is directly useful to the human) orientation of both humanist and conventional theological wisdom.[8] The Trinity points beyond itself. It points, essentially, to God's freedom, and the experience of that freedom in and through God's participation in human life and creation. God's freedom in the Trinity is what opens up theology to peoples' local dramaturgies. This divine freedom is centrally embodied in the passion of Christ, and God's continuing creative work in the Spirit.

---

6 *Op cit.*, p.32.

7 Choan-Sen Song, Third-Eye Theology: Theology in Formation in Asian Settings. Guilford: Lutterworth Press 1970. In this book, Choan-Sen Song makes use of the Japanese Zen master Suzuki's teaching on the 'third eye' – the intuitive (non-conceptual, non-rational) eye that envisions realities beyond the familiar.

8 Gutierrez, Gustavo. On Job: God-talk and the Suffering of the Innocent. New York: Orbis 1987, pp.77-79 and 89.

God's freedom in the passion of Christ

God's freedom, the 'divine passion' as witnessed in the Hebrew Scriptures[9] became flesh in the suffering, death and resurrection of Jesus. This "free relationship of passionate participation"[10] initiated by God is what sums up the Christian gospel as well as what unravels the meaning of the Trinity. Now, what does this implosion of divine passion within the Godhead imply for worship? Specifically, what would this imply for the worship of subversive pilgrims, they whose *leitourgia*-mission is to bring about a new order?

Liturgically, God's *pasyon* would also mean the freedom to take a deep plunge into the ritualizations of the marginalised. The *masa* of the margins may be inarticulate or inchoate, syncretistic, militant and formally inadequate in their ritualizations,[11] but they are genuine in their cries for redemption. The marginals seek in their liturgical encounters the emancipation of their bodies and souls (i.e. in the external and internal dimensions of their being and becoming in the struggle).[12] They speak the same language as those marginals and outcasts Jesus lived with in his time. *Kristo*logical worship is one that locates itself also in profane spaces, and specifically where the faith criss-crosses with revolutionary politics. Drawing from the fact of incarnation, the Iona Community, for example, believes and so states "that there is no part of life that is beyond the reach or outside the scope of faith. The word of life, which we attend to seek, discern and interpret in worship," the community affirms, "is as much for our politics as for our prayers."[13]

The sight of a resisting mass rallying around the iconic symbols of the Christian story emphasises how 'God's overflowing love' is dug deep into the crevasses of the human situation. *Kalbaryo ng Maralitang Taga-Lungsod* (Calvary of the Urban Poor), an annual paraliturgy of Metro Manila's resisting urban poor communities typifies that forlorn world God is being pulled into. It is one space where the church may overzealously protect God from, or one liturgical gathering that the church may choose to ignore with disdain. But the story of the incarnation suggests otherwise. What *Kristo*logy is meant to be and become [as visually illustrated in many of Emmanuel Garibay's works] is precisely that of a liturgical relocation of the Christ into the struggle. One of the

---

[9] Moltmann, *op.cit* p.75.

[10] Moltmann, *op.cit* p.25.

[11] As presented in Benigno Beltran, The Christology of the Inarticulate: an inquiry into the Filipino understanding of Jesus the Christ, Manila: Divine World Publications 1987.

[12] Everett Mendoza. Radical and Evangelical: Portrait of a Filipino Christian. Quezon City: New Day Publishers 1999.

[13] George McLeod as quoted in Kathy Galloway's 'The worship of the Iona Community' in: Thomas Best and Dagmar Heller (eds.), Worship Today: Understanding Practice, Ecumenical Implications, Geneva: WCC Publications 2004, pp.222-228 and 228.

central liturgical icons of the Christian story was that of the Christ crucified between 'two thieves' in a desolate space outside established liturgical spaces.

Trinitarian worship is the encounter between God's and suffering communities' *pasyones* (passions) in Christ. Radically incarnational, spatial and political, such an encounter also takes place, literally, in garbage heaps. The 'Kristo' is what places worship, not at the edge but at the centre, right in the grim squalor of the human condition. During the eighties and nineties, garbage heaps (*bundok ng basura*) like Smokey Mountain in Tondo, Manila were among the more popular images of suffering and resistance in the Philippines. The *bundok ng basura*, in fact, has become a favoured setting to several of the *Kalbaryo ng Maralita* (*Kalbaryo*) paraliturgies. It is the *Kristo*logical that mediates between the Christ in the grimness of every day resistance and the Christian. The urban poor's *Kalbaryo* being a community rite may be inadequate, or worse, 'utilitarian' and 'idolatrous'. But this needs to be assessed more from the perspective of the marginals than from the concern for the law and the preservation of the integrity of tradition. God in God's participation in human life has decided to "employ humankind's cultural forms and modes of expressions in spite of their manifest inadequacy to reveal Godself."[14]

A Trinitarian worship is borderless and cannot be confined within the perimeter walls of imperial liturgiology. 'Borderlessness' in worship, however, is defined for the Filipino Christians by the *Kristo*logical, and thus looks at the incarnate Christ as its epitome of spiritual freedom.

God's freedom in the Spirit

God's freedom needs to be seen also as defined by the third person in the Godhead. In the New Testament, it is 'in the Spirit' that the church grew and expanded from Jerusalem to Judea and beyond. If Christ is the vertical breaking of space, it is 'in the Spirit' that the horizontal spatial boundaries are similarly collapsing. The two however are not separate outworkings of God's grace, but a single reality within transformative human processes. It is also on this basis that liberation and inculturation need to be viewed as a single pastoral theological focus and task rather than two disparate if not contesting approaches to living out the faith in the world.

The freedom to explore potentials of and possibilities for the faith in various living contexts has drawn its inspiration mostly from the pneumatological in the Trinitarian economy. Contextualisation of the faith in contemporary multi-religious Asia, for example, has been more emphatic on the theme of the Spirit. Tan Yun-Ka writes of the Pentecost event as an inspiration to the whole enterprise of 'Asianising' Christianity. Specifically on liturgical renewal,

---

[14] See Tan Yun-Ka's 'Constructing An Asian Theology of Liturgical Inculturation' from the Documents of the Federation of Asian Bishops Conference, 1999.

Pentecostal pneumatology, adds Tan Yun-Ka, is what makes Christianity more relevant to Asian realities.[15]

Asian theology and practical liturgiology have been very much grounded on the twin concerns of inculturation and liberation. This is reflected in the various modes of contextualisation that arose out of the process of 're-Asianising' Christianity. For example, Jose de Mesa, a Filipino Jesuit theologian, blends everything that can be subsumed within Christian tradition, and liberation and inculturation concerns.[16] Also, speaking on the theme of the World Council of Churches' seventh assembly in Canberra, "Come Holy Spirit –Renew the Whole Creation," Chun Hyun-Kyung, the Korean feminist theologian, called on the "use of the energy of the Holy Spirit" to build solidarity in the struggle to bring about a better quality of life.[17] But what made her presentation controversial was her starting with a Korean harvest dance invoking the "spirits of the oppressed in history" using the *Han* (restless spirit) principle – calling them the "icons of the Holy Spirit." In reply to charges of syncretism from a section of the Assembly, Chun argued for the case of a feminist, Third World and Asian Pentecostal theology:

> We have been listening to your intellectualism for 2,000 years ... listen to us for 200 years or if that is too long, 20 years. Is it not time to listen to our voices? We are new wine; you cannot put us into old skins. Yes, we are dangerous but it is through such danger that the Holy Spirit can renew the church.[18]

Worship 'in the Spirit' is a celebration of freedom in God. Freedom does challenge the borders of tradition if only to free the voices that have been repressed, caged and marginalised for so long. This is the broader political theological context of paraliturgies like the *Kalbaryo* or Chun's theological liturgical performance. It is also 'in the Spirit' that 'interconnectionalism' supplants the 'dualism' that has kept the church 'free' and 'safe' from the world.[19] With the Spirit bringing all spheres of the *oikoumene* together, the praxis of Christian freedom and *leitourgia* also converge. Chun's dangerous pneumatological liaison with the edges in the quest for ecclesiastical reform is not an unfounded imperative in fundamental Protestantism. Everett Mendoza, for example, defines the Spirit-inspired freedom of the Christian as including:

> the boldness to venture, everything that needs to be done. Because Christians have been freed from all kinds of work, they can dare to do any kind of work. ... The

---

[15] *Ibid.*

[16] Stephen Bevans, Models of Contextual Theology: Revised and Expanded Edition. Manila: Logos Publications 2003, pp.95ff.

[17] CCA News, Volume 26. Number 1/2/3. January-March 1991, pp 16-18, 17.

[18] *Op.cit.*, p.18

[19] Ibid.

freedom of the Christian is so radical that nothing but the conscience stands between him / her and a particular kind of work.[20]

Toward a Pentecostal liturgy of struggle

Asian churches' pneumatological emphasis on the Trinity derives much of its inspiration from the Pentecostal experience of the ancient church. God's freedom, empowering and activating presence were the basic elements in the Lukan account of the Pentecost event. A Pentecostal liturgy is hegemony-breaking language from and for God. It is a statement of faith that needs re-affirmation in situations where freedom and human rights are curtailed and the church hierarchy maintains its silence and apathy – if not fear – to speak out in public the subversive and 'strange' Word of God.

Moreover, a Pentecostal liturgy of struggle also builds on both the prophecy of Christ and the identity politics of Pentecostals.[21] 'Speaking in tongues' is prophetic speech. It speaks languages other than the dominant one. The languages point to a world other than the present, or 'kingdoms not of this world,' indicting the 'Babel' humanity is building for its self-elevation. On the historical, practical level, 'speaking in tongues' is a lucid, even a literal case of a people's insurrection and resurrection, of a people breaking free from the hegemonic language and culture of domination. It is 'in the Spirit' and in spiritualities of struggle that protest marches (*rali*), Mendiola (the popular site of protest in the Philippines), and other spatial icons constituting the dramaturgy of a people's struggle are seen, for example, as integral to the Christian imagination. As suggested in Chung Hyun-Kyung's assertions, the 'icons of the Spirit' are also the 'strange tongues' or the Christological that irrupts from outside and below resurrecting hope among those on the margins.

The evolving faith and spirituality of Pentecostal communities is another source of reflection for resistance liturgies. The Pentecostal experience can also be viewed as a liturgical phenomenon, and a considerable challenge to the praxis of liturgical reform in the ecumenical churches. It does not help that engaged Protestants dismiss them merely as "epiphenomenona of capitalist ideology or pawns of US imperialism."[22] The Pentecostals and new religious movements are so adept in translating their 'prosperity gospel' into ritualizations that are electrifying and contemporaneous to geographically, socially, bureaucratically dislocated peoples and individuals.[23] These ritualizations are as indigenous, contemporary and potentially revolutionary as

---

[20] Everett Mendoza, *op.cit.* p.5.

[21] Bobby Alexander, Victor Turner Revisited: Ritual As Social Change. Georgia: Scholars Press 1991, p.68.

[22] Lanuza, Gerry, Christian Fundamentalism in the Philippines, Quezon City: UCCP 2001, pp.31-32.

[23] Alexander, o*p. cit.*, p.25.

they are alien, traditional and reactionary. Mainline Protestant churches need to equally heed the liturgical challenge emanating from these revivalist groups.

The tradition within the Pentecostal movement that traces its roots from the 1906 Azusa assembly particularly informs reflections on the faith and politics of the marginal mass.[24] Recent studies on Pentecostalism have ascertained some helpful ways to understand the potential of Pentecostal theology and practice as resources for the life-rite of peoples' struggles. Bobby Alexander identified at least two directions in Pentecostalism: the "normative" and the "ideological."[25] The former explains the reactionary disposition of Pentecostalism while the latter its revolutionary potential. Cox similarly identifies the "fundamentalist" and "experiential" courses within the movement, and the latter, Cox suggests, should be harnessed to release the transformative and creative energies of Pentecostalism.[26] A liturgiology of resistance can gain much insight from the more 'ideological' and 'experiential' modes or dimensions of the Pentecostal movement as these relate more directly to the object of the Christian's subversive pilgrimage: the anti-empire reign of God.[27]

Furthermore, in the practical realm, Pentecostalism is also reaching out beyond its traditional constituency. The movement has now successfully penetrated the enclaves of the urban middle class. It has been extraordinarily effective in bringing to this increasingly alienated class a real 'good news' that speaks to them and their situation.[28] Central to this act of communication are worship assemblies that are generative of new identities, bringing the disenfranchised mass to a *liminal,* self-transcending and self-identifying state.[29] It is from these gatherings that "mythologies of the new self" are constructed, aiding transformative processes, especially in domestic situations[30] as well as, anticipatedly, in larger social situations. The empowerment of those on the margins, the task of any conscientization and community organising work, has now, ostensibly, gone through and beyond Freire's popular education method. As proposed by students of the Pentecostal phenomenon, the same task of people empowerment is now being pursued through another approach – the 'Pentecostal route.'[31] "Far from being an escapist ghetto for the powerless," the Pentecostal communities, writes Bernice Martin "offer a route to new

---

24 Harvey Cox, Fire From Heaven: The Rise of Pentecostal Spirituality and the Reshaping of Religion in the Twenty-First Century, London: Cassel 1996, p.30.

25 *Op. cit.*, pp.58ff.

26 *Op. cit.*, p.319.

27 Alexander, *op. cit.*, p.60.

28 Lanuza, *op. cit.*, *pp.*25ff.

29 Mercado, Leonardo. El Shaddai: A Study, Manila 2001, pp 7ff.

30 Bernice Martin, From Pre- to Post Modernity in Latin America: the Case of Pentecostalism, in: Paul Heelas (ed.), *Religion, Modernity and Postmodernity*. Oxford: Blackwell Publishers 1998, pp.102-146.

31 Cox, *op. cit.* p.319; Martin, *op. cit.*, pp.102ff.

possibilities, to new experiences of selfhood."[32] They are, she adds, "a boundary-breaking movement; just as tongue-speaking itself breaks the bounds of languages, so Pentecostals everywhere are prepared to attempt the impossible in all kinds of eminently practical ways."[33]

This is a crucial threshold point that at any given time, as pointed out by similar studies, could bring about a 'saturnalia of power' that has the people's veiled resistance, or the 'hidden transcript', exploding in public.[34] Harvey Cox, from various sociological and theological studies, paints an optimistic scenario of Pentecostalism's fusing with the revolutionary:

> Much to the chagrin of the political right-wingers, a kind of Pentecostal theology of liberation is now emerging… the genius of Pentecostalism is an encounter with the power of the 'liberating Spirit' … That this Spirit has a 'project' that is being worked out within human history. … The difference between them (base communities) and Pentecostal congregations is diminishing rapidly. If these two powerful movements, both of them on the 'experientialist' side of the ledger, were somehow to combine their strength … the result would be extraordinarily potent. If the Pentecostals … lead, absorb something of the social vision of liberation theology, and the Catholic base communities shed the residual elements of vertical authority they still sometimes retain, the offspring could be more powerful than either of its parents.[35]

The above projection by Cox, as prototyped in the religious faces of the American civil rights movement and the Black struggle in apartheid South Africa, can happen initially and most demonstrably through protest rites and resistance liturgies.

Conclusion: the Trinitarian logic of the liturgies of resistance

God's 'three-ness' helps inform, substantiate, bind, and 'bound' the freedom of the Christian in the world and in the act of worship. A doxology to the Triune God is at once a prophetic assertion that there is nothing absolute and sacrosanct but God. Empires, ideologies, liberation movements, laws and canons are exposed as fallible human institutions and continuing constructs. It is when human activities and institutions like *pakikibaka* are stripped of their sacred moorings that they live more fully their freedom and recover what it means to live an existence shared and celebrated with the sacred. The Trinity allows the human in her / his exercise of freedom to encounter in both historical and liturgical spaces God's wholly other-ness. This is particularly true in the

[32] Martin, *op. cit.*, pp.132-133.

[33] *Ibid.*

[34] Phraseologies introduced in the seminal work of James Scott. See Scott, James. Domination and the Arts of Resistance. New haven: Yale University Press, 1990.

[35] Cox, *op. cit.*, p.318-319.

context of worship where the profane and the sacred, the now and the not yet, the earth and heaven meet.

Finally, the Trinity, vis-à-vis the issue of liturgical renewal in the struggle, speaks of free liturgical leaps and explorations beyond the confines of orthodoxies. Traditional liturgy has been critiqued in feminist liturgiology as a 'man's liturgy', i.e. "exclusive, sexist, misogynist, patriarchal, androcentric, imperial, hierarchical."[36] Confinement to this marginalizing and repressive tradition not only consents to the culture of male domination and the continuing perversion and impoverishment of the Christian tradition, it also re-creates God 'in man's image.' The freedom of God in the Trinity commences the praxis of freedom in worship and in all areas of Christian living. To affirm God as 'Creator, Redeemer and Sustainer,' or the 'Father, Son and Spirit' is to affirm and celebrate freedom and creativity in our worship and in our work.

---

[36] Teresa Berger, Women's Ways of Worship: Gender Analysis and Liturgical History. Minnesota: The Liturgical Press 1999, p.116.

Part Three

The Charismatic Challenge

The Challenges of Charismatic Movements To The Mainline Historical Churches in Africa

Abednego Keshomshahara

The fast growth of the church in Africa

The church is growing very fast in Africa. This shows how mission work in Africa has been successful in one way or another. But we have to go beyond this achievement and ask ourselves whether this growth is without problems. Although the mainline historical churches (Anglican, Lutheran and Roman Catholic) are growing, the Pentecostal and Charismatic churches are growing faster.[1] Many Christians from the mainline historical churches join the Charismatic churches in order to quench their spiritual needs.[2] This challenges the mainline churches to know what has gone wrong in their approach to doing mission in Africa and elsewhere in the world.

The Charismatic churches emerged mainly in the African cities and towns in the early 1980's. Most of these churches have had financial support from the USA, Canada and Scandinavian countries.[3] These movements attracted many people with modern media and communication systems while addressing people's needs and expectations. As far as Tanzania is concerned, this movement came when the country was experiencing economic hardships which resulted from the oil crisis and the failure of African socialism. These Charismatic churches promised people a good life if they believed in Jesus Christ, fasted and prayed for healing miracles. They went on to say that even students could pass their examinations if they prayed. Since people were needy, they joined these movements with expectations that their needs would be met. In fact, when you tell people who have no food to fast, such people will accept your appeal not only because of religious factors but also because of economic

---

[1] Klaus Koschorke, "Introduction" in Klaus Koschorke (ed.) *African Identities and World Christianity in the Twentieth Century*, Hamburg: Missionshilfe Verlag, 2002, p.233-234.

[2] Edward D. O. O'Connor, *The Pentecostal Movement: In the Catholic Church*, Notre Dame: Ave Maria Press, 1971, p.239-262.

[3] Jesse Mugambi, *From Liberation to Reconstruction: African Christian Theology after the Cold War*, Nairobi: East African Educational Publishers Ltd, 1995, p.68-70. Also Wilson Niwagila, "Charismatische Bewegung in Tansania", p.1-9, in: *Das andere Afrika: Impressionen, Reflexionen und auch Visionen aus dreißig Jahren kirchlicher Arbeit in Afrika,* ed. by C. Friedrich Durst, Neuendettelsau: Erlanger Verlag für Mission und Ökumene, 2004, p.168-171.

hardships as they will take fasting as a way of economising their consumption of food.

Again, when you tell people who have no possibility of accessing health services to pray only for healing miracles, your message will be accepted since people have no access to medical facilities anyhow. They are even not ready to go to the traditional healers who charge them money for their healing practices. This was already a challenge to the mainline historical churches which had established centres for health services that serve those who can pay for medical treatments.

The mainline churches stress medical services with less emphasis on prayers for healing, a weakness that makes their Christians leave their denominations and join the Charismatic movements. Moreover, the challenge that faces the mainline historical churches is to empower people to be in a position of improving their economies so that they may be able to pay for health services. At least nowadays the mainline historical churches empower the Christians and the entire community through savings and credit cooperative societies (SACCOS) through which members can access credit and produce to meet their daily needs including health services.

Religion and society are inseparable. The question is how this relationship can be well utilized to bring about social, mental, economic and spiritual development without jeopardizing the integrity of people. This leads us to the challenge of doing mission in a holistic way, addressing both the spiritual and material dimensions of the people. Both the Charismatic churches and mainline historical churches are challenged to address the needs of people without concentrating on one aspect of life, since people have spiritual and material dimensions of life. A good example can be taken from Jesus Christ who preached to people the good news of salvation for the forgiveness of sins while at the same time feeding and healing them.

Theological differences between the mainline historical churches and the Charismatic movements

The role of the Holy Spirit

The difference between the mainline historical churches and the Charismatic movements is mainly found in their understanding of the Holy Spirit and his functions in the church. The mainline historical churches have mainly emphasized the person and work of Jesus Christ with less emphasis on the person and work of the Holy Spirit.[4]

Marie-Henri Keane poses a similar challenge:

[4] Lesslie Newbigin, *The Relevance of Trinitarian Doctrine for Today's Mission,* London: Edinburgh House Press, 1963, p.77-78.

> "Christ was never forgotten, the God who sent him was never overlooked, but what is surprising is that we who believe in a triune God should have grossly neglected the life-giving Spirit, especially since we know that we cannot say 'Jesus is the Lord' or call God 'God' unless this grace is given to us through the Spirit."[5]

In showing how pneumatology has been neglected or marginalized by some churches, Elizabeth Johnson quotes leading theologians who comment that the Holy Spirit has become "half known God" (Yves Congar); "watered down from its Biblical fullness" (Wolfhart Pannenberg); "homeless in the West" (Joseph Ratzinger); "faceless" (Walter Kasper) and "shadowy" (John Mackuarrie).[6] At least Reformation theology puts it very clearly that people by their own reasoning ability and strength cannot believe in Jesus Christ except through the Holy Spirit. The Holy Spirit is responsible for calling, enlightening, sanctifying and preserving the believers in the true Christian faith. Moreover, the Holy Spirit forgives sin and is expected to resurrect and provide the believers with eternal life.[7] The Danish scholar Regin Prenter argues that Lutheran theology gives much attention to the Holy Spirit since it maintains that both justification and sanctification are the work of the Holy Spirit.[8]

However, other functions of the Holy Spirit such as healing through prayers, speaking in tongues, and prophesy (charismatic gifts) have been marginalized or even neglected by Lutheran theology because charismatic gifts are not central to the salvation of people and are not upholding the theology of the cross, instead, they are confined within the theology of glory.[9] But the theology of the cross is not only meant for those who suffer but also those who prosper since both sides are challenged to go beyond their situations and reflect on God's grace of saving humans through Jesus Christ. In addition, the cross does not only imply spiritual aspects of life but also socio-economic and political arenas of life since Jesus' death on the cross was caused by his challenging

---

5 Marie-Henri Keane, "The Spirit of Life" in: *Doing Theology in Context: South African Perspectives*, edited by John W. de Gruchy and Charles Villa-Vicencio, New York: Orbis Books, 1994, p.69.

6 Keane, 72.

7 Martin Luther, "The Small Cathechism" in: *The Book of Concord: The Confessions of the Evangelical Lutheran Church*, ed. Theodore G. Tappert, Philadelphia: Muhlberg Press, 1959), p.345.

8 Benard Holm, "The Work of the Spirit: The Reformation to the Present" in: *The Holy Spirit in the Life of the Church*, edited by Paul D. Opsahl, Minneapolis: Augusburg Publishing House, 1978, p.100-103.

9 Karlfried Froehlich, "Charismatic Manifestations and the Lutheran Incarnational Stance" in: *The Holy Spirit and the Life of the Church*, edited by Paul D. Opsahl, Minneapolis: Augusburg Publishing House, 1978, p.136-145.

actions and constant sermons about God's kingdom that challenged exploitation, oppression of people and religious legalism.[10]

But as people, we encounter diseases, pain and death. Jesus himself prayed in Gethsemane to avoid torture and death, but he prayed while letting the will of God to be done.[11] That is what he taught his followers to pray by saying "Thy will be done". In spite of his prayer, he was confronted by torture and death that was meant for the salvation of humans. On the cross he complained to God as to why he had forsaken him (Mark 15:34-36). But afterwards he placed his soul in the hands of God (Luke 23:46) and died. In this context, we ought to accept the reality of being humans who ought to carry the cross with the hope of resurrection. Otto Markmann says that the Charismatic movements tend to overlook the cross and live as if Christian perfection was possible here on earth, while in reality Christian perfection is expected after resurrection of the body and life everlasting as we read from Philippians 3:12 and 1 John 3: 2.[12]

Some Christians in the Charismatic movements have been tempted to perceive healing as a necessary phenomenon to those who pray and believe. They forget that even those who believe cannot avoid the reality of death. The teachings about charismatic gifts need special theological attention and clarification in doing mission in the light of the Biblical teachings and evangelical theology, lest people are misled by wrong teachings.

Other theological differences

Another problem is related to the understanding of God from the perspective of the Trinity, whereby every denomination tends to emphasise only one aspect of the Triune God with less emphasis on the other aspects of the Trinity. For example, while Lutherans put much emphasis on the person and works of Jesus Christ (solus Christus), the Roman Catholic Church emphasises the aspect of God as Father. The Charismatic churches stress the works of the Holy Spirit who is associated with the events of healing, prophecy, speaking in tongues, visions and dreams without attention to the other persons of the Trinity. As such, Lesslie Newbigin challenges all denominations to have a Trinitarian approach in doing mission, an approach that will help the Christians to have confidence in God as creator, redeemer and sanctifier. The balanced Trinitarian aspects in the task of doing mission will also help the church to overcome the challenge of secularism[13] as long as God is involved in all dimensions of life as creator, redeemer and sanctifier.

---

[10] Jürgen Moltmann, *The Crucified God: The Cross of Christ as the Foundation and Criticism of Christian Theology* translated by R. A. Wilson and John Bowden, London: SCM Press, 2001, pp.46-50, 128-147.

[11] Mark 14:36- 15:47.

[12] Otto Markmann, "Die Charismatische Bewegung", Berlin, 1987, p.31.

[13] Newbigin, *op. cit.*, p.77-78.

Hans-Peter Grosshans observes that the Charismatic churches emphasize living out the faith without focus on the theological reflections about faith. For them theology is unnecessary and seems to be a disturbing activity. He admits that there are ways of doing theology which are far away from living out faith, but he maintains that there is also good theology that does not oppose faith. This kind of theology, he adds, is part of faith or its instrument. Grosshans points out that we need some distance from living out the faith and experiences of the Holy Spirit in order to see and understand what is going on in the church and society. Theology is necessary if at all we want to know and reflect the foundations of our faith. Charismatic churches are interested only in the immediate, direct experiences of the Holy Spirit without theological reflections on the foundations of what they are believing in.[14] Since the Charismatic movements have a negative attitude towards theology and theologians, there has been tension between Charismatic Christians and mainline clergy or theologians. In this context there is a need for dialogue in which the clergy ought to listen carefully to the challenges of the Charismatic Christians who want to freely express their faith and experiences of their lives in the Spirit. At the same time, Christians in the Charismatic movements should be able to see the relevance of theology in clarifying the foundations of the Christian faith. Church history tells us that there are times when faith without theological reflections leads to danger and death of people. A good example of faith without reflection is when some Charismatic preachers tell people to only pray for healing without going to hospital. As a result, some people have lost their lives because of faith that lacks theological reflections. Thus, Christian faith must be based not only on the immediate experience of the Holy Spirit but also on the theological reflection for the sake of clarity, certainty, pursuit of truth, salvation and liberation of humans from obstacles of life by relating faith to socio-economic and political aspects of life.

The context of African traditional spirit beliefs

The challenge which faces the church in Africa today is caused by what John S. Mbiti observes, namely that Christianity has failed to relate and interpret the Gospel in the context of African spirituality.[15] Since the Gospel was not interpreted in the African cultural and religious context, African Christians became Christians during the day but in the night they became adherents of

---

[14] Hans-Peter Grosshans, "The Work of the Holy Spirit in Christian Life and in the Church: Lutheran Theological Reflections" in *Lutherans Respond to Pentecostalism*, ed. by Karen L. Bloomquist, Mineapolis: Lutheran University Press, 2008, p.119.

[15] John S. Mbiti, *African Religions and Philosophy*, London: SPCK, 1969, p.237-238.

their African Traditional Religion (ATR).[16] In African Traditional Religion every aspect of life has connection with the spiritual world hence there is an interrelationship between the material and spiritual dimensions of life.

The emphasis of the Charismatic churches on the functions of the Holy Spirit appeals to many Africans whose traditional spirit beliefs are associated with the miraculous aspects in life.[17] This leads us to the need of interpreting the doctrine of the Holy Spirit in the socio-religious settings of Africans without jeopardizing the essence of the Gospel. Gwinyai H. Muzorewa argues that the role of the Holy Spirit correlates with that of the ancestral spirits in the African Traditional Religion.[18] This implies that Africans whose traditional religion maintains that the ancestral spirits can heal people will likely feel at home when the Charismatic movements emphasize that the Holy Spirit is responsible for healing sick people. The same applies to the functions of the Holy Spirit in prophecy, speaking in tongues, counselling etc. African ancestral spirits are also involved in prophesying in the sense that they enable those who are possessed by them to predict what will happen in the future. In addition, there are beliefs among Africans that the ancestral spirits can make people speak in a language that is foreign to the hearers.[19] The traditional healers use the ancestral spirits to acquire knowledge for counselling people regarding their needs in society.

When the Bible talks of the Holy Spirit as the one who has power to counteract the evil spirits, African traditionalists talk of good spirits as protectors of people against them. When the Charismatic preachers emphasize the role and functions of the Holy Spirit against the evil sprits and other calamities in life, their message is well perceived.

The question is why are Africans interested in the Holy Spirit if they already have ancestral spirits which play a great role in their lives? The Christian message attracts Africans when the Holy Spirit is presented as God, a message that shows that the ancestral spirits are inferior to God. While the Holy Spirit is the Spirit of God, the ancestral spirits are spirits of humans. This is accepted in African Traditional Religion in which the spirits are graded below God. Thus, the traditional ancestral spirit beliefs should not be an end in themselves, rather, they should be perceived as a background through which the doctrine of the Holy Spirit as God can be interpreted in our endeavour of doing mission in

---

[16] Israel Katoke, "The Coming of the Gospel and African Reaction" in *Essays on Church and Society in Tanzania*, ed. by C. K. Omari, Arusha: Evangelical Lutheran Church in Tanzania, 1976, p.112-113.

[17] Abednego Keshomshahara, "The Lutheran Doctrine of the Holy Spirit and the Challenge of the Traditional Spirit beliefs among the Haya People", M.Th Thesis, Makumira, 2000, p.1-6.

[18] Gwinyai H. Muzorewa, *The Origins and Development of African Theology*, New York: Orbis Books, 1985, p.43.

[19] Keshomshahara, *op. cit.*, p.50ff.

Africa and elsewhere in the world where people still have ancestral spirit beliefs. While there are special traditional spirits for specific purposes like hunting, fishing, farming and having children, the church failed to address the needs of people by asking the Holy Spirit to guide and help them in such daily needs.

African theology has tried to express Jesus as a "proto-ancestor" bearing in mind that the ancestors play an important role in the lives of the Africans. But the task which ought to be given attention as far as the Charismatic movements are concerned is the correlation between the Holy Spirit and the ancestral spirits. When we do mission in Africa we should always be careful regarding the aspect of salvation and miracles in view of the role of the Holy Spirit. Although the Bible talks about the aspects of miracles, its essential message is about the liberation and salvation of humans in and beyond history; it encompasses history and eschatology. It is here that we should differentiate between the temporal and eternal needs of humans.

We have to understand that the Holy Spirit provides for temporal and eternal needs in life. Ibrahim Bitrus challenges the historic churches to review their curricula in theological seminaries and universities in order to encounter the challenges of Charismatic and neo-Pentecostal movements by adding courses concerning *charisma*, Spirit baptism, speaking in tongues, healing and deliverances, dynamics of worship, job and wealth creation and capacity building.[20] Galana Babusa Yako depicts how the historic churches in Kenya have started to adjust themselves to the challenges of Charismatic movements by praying for people who have special problems during worship services. He adds that once per month during Sunday sermon, the preacher leads a discussion with members of the congregation on topics such as the Holy Spirit whereby they are given a chance of sharing their views and understanding with one another. Other strategies include allowing lay Christians to preach and the opportunity for afternoon fellowships in which pastors are present to learn from people and help them in their spiritual growth.[21] It is very interesting to note that historic churches which respond to the spiritual needs of their Christians have succeeded in retaining their Christians. Even some of the Christians who leave historic churches and join the Charismatic movements come back when the spiritual needs are met.[22]

---

[20] Ibrahim Bitrus, "The Influence of Neo-Pentecostalism in Nigeria" in: *Lutherans Respond to Pentecostalism*, edited by Karen L. Bloomquist, Mineapolis: Lutheran University Press, 2008, p.88.

[21] Galana Babusa Yako, "One Church's Response to Pentecostalism" in Karen L. Bloomquist, *op. cit.*, p.89.

[22] *Ibid.*, p.89.

The attractiveness of Charismatic movements

Other reasons that make African Christians leave mainline churches and join the Charismatic movements include that of seeking a place where they can freely participate in the worship services without depending on pre-determined liturgies. Ibrahim Bitrus observes that liturgies in the mainline churches are associated with cold formalism rather than vibrant worship that is found in the Charismatic and Pentecostal churches. He adds that many worship services in the mainline churches are still centered on the pastor rather than the whole congregation. As a result, the congregation becomes passive rather than being active participants in the whole process of worshipping God.[23]

Worship services in the Charismatic movements have room for simple songs that can be sung without hymn books. Such songs can be sung while dancing, twisting, moving and clapping hands, creating an atmosphere of joy and participation. Such worship services attract many youths who like dancing and singing. This, again, is a challenge to the historic churches. It is in this context that creativity and innovation of things that are attractive to Christians in worship should be encouraged to avoid worship services that are boring. Such innovations include liturgies that are flexible and appealing to people. This should go hand in hand with encouraging active participation of all Christians in the worship services. The priesthood of all believers as upheld by the Lutheran doctrines seems to have been marginalized since the participation of all Christians in the Lutheran churches and other historic churches is not encouraged.[24]

Christians in the Charismatic and Pentecostal churches encourage relationships in the sense that they care for one another, unlike some large established historic churches which may not even know their church members. In addition, Charismatic churches are concerned with solving individual socio-economic and spiritual problems.[25] The fact that Christians in the Charismatic movements participate in the ministry and feel responsible to visit the sick people and pray for them makes Christians in the historic churches leave their churches and join a Charismatic movement. This is a challenge to the mainline historic churches, which ought to involve the Christians in the ministry by encouraging them to visit, counsel and care for one another without waiting for their pastors to do such duties.

---

23 Bitrus, *op.cit.*, p. 86-87. *Cf.* Musawenkosi Biyela, "In Spirit and Truth: Liturgy in Dialogue with Pentecostalism" in: Karen L. Bloomquist, *op. cit.*, p.95.

24 *Ibid.*, p.87.

25 *Ibid.*, p.87.

Critiquing the Charismatic movements in Africa

We have seen how the Charismatic churches respond to the social, material and spiritual needs of the people. However, the Charismatic churches which have tried to emphasize the role of the Holy Spirit and his gifts to meet the challenge of African traditional spirit beliefs have created some theological problems which ought to be criticized. For example, while they stress the miracles of healing through prayers, they marginalize Western and African traditional medicines[26] as if the Holy Spirit is limited to one form of healing. Moreover, in those churches, prayers to God have predictable results which depend on one's observance of laws and taboos. Failure to follow the rules leads to unsuccessful prayers according to the teachings of these churches.[27]

Another problem is associated with lack of order in the church, especially when every Christian claims to be guided by the Holy Spirit which has led to split of the churches in various small groups and movements of people from one denomination to another. The same applies to the Pentecostal and Charismatic movements' views concerning social miseries, which are attributed to individual sins only without consideration of socio-political and economic structures of evil.[28] All these problems ought to be addressed and solved so that African Christianity may not disassociate people from political engagement.[29]

Charismatic and Pentecostal movements are criticized for reading the Bible literally.[30] It is in this context that we see the relevance of exegetical work in which we are enabled to understand the social, religious, cultural and historical context of the text before we apply it to our life experiences.[31] However, exegesis should be done in a way that does not take over the place of faith, especially when exegesis makes some ordinary Christians doubt if what they read and hear is really God's word or people's words.[32] The Bible is not a book of science but a book which requires us to believe beyond what we can verify scientifically. Paul Tillich warns believers against the problem of literalism and science with regard to faith. He says that reading the Bible literally is superstition, and replacing religious language with science is also superstition.

---

[26] Mbiti, *Bible and Theology in African Christianity*, Nairobi: Oxford University Press, 1986, p. 74-78. *cf.* Keshomshahara, *op. cit.*, p.3.

[27] E. Ikenga-Metuh, "The Revival of African Spirituality: A Leaf from African Instituted Churches" in: *Encounter of Religions in African Cultures*, Geneva: LWF, p.37.

[28] Keshomshaha, *A Theology of Poverty Reduction in Tanzania: A Quest for Christian Socio-Economic and Political Vision*, Ph.D Dissertation, Kirchliche Hochschule Wuppertal/Bethel, June 2008, p.151.

[29] *Ibid. Cf.* Mmugambi, *op. cit.*, pp.72-85, 149-160.

[30] Bitrus, *op. cit.*, p.83.

[31] *Ibid.*

[32] *Cf.* Naaman Laiser, Lutheranism in Africa" in: *The Theology of the Cross: Second International Lutheran Confessional Conference*, 14-18.3.1994, ed. Reijo Arkkila and R. O. Olak, Helsinki: Sley-Kirjat Oy, 1994, p.146. *Cf.* Keshomshahara, *op. cit.*, p.90-91.

Rather, religion should continue to have its own language and symbols which should not be replaced by science, bearing in mind that religion and science address different fields of human life.[33]

The challenge of modernity

Another problem which faces the doctrine of the Holy Spirit is modernity that has made some theologians like Rudolf Bultmann to understand the Holy Spirit as a myth which is unintelligible and useless to modern humans without demythologization.[34] The same applies to the spirits or ancestral spirits which are viewed as myths which ought to be demythologized.[35] From the time of enlightenment rationalism, the reality of spirits has been denied in the light of natural science.[36] Some Western missionaries in Africa were greatly influenced by the enlightenment worldview and therefore they rejected the existence of spirits[37] although the Bible accepts the existence and miraculous powers of these spirits while warning people not to depend on them except God alone.[38] Michael Green warns that if we reject the existence of the evil spirits on the basis of science and rationalism, there is a danger of not accepting the existence of the Holy Spirit on the basis of science and rationalism since we cannot prove the Holy Spirit's existence by human reason.[39]

However, it should be noted that evil spirits and Satan are not objects or articles of the Christian faith. Sometimes, Christians in the Charismatic movements focus more on Satan and evil spirits to the extent of marginalizing the almighty God. The Nicaean and Apostles' Creeds are very clear on this, especially when they are concerned with God the Father, Son and Holy Spirit. Nothing is said about Satan except the reality and forgiveness of sin.[40]

The influence of modernity on contemporary African theologians affects communication between them and ordinary African Christians who take

---

33 Paul Tillich, *Systematische Theologie Band II*, 7. Auflage 1981, (erschienen 1958) Stuttgart: Evangelisches Verlagswerk Stuttgart, pp. 121-128; 151, 164 ff.

34 Holm, *op. cit.*, pp.121-125. *Cf.* Keshomshahara, *op. cit.*, pp.89-90.

35 Michael Green, *I Believe in Satan's Downfall*, London: Hodder and Stoughton, 1981, pp.15-20, 84-99. *Cf.* Keshomshahara, *op. cit.*, pp.90.

36 Richard Gehman, *African Traditional Religion in Biblical Perspective* (Kijabe: Kesho Publication, 1987), 106-119,171; Green, *op. cit.*, pp.15-20, 84-99.

37 Mbiti, "Eschatology" in *Biblical Revelation and African Beliefs* ed. Kwesi A. Dickson and Paul Elingworth, Maryknol: N.Y, 1969, p.183. *Cf.* Gehman, *op. cit.*, pp.171.

38 Gehman, *op. cit.*, pp.176-183. *Cf.* Kurt E. Koch, *Demonology Past and Present: Inaugural Lecture at the Swaziland Christian University of Theology* (Neuhausen: Hanbler, no date), 4. *Cf.* I Samuel 28:3-22; Leviticus 19:31; Deuteronomy 18: 10-18; Isaiah 8: 18-20. Keshomshahara, *op. cit.*, p.52-53.

39 Green, *op. cit.*, p.20.

40 Keshomshahara, *op. cit.*, p.95.

seriously the reality of the spiritual world in the light of their African religious heritage and the Bible.[41] Thus, African pastors and theologians find themselves in a conflict between Western and African theology.[42] But all theologies are bound up with the cultural contexts in which they are made although learning from different cultures is of cardinal importance. Even when modern science regards the impact of charismatic gifts as sociological and psychological phenomena, some theologians argue that God operates also in the context of sociological, psychological, and natural means to fulfil his purpose of addressing the needs of humans.[43] This echoes what was said by the Lutheran Church in the USA regarding the functions of the Holy Spirit and psychological interpretations. This Lutheran Church states that:

> "A combination of personal magnetism of healers and the suggestive atmosphere of the gathered congregation can be explained psychologically, but they can also be seen as God's gift. That a phenomenon has psychological explanation does not prevent it from being a gift of the Spirit."[44]

When the church explains faith and addresses human needs in terms of science and reason only, there is a danger of failing to address needs that are beyond what we can see and verify. As a result, people who have failed to get peace through science and reason tend to find solutions to their problem outside the church. That is why some have resorted to occultism and horoscopes in spite of scientific and technological developments in the world.[45] Although science and technology have improved people's lives, they have also created some problems that need solutions outside of the field of science and technology.[46] These are the challenges which our churches ought to tackle in the

---

[41] Muzorewa, *op. cit.*, p.12. Also T. G. Kihogora, "Angels, Demons and Spirits in African Christianity" in *Mission in African Christianity: Critical Essays in Missiology*, ed. A. Nasimiyu-Wasike and D. Waruta, Nairobi: Uzima Press, 1993, p.53. Gehman, *op. cit.*, p.107. Mbiti, *Bible and Theology in African Christianity*, Nairobi: Oxford University Press 1986, p.76. *Cf.* Keshomshahara *op. cit.*, pp.5 & 90. *Cf.* Laiser, *op. cit.*, p.146.

[42] Mika Vähäkangas, *Genuinely Catholic, Authentically African? The Encounter between Neo-Thomism and African Thinking in Charles Nyamiti's Methodology*, Ph.D Dissertation, Helsinki, 1997, p.9.

[43] Stanley Benson, "The Conquering Sacrament: Baptism and Demon Possession among the Maasai of Tanzania" in *African Theological Journal* Vol.9, No. 2, Makumira, July 1980, pp.58-60.

[44] Paul D. Opsahl (ed.), *The Holy Spirit in the Life of the Church*, Minneapolis: Augusburg Publishing House, 1978, p.262.

[45] *Spirits, Ancestors and Healing: A Global Challenge to the Church, A Resource for Discussion*, Geneva: LWF, 2006, pp.14-17.

[46] A. Keshomshahara, *A Theology of Poverty Reduction in Tanzania. A Quest for Christian Socio-Economic and Political Vision*, Dodoma: Central Tanganyika Press, 2008, p.12, footnote no.84.

sense that our mission is holistic in covering the spiritual, psychological, sociological and material needs of humans, without deviating from the Biblical and theological foundations of the Christian faith.

Healing in Relation to Ministry and Evangelism

Kingsley Weerasinghe

Introduction

The word "healing" is used in the Bible in a broader context than in common parlance. The mission to heal that was given to the church is now being revived all over the world. It is obvious that especially the new 'Evangelical' groups use this ministry a great deal in their activities. This results in drawing non-believers or complacent / slumbering Christians into the fold, or at least in getting their attention focused to 'see' God's abilities and power through miraculous healings. Even members of mainline church communities realize that God's healing is one of the most important ways by which congregations could be kept alive, and thus concentrate on this ministry. Faith in divine healing is increasing rapidly among the Christians in Sri Lanka, and through them to our non-Christian brothers and sisters in their social and family circles as well as in their neighbourhoods. As a minister of the Methodist Church of Sri Lanka, what I will share here are my personal experiences in the healing ministry and my observations. Therefore, this is a narrative report rather than an academic paper, even though I will avail myself of some Biblical verses and theological reasoning.

Healing in the Bible

The Bible, both in the Old and the New Testament, reveals our God as the God who gives healing to His people. In fact, God revealed Himself as 'The Lord who Heals' (Ex. 15:26), quite early in the Bible. Thus, with healing as a component of His very nature, it is not surprising that in examining these instances of healing carefully, we discover that this God of the Bible gives not only spiritual or mental healing, but physical healing too. When we read passages like Exodus 15:26, 21:19, Numbers 12:13, 2 Kings 20:15, 20:18, 1 Chronicles 21:18, 28:15, 36:16, Psalms 103:03, 147:3, Proverbs 3:8, 4:22, 6:15, 12:18, 13:17, 15:4, 16:24 etc., it is obvious that the Bible discloses God as the God who has the power to heal, and that this divine healing becomes a tool of His mission on earth. If we are to obey the Great Commission, we need all the help we can get. This is why the Holy Spirit will help us in the mission field to engage in the healing ministry as well. Thus, God has given us the ability to carry His command through with divine healing as a door that opens hearts to grow into faith and love of God as Jesus used this divine power.

The New Testament shows us that Jesus healed people who suffered from a variety of diseases. He gave equal importance to the healing ministry as to other ministries and he healed the sick wherever he went, which resulted in people being drawn to him. What we must remember is that some of those who came may have come just for the healing – out of sheer desperation or to see a miracle taking place, or to check whether all they had heard was true. But his healing ministry would have opened the door for even those people to hear his teaching as well. Three words describe Jesus' ministries: teaching, preaching, healing. The Gospel of John describes miracles as signs of the kingdom of God. Healing made a great impact in the lives of people of that day, and the healing ministry opened a pathway for Jesus to preach and teach the good news, just as it is for us today.

Jesus also imparted the healing ministry to his disciples through the Holy Spirit. Matthew 10:1 says, "and having called to him his twelve disciples, he gave to them power over unclean spirits," so that they could cast them out. Thus, they were able not only to heal sickness and disease as we refer to them, but every sickness and every malady in a broader sense. It was the Lord Jesus who gave this power to heal the sick, not that this power was inherent in them. This power to heal the sick was given to them to use in their ministry. Only when they had received the power of the Holy Spirit they were able to heal others.

The Book of Acts furnishes plentiful evidence of the apostles and others in the early church exercising this gift (Acts 3:7, 5:12-16, 8:7, 19:12, 28:8) and the epistle of James refers to a ministry of healing carried out by the elders of a local church acting collectively (James 5:14). Among the spiritual gifts enumerated in 1 Corinthians 12:4-11, 28 is the gift of healing. Paul speaks of the gift of healing as being distributed along with other spiritual gifts among the ordinary members of the church. There were people, it would seem, who occupied no official position in the community, and who might not otherwise be distinguished among their fellow members, but this special charisma of healing had been bestowed upon them.

Healing: my personal experience

In the year 1996, I was appointed to a church at Bandarawela in the mountainous region of the country. One day a lady, a Buddhist, came to see me. She shared with me all her physical pain due to a disease she was suffering from, and she pleaded for me to do whatever possible according to my religion. I invited her to come back the next day. The following day, I asked one of my church workers to join me as I did not really have faith in healing through prayer. I asked him to pray for her. While he prayed, I heard this lady making a strange noise, and then she fell to the ground. I was amazed to see this. The church worker who prayed for this lady said that it was necessary to pray for her the next day too. Because I realized that what happened was due to prayer I became convinced of the efficacy of divine healing. When the lady came the next day, I laid my hand on her head and prayed for her. Again she fell to the ground, but there was a severe backlash on my body too. I felt as if I had been pummelled and was being throttled. So I went to the Word and found that it was necessary for me to fast before such a prayer. On the third day, my wife and her grandmother also joined in the prayers. I had of course fasted. This lady fell to the ground and made a very strange noise. Finally she gave a great cry, "Jesus, don't come. I am going!" Then she came to her proper senses and asked what had happened to her. I asked her how she was, and she said, "I have no more pain." Hallelujah, God had delivered her from the demon which caused her disease, and he had delivered me from my lack of faith! This incident changed my heart and my thinking totally. I was convinced that this lady was liberated solely through the power of prayer. This altered my approach towards my ministerial service, and I hoped for the Holy Spirit's gift of healing to be operated through me.

God convinced me that he was turning me in a new direction. I found fairly soon after that he was using his power to heal through me. God used the consequences of this lady's actions to prove this change to me. She began to spread the news of her healing everywhere she went, and people started to visit me asking me to pray for them. I prayed and I found people receiving miraculous healing. This was just the beginning of God's work of healing through me.

There was another experience. One day, a lady, again a Buddhist, came to see me with her little daughter and said that her daughter was suffering from a disease called meningitis, and that this child had been discharged from the hospital after being there a whole month but now she had a high fever again. She also said that she took this child to a physician in the area and he had advised her to admit the child to the hospital as soon as possible. She was terrified at what the physician had told her about the consequences of this disease which could leave her child disabled. This mother was helpless and confused, so she begged me to pray for the child. I took the child in my arms and prayed for her. After praying I gave the child to her mother. After about ten minutes we noticed that the child's body was wet. She was perspiring! Quickly the fever went down. Praise God! The next day the lady came to see me with the child and shared with me what had happened. She said that after they went home, her daughter had begun to play with her toys and had continued to play until midnight. That disease never returned to her. The child was delivered and she was not beset with physical disabilities. She was perfectly healed. The proof that when God heals, his healing is permanent is clearly seen through this healing.

Healing: its relationship to the ministry and to evangelism

I would also like to share how healing through prayer is a support to the teaching / preaching ministries and the evangelist ministry of the church.

As I said earlier, in 1996, I was in Bandarawela, a town in the mountains in the central province of the country. One day a man named William, a father of three children and the head man of his village, came to see me. His wife had suffered from womb cancer for a long period and at this stage she had started to bleed – profusely and non-stop. After seventeen days of this bleeding, some one had told him to come to our church. The next day he brought his sick wife to our church for prayer. I prayed for his wife. After praying, I asked, "Did you feel anything while I prayed?" and she said, "I feel as if the bleeding has stopped," and it really had! She had received healing. All the members of that family acknowledged that she had been healed. The result of this healing was that this whole family accepted our Lord and Saviour Jesus Christ as their Lord as well. Because of this miraculous experience, this family began to spread news of this happening everywhere in the village. They boldly shared with people how Jesus had healed their mother. To God be the glory.

This healing experience released them from a great burden and resulted in their becoming strong Christians. Because they shared this experience with others it automatically opened doors to evangelism among so very many people. Also because of this occurrence, not only did many people begin to come for prayer to me, but they gathered in one place for worship. Today it is a big Christian community where a new church worker is ministering. All glory is to God.

Through this healing, I was able to reach uncharted areas for new ministry. Because of their new experiences with God and also because they were able to hear of other people's experiences, they invited me to their homes. I praise God that this opened the way for me to reach non-Christian communities and to build up fellowships in those areas.

In the year 2000, I was sent to a city called Galle in the south of the country. There I had to minister to two churches, one of which was more than one hundred years old but did not have a single member attached to that church anymore. This church, situated in a historically famous area called the Galle Fort, had been closed for more than 50 years due to the lack of members. The other church, where I resided, had a fairly good membership. In the year 2001, I started to pray with them and in answer to our prayers God healed some church members miraculously. The news began to spread. With these new happenings, I started to worship in this empty church.

With the news of people's healing experiences being spread in the area, people started to come for healing. One day, members of a strongly Buddhist family, a mother with her 18 year-old daughter, Nelka, came to see me. Nelka had cancer and at the time she came to the church, she was extremely ill. I prayed with her after the service laying my hand on her head. Suddenly she fell to the ground. When she got up, I asked her what happened to her. She said that something like a big electrical shock went through her and that she did not know what happened after that until she awoke on the ground. Two weeks after this she was again taken to the hospital by her family as scheduled. It was then that they got to know that a miracle had taken place. The test reports found that the cancer was healed. Praise the Lord.

There was a certain high placed gentleman, Angus, and his wife, Mithila, both Anglicans, in Galle who had no children. This was due to the husband having been a victim of the disease called mumps, and as a result had to suffer its after-effects which caused him to become infertile. Doctors had informed him that they would have to go to Singapore for treatment but even with treatment there was no guarantee of success. They had gone to Singapore, but ultimately even that treatment failed. One day they invited me to pray for them, and I went to their home. About one month after the prayers, Mithila gave a telephone call to me to say she had conceived. Hallelujah Jesus. Now they have a daughter who is five years old.

The church that had been closed now has a healthy congregation with a church-appointed worker to look after the flock. During my time there, as a result of this healing ministry, I was able to reach many areas and form about seven worship groups. The final outcome was that these worship groups were accepted by the Methodist Church as a circuit.

A most recent experience is that of a three month-old baby girl who had a hole in her heart and could retain very little of her mother's milk or any baby formula. She used to vomit copiously and scream, scaring the whole family. This baby received God's miraculous healing and because of this healing now fifteen to twenty Catholics, most of whom had not read the Bible before, gather in their home every week to praise, thank and worship God, pray and study the Bible. It was here that I learnt about the efficacy of song while I prayed. Having someone to sing choruses while I was praying for healing helped me in the praying and increased the power of the Holy Spirit in the place.

There were many similar healings. People talked about them, and the healing ministry became very popular among the Christians as well as the non-Christians. All these experiences opened gates for me to build up a fellowship with non-Christians and Christians who were churchgoers but with no real relationship with the Lord. This gave me the opportunity also to share the Christian message with all of them. There is no need to mention all the healings that have taken place and thus I have included only a few selected experiences in this report.

My observations

Sri Lanka's Christian population (Catholic and non-Catholic Christians together) is 7.5%. Praying for healing is well accepted in our church culture.

People believe in God's supernatural power and are therefore ready to receive divine blessings.

- Healing experiences help people to get to know the living God and grow in him.
- Because of these encounters, people become more alive in their faith.
- Their willingness to share their experiences with others makes it easy to use them more actively in ministerial work and to train them as leaders.
- The people who receive divine healing become highly responsive to the Good News. Their commitment to God is very high.
- These people become actively involved in various church activities. Subsequently the church too becomes a growing and living church.
- When non-Christians experience this power of healing, their attitude and approach toward Christianity change. They build up very close relations with the church and a good fellowship with the church members. This results in their giving their maximum support to carry out various activities in church work.
- The sharing of testimonies results in the formation of new worship groups, which can later become worship centres.
- Healing is often a major key in evangelism. It does not only bring a cure to people's sicknesses and diseases, but also changes their lives. There are many people who either have been healed or are from a family where a member has been healed who have been drawn to the Lord as a result. Some of them used to be engaged in activities that are totally unacceptable to society. There were some who were even addicted to alcohol and drugs. It is wonderful to see how God has changed their lives and what good Christians they have become. Thus, God's healing really prepares a basis for us to use these people more actively for kingdom work.

Conclusion

Prayer for healing is not the only ministry that the church has to carry out but all mission activities finally bring healing to the people and the nation. But concentrating on developing this ministry to pray for people's diseases and sicknesses and helping them to experience our living God will produce more results in church life. It can be used as an effective method to reach the non-reachable. It also builds up very good partnerships with non-Christians. There are several people whom I have met in my ministerial life (some of whom have experienced divine healing) who have not become Christians, but because of the healing they experienced they have become good friends of Christians. They even help and support the church.

There was a Buddhist couple, both teachers, whom, in answer to prayer, God blessed with a beautiful boy. They never became Christians, but whenever they have time, they go to church and also support church activities. Yet this is not the end but a beginning, for the Holy Spirit would do the rest and draw each of these persons to form an active relationship with our God. All glory and honor is to God.

Therefore, I recommend giving a prominent place in the church to practice the healing ministry and to use it effectively. It helps the whole congregation to become more vibrant and grow into a living church

Response by Chediel Sendoro

I am really thankful for this paper that reminds the church of the importance and place of the healing ministry. In most cases the mainline churches have forgotten or given the healing ministry a very marginal position. People need healing in both physical and spiritual spheres. However, in the process of giving the healing ministry the right position, I have two points of caution.

Firstly, we need to be careful that we do not fall into the trap of using the healing ministry as a bait for catching people and bringing them to our churches. In my opinion, this will be nothing less than proselytism. I know some churches in my country that have been using the healing ministry to advertise their churches on TV and radio. I pray that we do not take that direction. I like the example given of the Buddhist couple who have not become Christians, but good friends of the church. Such people, since they are not persuaded / pushed to join Christianity, if they happen to decide to be converted, will be very strong in their faith.

Secondly, the paper recommends giving the healing ministry a prominent place in the church. My caution here is that we should not elevate the ministry to an extent that it overshadows all other ministries like preaching and teaching. This may lead to having members who come to church only because of miracles, but without roots in their faith. The apostle Paul insists that faith comes from hearing the message through the word of Christ (Rom. 10:17).

Apart from the two cautions, I concur with Weerasinghe that a healing ministry is an important tool in evangelism and needs to be given more space in the church.

Response by Mangisi Simorangkir

Kingsley Weerasinghe shares his experience with us, of his experiences with Jesus' power, when Jesus is successful in healing. Through his healing power, he would convince people in Sri Lanka that he is the Saviour, the healer of the world. I hear some stories like this in our country, Indonesia, as well, but there is a difference: Weerasinghe prays together with his congregation. He believes it is a gift to the church, not to a person, but the real church's experience, not that of a special man. In his sentence: "to build up fellowship with non-Christians and Christians."

In the Bible we see that God sometimes tested sick people, and their faith was rewarded by the healing of their body and soul, to show that the effects of faith may extend beyond our logic. The power of the Saviour and his miracles produce faith.

Jesus said that if you have faith the size of a seed, you would be able to move mountains. But why didn't we see any mountains moving, and see many Christians praying to be healed, but most were not healed? Is the word of Jesus wrong or do we have no clue about what faith is? I think here we have seen the meaning of faith and how to ask Jesus for giving us faith.

Weerasinghe and his congregation can move mountains. He and his congregation have experiences with the power of faith and prayer. They have experiences of how to increase the prayer level to the maximum; they heard answers to their prayers and dissipated worries about sickness. The point is, through prayer in faith people's lives have dramatically changed.

Weerasinghe tells stories of healing prayer that in turn inspire prayers for the healing of the soul and body, for spiritual and physical well-being. Everybody, not only people in Sri Lanka, needs to bring his or her vulnerability and suffering before the Lord. Physical and psychic pain have no regard for age or race. Anxiety and depression rob us of health and happiness, but Jesus wants to lighten our load when we turn to him with childlike humility. The power of God's love can break through any pain and suffering we encounter.

Part Four

Mission and JPIC

Our Common Mission: To Protect Human Dignity by Promoting Human Rights and the Rule of Law

Jochen Motte

All human beings are born free and equal in dignity and rights (Art. 1 - Universal Declaration of Human Rights)

Human dignity and human rights belong together and are indivisible. It is not just by chance that the Universal Declaration of Human Rights was passed by the United Nations (UN) on December 10th 1948, only a few years after the end of the Second World War with more than 56 million dead, the murder of six to seven million Jews and innumerable other criminal acts.

It seemed that after the unbelievable crimes of National Socialism and their repercussions and consequences throughout the world, for the first time in history the time had come to establish universal and indivisible rights for all human beings and to make these an integral part of international law.

The experience of a million-fold abasements and degradations led to the growing conviction that human dignity must be protected by human rights, and that all human beings have the right to human dignity, irrespective of race, colour, sex, language, religion, politics or other opinions, national or social origins, property, birth or status.

In view of the present challenges facing the world community more than 60 years after the adoption of the Universal Declaration of Human Rights, it is helpful to remember what global answers, which today still form the basis for our rule of law, were given to the global challenges of terror and injustice at that time. It is necessary to continue to re-interpret these and to develop them further, depending on the prevailing threats to human dignity that we encounter in old and new forms in our changing world today.

The Preamble of the Universal Declaration of Human Rights states:

> "Whereas recognition of the inherent **dignity** and of the equal and inalienable **rights** of all members of the human family is the foundation of freedom, justice and peace in the world,
>
> Whereas disregard and contempt for human rights have resulted in barbarous acts which have outraged the conscience of mankind, and the advent of a world in which human beings shall enjoy freedom of speech and belief and freedom from fear and want has been proclaimed as the highest aspiration of the common people, now, therefore the General Assembly proclaims this Universal Declaration Of Human Rights, article 1: **All human beings are born free and equal in dignity and rights.**"

The commitment to guarantee life in dignity and to uphold human rights is the duty of the states. It is their task to establish the rule of law and to maintain it. It is essential to maintain absolutely the universality and inalienability of human rights whenever any attempt is made to relativise them. Nor may civil and political rights be played off against economic, social and cultural rights or vice-versa; they are both dependent upon each other. The importance of social rights is particularly of note to the churches, on account of their own biblical traditions.

"But let justice roll down as waters, and righteousness as a mighty stream" (Amos 5:24)

Although the churches remained rather sceptical and disapproving of human rights until the end of the Second World War, they then became actively involved in the discussions about the formulation of the Universal Declaration and in the continuing process of its implementation. This particularly applies to the World Council of Churches which was able to exert direct influence on certain formulations of the Declaration through its Commission for International Affairs. All this took place against the background of a growing awareness of solidarity within the church's own global community whose members in many countries in the South, but also in the Eastern Block countries at that time, were affected by human rights violations and poverty. The churches took up the challenge to themselves as a global and yet at the same time local community of people to stand up together against injustice, exclusion and violence. They raised their voices to admonish and protest to governments and the community of states on behalf of the victims of human rights violations.

In this way the churches re-discovered their own traditions and learnt to read them in a new way. Today they consider it their work to protect the dignity and human rights of people throughout the world as a contribution in accordance with the core message of the good news of God's revelation in Jesus Christ. In 1977 Emilio Castro, General Secretary of the World Council of Churches from 1985 -1992, expressed this very pointedly in the following way:

> "God invites every creature to new life in him, and the church is sent into the world to struggle against everything which keeps that invitation from being presented to them and everything that hinders their freedom to respond to it. The freedom to respond to God implies more than what is normally called religious freedom, or even political freedom. The freedom to respond to God implies the liberation of man (*sic*) from everything that enslaves him, that deprives him of the possibility of standing as a free human being before God. Freedom from hunger, from want, from fear are aspects of that liberation. Such liberation creates

> community. ... 'Human rights' is not just the slogan of the political activist; it sums up the Christian missionary imperative.[1]

The God of the Bible as encountered by Israel is a God who leads from slavery to freedom, who on the way through the desert towards this freedom gives his people laws and legal statutes for a life in freedom, and with the gift of land guarantees the material foundation for a life in community with God and other human beings. It is not through violence and terror, but through justice and peace that Israel and Christianity shall become the "light of the nations".

It is remarkable in this context that the Old Testament law is particularly oriented towards the well-being of the weak, in other words, it declares precisely what we today understand as economic and social human rights to be the yardstick for justice and righteousness. Women and children, insofar as they are widows and orphans, are included among the groups of persons to be given special protection. "Thus saith the Lord: Do justice and righteousness, and deliver from the hand of the oppressor him who has been robbed. And do no wrong or violence to the alien, the fatherless, and the widow, nor shed innocent blood in this place." (Jer 22:3). God will give justice to those who live in injustice. "He shall defend the cause of the poor of the people, give deliverance to the needy and crush the oppressor!" (Ps 72:4)

"But let justice roll down as waters, and righteousness as a mighty stream." These words of the Prophet Amos (5:24) express God's just intent for a social community called to a life in freedom, and it is the representatives of the state with the king at their head who are made responsible before God that this law shall be applied.

Prophetic criticism is directed in very harsh words against perversions of the course of justice, of corruption, exploitation of the poor, the selling of people into slavery, fraudulent profit and other crimes, and the growing gap between the rich and the poor. Almost 3000 years after Amos, these phenomena that exclude people and prevent a life in dignity are not new, even if they encounter us today in a global context.

In the New Testament God encounters us in the person of Jesus of Nazareth. He is the true image of God. Through his death and resurrection we are freed from guilt and have a share in a new life in dignity and freedom. In his image all people - Jews and Christians, women and men, rulers and servants become brothers and sisters (Gal 3:28). The sanctity of all people and their inviolable dignity is grounded in Christ and in our relationship to him. For in his life and message Jesus directs us to act mercifully and in a healing way towards our neighbours, especially towards the weakest and most threatened members of the community, to protect them and give them back their dignity and rights. A

---

[1] Emilio Castro, *Human Rights and Mission*, IRM 56 / 263, 1977; p.215f.

good example of this is Jesus' parable of the Good Samaritan, where the Samaritan gave help in spite of the barriers of nationality and religion:

> "We are all one in Christ Jesus. And when we truly believe in the sacredness of human personality, we won't exploit people, we won't trample over people with the iron feet of oppression, we won't kill anybody."[2]

That was what Martin Luther King preached in a Christmas sermon on peace in 1967 in which he spoke out strongly against racial discrimination, and justified the dignity of all human beings, and therefore, with our fellowship and community in Christ.

It is with this understanding of dignity and justice that come from God and God's liberating and merciful action towards us that the churches participate in the discussions to bring about peace and justice in the age of globalisation. However, the churches do not exclude any other religiously or secularly motivated justification for action, but rather consider them constructively and are open for alliances and coalitions to enforce the implementation of human rights and the protection of human dignity wherever they are threatened. In the prophetic tradition, churches will raise their voices wherever people suffer under injustice and violence. They will remind the governments and states of their responsibility to enforce the rule of law and to make a life in dignity possible for all people.

Current missionary challenges for the churches to stand up for God's justice and righteousness

In many of the countries where there are member churches of the UEM, people suffer today under conditions such as the prophet Amos described 3000 years ago. For example, people in the Philippines are executed on account of their political convictions. The perpetrators are suspected in government and military circles and the judiciary fails to search for the perpetrators. According to various reports from human rights organisations in Sri Lanka, during the war between the Singhalese armed forces and the Liberation Tigers of Tamil Eelam, which ended in May, 2009 with the defeat of the LTTE, various war crimes have been committed by both parties. Civilians were trapped between the frontlines and attacks on civilians were launched by government forces and LTTE. Thousands of people have lost their lives. More than 200,000 refugees were kept in refugee camps with shortage of food and water even months after the defeat. In West Papua in Indonesia, people are discriminated against on account of their origin and colour and pushed to the fringes of society without

---

[2] J.M. Washington, (ed.), *Martin Luther King, A Testament of Hope. The Essential Writings of Martin Luther King Junior*, San Francisco: Harper San Francisco 1991, p.255.

the state doing anything to effectively protect the rights of the minorities. In Congo, countless women are raped and children misused as soldiers while perpetrators hardly need to fear that they will ever be called to account. Under such circumstances there is scarcely any chance that state structures will be set up to protect the poor and to implement law and order.

In view of the financial and economic crisis, the millions of poor people in Cameroon, Namibia, Tanzania and elsewhere have even less chance of an improvement in their situation.

In many countries where the UEM is affiliated to the churches, human rights are recognised on paper while insufficiently protected in practice. Often these states lack the will or the means to implement justice in face of corruption and a lack of resources.

In Germany, people are asking whether the state is fulfilling its duty to enable life in dignity and to enforce the rule of law in view of a collapsed finance and banking system with its excessive profit seeking, golden handshakes and incomes of millions for managers and the liberalisation and abolition of regulations and laws in this field. Everyone now has to bear the consequences, especially of course those who lose their jobs or were already on the fringe of society beforehand. Churches have also criticised the states of the European Union for the way they deal with refugees who are drowning in their thousands in the seas around Europe's coasts, and they have demanded the protection of refugees and more correct behaviour towards them.

Further challenges for current work on human rights can be listed as follows: the undermining of the ban on torture by the USA in its "war against terror"; the limitation of the right to freedom of speech by Islamic countries who refer in an unacceptable way to the right of freedom of religion, thereby turning the individual right into a right of the religion itself; the political instrumentalisation of human rights by various groups of countries in the Human Rights Commission of the United Nations.

In view of this situation, it is and remains part of the mission of the churches in the UEM with their proclamation of the liberating message of the Gospel to protect human dignity, to stand up for human rights and to remind those in power of their duty to ensure that there is justice and peace.

There can be no going back from the Universal Declaration of Human Rights or the Agreements and Conventions for the protection of human dignity that have so far been passed by the United Nations. We must make far more effort to further develop the norms for the international protection of Human Rights, and in particular to do away with the great deficits in their enforcement. At the same time it is necessary to constantly debate and justify anew the basis for the universality and indivisibility of human rights in discussions with other religions and ideologies, to work against fundamental tendencies within our own religion as well as in other religions and ideologies and to seek for common convictions. In this context the question of religious freedom is of particular importance for the churches.

Today the churches face the task of opposing clearly any undermining of the standards for human rights, naming states that violate human rights or indirectly contribute towards such violations, and campaigning for the setting up of international structures for the protection of human rights that are capable of coping with current global challenges.

In the process of globalisation, private protagonists and huge national and internationally operating companies and banks have gained a position of power that limits the scope of action of individual states and has dramatic effects on the living conditions of people throughout the world. Not only people in countries of the south but also people in the north see themselves more and more as victims of globalisation, when jobs are lost or people have to live and work in production under inhuman conditions. As in 2008, at an international conference of the UEM on justice, peace and the integrity of creation held in Batam / Indonesia, churches are raising their voices and demanding that companies, banks and international institutions such as the World Bank and the IMF must be integrated effectively into the responsibility for human rights.

In view of the situation that, this year, the number of hungry people in the world will reach the billion mark, and that over 30,000 children die every day of curable diseases, extreme poverty remains one of the greatest challenges that prevent a life of dignity. The churches welcomed the fact that in the year 2000, 189 states committed themselves to halve poverty throughout the world within 15 years. Due to the consequences of climate change and the international finance and economic crisis, the achievement of this goal has moved into the distant future. The churches will continue to speak out emphatically that more must be done to abolish poverty. How much more could be done if only a fraction of the money that is now being pumped into securing the financial systems were to be made available for fighting poverty, for education, health care and rural development!

These examples show that human dignity and human rights can only be protected effectively where there are structures under the rule of law, and where the state does not, through absence, looking away, toleration or even active support, violate human rights. For this reason the churches will speak out for the setting up of state structures where this is necessary, and will warn people that there is danger of the state being weakened where its scope of action to guarantee the law and to protect human dignity is reduced. In doing this the churches can and must refer back again and again to their own fundamental principles stemming from God's liberating action and God's will for justice and righteousness for the world. When the churches understand this they can give good reasons for the cause of human dignity. Based on God's commandment they will explain the task and the duty of the state to protect human dignity and to enforce human rights.

In 1977, Emilio Castro named the championing of human rights as the missionary imperative for the churches. I believe that this is still valid today and finds a visible expression in the mission understanding of the UEM member churches. The churches in the worldwide ecumenical movement stand, in their mission work, on the side of those who have fallen among robbers. As UEM we remind those in power of their responsibility to respect human dignity and to enforce human rights. At the same time we stand together with those in our society who suffer and are in need. We do this by sharing and helping others, by showing sympathy and fellowship to them and through intercessions and trust in God, to whom we pray: „Your kingdom come. Your kingdom of justice and of peace."

Response by Victor Aguilan

What struck me after reading this paper was the similar theme(s) I was developing in my paper. I agree with Motte that the protection of human dignity today will depend on how human rights and the rule of law are promoted and fulfilled. Hence any non-fulfilment is a violation of human rights and a denial of human dignity. The question now is who is required to fulfil human rights? Respect for human dignity cannot flourish under totalitarianism, anarchy, failed-states and tyrannical regimes. Human rights cannot be fulfilled in the absence of the rule of law. As church's mission becomes more involved in human rights advocacy, development and justice work, it is increasingly clear that churches may need to confront government and work with those who have the power to bring about change. There is a challenge for us to revisit our theology of the state in relation to the notion of the rule of law and human rights. Motte's paper has brought back to the discussion the question of church (religion) and state relation in the context of mission.

CHRIST, CREATION AND COMMUNITY: BIBLICAL WITNESS AND PRAXIS

Yak-Hwee Tan

"If icebergs break off and float past the south coast of New Zealand we wonder what is coming next." Rev. Asora Amosa[1]

Rev. Amosa, a Samoan-born pastor of the Presbyterian Church of Aotearoa, New Zealand made the above comment at the 16-21 November 2008 United Nations Advocacy Week of the World Council of Churches (WCC). Together with Christians from the Pacific Islands, Rev. Amosa was stressing the effects of climate change that are affecting the lives of their communities. That is to say, the issue is about life and death for the communities whose island nations would disappear under the rising waters. For the past twenty years, the sea level around the Carteret Islands has risen ten centimeters, damaging plantations and threatening homes. In fact, a Papua New Guinea community from the Carteret Islands (an atoll of Bougainville) is being forced to leave their homes to resettle in Bougainville because of the rising waters that threaten to engulf their island. They are the "first global warming refugees."[2]

Rev. Amosa also appealed "for worldwide solidarity with regard to climate change."[3] In other words, the ecological crisis that confronts the Pacific Christians is also the crisis of the worldwide Christian community. The crisis is *glocal. Glocal* is a term used in "global and transnational cultural studies to indicate the notion of how the local and global are co-complicit, each implicated in the other."[4] The ecological crisis is not only "local," that is the concern of the Christians of the Pacific Islands but also has an impact on the world. It is "global." The interconnection between the "global" and the "local" is inevitable, especially in the face of intense globalization when nations are interdependent upon each other for survival and life.

---

[1] *World Council of Churches News Release,* 24 November 2008 "Climate Change: It is too late to save our island, but not too late for the world, say Pacific Christians."

[2] *Council for World Mission News*, 6 November 2008. CWM received this information about "global warming refugees" from People First Network who reported it on 5 November 2008.

[3] *World Council of Churches News Release,* 24 November 2008, *op. cit.*

[4] Susan Stanford Friedman, "Locational Feminism. Gender, Cultural Geographies, and Geopolitical Literacy," in: Marianne Dekoven (ed.), *Feminist Locations. Global and Local, Theory and Practice*, New Brunswick, Rutgers University Press, 2001, p.31.

Voices from the fields of science, politics and economics have articulated their concern for the current and future situation of the earth and humans. Some scholars from the field of Bible and theology have broached this issue, raising some critical questions for the academy as well as for the church. This paper reflects my ongoing interest in the relationship between ecology and the Bible, and its implications for Christian witness and mission in the area of justice, peace and the integrity of creation.

Ecological crisis, saying it again

Much has been said regarding the ecological crisis that threatens the earth and humanity at large, and there are facts and figures from different non-governmental organizations to vouch for the severity of the situation. Christian Aid claims that according to the research done by the United Nations Intergovernmental Panel on Climate Change (IPCC),[5] the global temperature will rise by 2 centigrade by 2050 if the current rate of carbon emissions persists. They state that unless some action is taken, millions of people will face a shortage supply of food and water.[6]

While natural causes such as volcanic activity and the natural decay of plants and animals contribute to the emission of greenhouse gases, human activity also contributes to the change of climate. The emission of greenhouse gases, primarily carbon dioxide, is caused by the burning of fossil fuels which are used to generate power to heat or cool homes and offices, as well as to provide fuel for production and transportation. The greenhouses gases gradually raise the average temperature of earth and hence affect the weather patterns.

Whether it is human activities or natural processes that are causing climate change, one must not discount the impact globalization has upon the earth and humans. Larry L. Rasmussen identified such an impact as in three waves namely, "colonization, development and free trade global capitalism."[7] To put it differently, the discussion of ecological crisis must take into account that machines and money "deeply altered the biotic community, locally, regionally,

---

[5] The IPCC is a scientific intergovernmental body set up by the World Meteorological Organization (WMO) and the United Nations Environment Programme (UNEP). It was established to provide the decision-makers and others interested in climate change with an objective source of information about climate change. For more information about IPCC, check their website, http://www.ipcc.ch.

[6] http://www.christianaid.org.uk/issues/climatechange/facts/index.aspx, accessed on 11 February 2009. Some of the consequences of climate change are i) 250 million people will be forced to leave their homes between now and 2050; ii) with the rise of 1 centigrade, expected by 2020, an extra of 240 million people will experience water 'stress' and tens of millions more will go hungry due to falling agricultural yields and rising global food prices.

[7] Larry L. Rasmussen, "Global Ecojustice," *Mission Studies,* VVI-1, 31, 1999.

globally"[8], especially for people who are living in poor economies. They are the ones who suffer most from the effects of a global ecological crisis. As such, the inter-relationships between economy and ecology and empire must not be overlooked. In the church's approach towards mission, the question of justice, peace and the integrity of creation, therefore, must be addressed as part of the holistic nature of mission. A brief study of some biblical texts will help us to understand the inter-related relationships of creation, God, Christ and community.

Some biblical bases

In the field of biblical scholarship, there is an increasing interest in reading the biblical text with empathy for the natural world. In the recent years, the Society of Biblical Literature (SBL) has included a section "Ecological Hermeneutics" in their Annual Meetings.[9] Such an interest in the academy, I believe, is also triggered by the ecological crisis. Some biblical scholars and theologians have articulated a biblical understanding of creation, Christ and community from an ecological perspective. They examined passages from the Bible that speak of the integrity and dignity of creation, the role of God and humans in creation, and also its redemption and restoration.[10] In this section, I will discuss briefly some of these contributions and their implications for mission.

Old Testament

On the perspective of creation, Gene McAfee states that creation is "radically theocentric: 'The earth is the Lord's and all that is in it, the world, and those who live in it (Ps 24:1).'"[11] Every area of existence, the historical, the social and the cultural as well as the physical natural area is a "seamless whole created by God."[12] Therefore, McAfee argues that the relationship between the natural world (creation) and the supernatural (God) is not disconnected. God's self-revelation to God's people was oftentimes accompanied by natural phenomena

---

8 Rasmussen, "Global Ecojustice," *op. cit.,* p.127.

9 http://www/sbl-site.org./meetings/Congresses_CallForPaperDetails.aspx, accessed on 14 February 2009. In the 2009 Annual Meeting in New Orleans, a session in the "Ecological Hermeneutics Section," will look at "responses to natural disasters in the earth community (human and non-human), in the Bible and the Ancient Near East."

10 An example is an article by Gene McAfee, "Ecology and Biblical Studies," in Dieter T. Hessel (ed.), *Theology for Earth Community, A Field Guide*, Eugene (OR): Wipf and Stock Publishers, 2003, pp.31-44. McAfee gives a brief overview of studies of the creation account and their contribution to theological education, and propose areas for future exploration on the subject.

11 McAfee, *op. cit.,* p.36.

12 *Ibid.*, p.37.

such as fire, thunder, lightning, mountains, and trees,[13] exemplified in God's revelation to Moses at the burning bush (Ex 3). The relationship between creation and God is also intertwined when the psalmist affirms that God is the owner of creation, "for all the world and all that is in it is mine" (Ps 50:10-12),[14] and humans are given "dominion" over creation (Gen 1:26-28). However, the word "dominion" is problematic as it suggests that humans could trample over the earth and use up all its resources. Therefore, Jacobson suggests that "dominion" is to be read as oversight of God's divine kingdom and as such, humans are "God's royal representatives."[15] As "God's royal representatives," humans must know that the shape of God's reign is "justice and righteousness" and that they are to exercise it by "service and sacrifice" (*cf.* Ps 97:1-2; 99:4).[16] Therefore, in the light of God's creation, humans are to protect and safeguard earth and all its resources from degradation and destruction.

Furthermore, the motif of the land is closely connected with the people of Israel. Both the land and the people are bound up in their relationship to God. The prophet Ezekiel declares that God took away their land even though they are God's people (Ezek 36:20). Their land was taken away because God, who is the rightful owner, seeks justice and peace over God's creation, which apparently God's people did not exercise. However, the land would be restored to Israel when Israel acted rightly towards creation, neighbours and foreigners included, and all for the sake of God's name (Ezek 47:22-23).

Therefore, creation and God is holistic - a "seamless whole" whereby the continued existence of earth and humans and God is interconnected. When earth and humans suffer, God suffers too. However, God's intention is *shalom* for God's creation, both earth and humans. These similar perspectives are also found in the New Testament such as in Jn. 1:1-14, Rom 8:19-24 and Rev 17-18, 21-22.

New Testament

In the life and ministry of Jesus, the Gospel writers show Jesus' relationship to creation. For example, Jesus reaffirms God's care and concern for the birds of the air and the lilies of the field (Matt 6:26-30; *cf.* 10:29). Moreover, in the stilling of the storm (Mk 4:35-41) and walking on the water (Mk 6:45-51), Jesus is the Lord of creation.[17] The disciples expressed in wonder and questioned, "Who then is this, that the wind and the sea obey him?" (Mk 4:41). The fourth evangelist has an answer for them - Jesus is the Word.

---

13 *Ibid.*

14 *Ibid.*

15 Diane Jacobson, "Biblical Bases for Eco-justice Ethics," Dieter T. Hessel (ed.), *op.cit.*, p.46.

16 Jacobson, *op. cit.*, p.47.

17 Celia Deane-Drummond, *A Handbook in Theology and Ecology*, London: SCM Press Ltd, 1996, pp.28-29.

In the Prologue of his Gospel, the fourth evangelist emphasizes that Jesus Christ, the "Word was with God and the Word was God" (Jn 1:1). The preposition "with" in the phrase "with God" suggests a relationship, meaning that the Word is also divine.[18] Moreover, the Word is pre-existent since it existed from the beginning, even before creation itself (Jn 1:2). Another affirmation about the Word is that it is a partner in God's creation, "all things came into being through him, and without him not one thing came into being" (Jn 1:3). Therefore, in the Prologue, we see the inter-relationships of God, Christ and creation, a notion with which Paul concurs in his letter to the Colossians (Col 1:15-20).[19] Paul argues that, though creation is subjected to Christ and destined for Christ, creation is still in need of rescue "from the power of darkness" (Col 1:16, 13). This aspect he reiterates in his Letter to the Romans (Rom 8:18-23).

In his Letter to the Romans, Paul states that the whole creation waits to be liberated from the bondage of sin and to gain freedom of the children of God. The corrupted creation is likened to a parent who is in the process of giving birth (Rom 8:19, 22-23).[20] Consequently, the suffering of creation will result in a successful birth, that is, its redemption. Paul affirms that in the death and resurrection of Jesus Christ, God's new creation of reality has occurred (Rom 8:19-21). "Creation, fallen with the human race, shows a hope nonetheless that it will share also in its restoration."[21] And this hope of restoration of creation is also found in the reading of the Apocalypse of John by Barbara R. Rossing.

Rossing seeks to link nature and human justice in the face of the exploitation of both people and nature as evident in the gap between rich and poor as well as the destruction of ecosystems. She argues that the whole of the Apocalypse of John leads up to the vision of the New Jerusalem in Rev 21-22 which offers a "profoundly earth-embracing vision in which God descends from heaven to earth to live with humans in a renewed urban paradise."[22] Moreover, in the

---

18 Robert Kysar, *John. The Maverick Gospel. Revised Edition,* Louisville: Westminster John Knox, 1993, p.32.

19 The Colossian Christological hymn declares that the cosmic order is being mediated through Jesus Christ who created "all things." And it is through Christ's death and resurrection that God reconciles "all things" to God. Therefore, Christ is the key to cosmic and human existence. See Lewis R. Donelson, *Colossians, Ephesians, 1 and 2 Timothy, and Titus,* Louisville: Westminster John Knox Press, 1996.

20 A. Katherine Grieb, *The Story of Romans. A Narrative Defense of God's Righteousness,* Louisville: Westminster John Knox Press, 2002, p.80.

21 Philip F.,Esler, *Conflict and Identity in Romans. The Social Setting of Paul's Letter,* Minneapolis, Augsburg Fortress, 2003, p.261. He quotes Brendan Byrne, *Reckoning with Romans: A Contemporary Reading of Paul's Gospel.* GNS 18, Wilmington, DEL.: Michael Glazier, 1986, p.166.

22 Barbara R. Rossing, "For the Healing of the Word: Reading Revelation Ecologically" in: David Rhoads (ed.), *From Every People and Nation. The Book of Revelation in Intercultural Perspective,* Minneapolis: Augsburg Fortress, 2005, p.166.

centre of the New Jerusalem is the river of the water of life flowing from the throne of God, water which is available for everyone, not just people with economic resources but also to the poor whose cries were heard by God (Rev 21:6, 22; 22:17).[23] However, there is also the city of Babylon representing political Rome with its exploitative political power over people and land (Rev 17-18). The cargo list illustrates Rome's military and economic might. The natural resources of conquered lands and the transportation of human captives were all for Rome's development and benefit (Rev 18:11-13).[24] In showing the contrasting pictures of the two cities, the Apocalypse calls upon readers (and us) to make "an ethical choice between two citizenships," that is, that of the New Jerusalem or that of the city of Babylon.[25] God's people must "come out" from the city of Babylon in order to enter into the New Jerusalem.[26]

Summary

Rossing's reading of the Apocalypse of John is an implicit call to the church to address the question of justice, peace and the integrity of creation in the church's missionary task. The corrupted state of creation, earth and humans, is the result of the sin as seen in the exploitation of earth's resources as well as humans. And this violence and destruction of earth and humans must be interrogated, especially in the light that God is the owner of creation and the agent is Jesus, the Word. Corrupted creation is in desperate need of redemption and restoration. The church is therefore challenged to appropriate these biblical insights in its missionary task with respect to justice, peace and the integrity of creation.

Implications for mission and JPIC[27]

The phrase "justice, peace and the integrity of creation" (JPIC) first surfaced at the World Council of Churches Assembly at Vancouver in 1983. It was a time when there was a proliferation of nuclear arms which was threatening world peace in addition to the widespread injustice in the world. Therefore, the Assembly issued an invitation to churches to "*confess anew their faith*" and to seek "*the biblical vision of peace with justice for all,*" grounded in the affirmation that Christ is "*the life of the world*" and resists exploitative and dehumanizing systems. Though issues of justice and peace have long been

---

23 Rossing, "For the Healing of the World," *op. cit.*, pp.178-179.

24 *Ibid.*, p.177.

25 *Ibid.*, p.167.

26 *Ibid.*

27 D. Preman Niles, "Justice, Peace and the Integrity of Creation" *Dictionary of the Ecumenical Movement*, Nicholas Lossky et al. (eds.), Geneva, Switzerland: WCC Publications, 1991, pp.557-559. In this short article, Niles charts the rationale, the goals the continuing process of JPIC.

discussed in the World Council of Churches circles, the addition of "integrity of creation" highlighted the issues of the degradation and exploitation of the environment and the survival of life that need attention. Consequently, discussions in ecumenical circles began to examine the doctrine of creation anew, to see God as the Creator first and hence, also Liberator and Sustainer. Therefore, instead of referring to justice, peace and the integrity as three separate issues, the Assembly intended them to be viewed as three aspects of one reality, namely, the threat to life. Justice, peace and the integrity of creation are interconnected and churches were asked to make a response to them. The Assembly called for a new understanding of the missionary task of the church then and the process continues,[28] "JPIC will continue to be a primary emphasis in the work of WCC."[29]

The church's commitment to justice, peace and the integrity of creation in its missionary task is not only necessary but imperative in the face of the global ecological crisis. If the church understands that mission is *missio Dei*, that is, mission as a characteristic of God rather than an activity of the church, then the church is to participate "in the movement of God's love towards people."[30] The church, redeemed by God's love, is to bear witness to that redeeming love in the world, earth and humans included. Furthermore, God's love for the world is matchless and God is "actively engaged in the reestablishment of His liberating dominion over the cosmos and all of humankind."[31] Therefore, the proclamation of the gospel of Jesus Christ is holistic, ecology included. Ross Langmead states:

> "Ecology is about a whole system in interrelationship, and then systems-of systems. Abundant life shares a similar scope. This means that missiology needs to be both comprehensive (taking all dimensions of the gospel into account) and holistic (integrating them and not just adding one to another)."[32]

In the globalized world that we live, the material and cultural life of the local is also connected politically and economically to that of another, namely the global. We live in a *glocal* world in which we are interdependent and

---

28 Niles, *op. cit.*, p.558.

29 *Ibid.*, p.559.

30 David J. Bosch, *Transforming Mission. Paradigm Shifts in Theology of Mission*, Maryknoll, New York, Orbis Books, 1991, p.390.

31 J. Andrew Kirk, *What is Mission? Theological Explorations*, London, Darton, Longman and Todd Ltd., 1999, pp.26-27. Kirk cites Johannes Verkuyl 'The Biblical Notion of Kingdom: Test of Validity for Theology of Religion," in: Charles Van Engen, Dean Gilliland and Paul Pierson (eds.), *The Good News of the Kingdom: Mission Theology for the Third Millennium* (Maryknoll, New York, Orbis Books, 1993), p.72.

32 Ross Langmead, "Ecomissiology," *Missiology. An International Review*, Vol. XXX, No. 4, Oct. 2002, p.509.

interconnected. As such, the theme of justice, peace and the integrity of creation must be underscored in the mission endeavour.

Creation is the totality of "all things"

If we understand that creation is the totality of "all things," and God is its Creator and dwells in it, to abuse and degrade creation is sacrilegious. Besides, the totality of "all things" also implies that the existence and survival of earth and humans are inter-dependent and inter-related, like an *oikos.* Rasmussen pictures creation as *oikos*, a "vast public household" where abundance is shared and managed. In this *oikos,* unity is fostered between earth and humans and its life and existence is holistic.[33] Whatever affects earth affects also humans. The devastation of earth has ramifications for humans, especially for the poor whose existence depends on earth. Liberation theology insists that the mission of the church includes its social location and commitment to the poor and the marginalized. Leonardo Boff has widened liberation theology to include the liberation of the poor earth and calls for eco-justice, "a respect for the otherness of beings and things and their right to continue to exist."[34]

On the one hand, we see Jesus Christ as the creator of "all things" yet on the other hand, Jesus Christ is also the incarnate One who had compassion for the poor and the marginalized. "This Jesus is wholly of earth."[35] God in Jesus Christ hears the cries of the people of Kiribati and walks with them who have already lost their homes and livelihoods as floods have become more frequent and intense.[36] God in Jesus Christ is affected by creation's chaos and suffering and bears them upon God Himself. While the suffering felt by the people of Kiribati is local, it is also experienced by the global church community. The integrity of creation is broken since the "value of all creatures themselves, for one another, and for God, and their interconnectedness in a diverse whole that has unique value for God" is ruined.[37] Where is justice when "all things" are broken and in disarray? In its missionary task, the church becomes an agent of liberation through its proclamation of the gospel that Jesus Christ came to liberate, and also to reconcile and sustain "all things."

---

[33] Larry L., Rasmussen, "Creation, Church and Christian Responsibility," in: Wesley Granberg-Michaelson (ed.), *Tending the Garden. Essays on the Gospel and the Earth,* Grand Rapids, William B. Eerdmans Co., 1987, pp.116-117.

[34] Leonardo Boff, *Ecology & Liberation. A New Paradigm,* Translated from the Italian by John Cumming, Maryknoll, New York, Orbis Books, 1995, p.77.

[35] Larry L. Rassmussen, *Earth community earth ethics,* Maryknoll, New York, Orbis Books, 1996, p.283.

[36] *World Council of Churches World News Release*, 24 November 2008.

[37] Rassmussen, *Earth community earth ethics, op. cit.,* p.99. Rasmussen quotes Jay McDaniel, "'Where is the Holy Spirit Anyway?' Response to a Sceptical Environmentalist," *Ecumenical Review* 42, no. 2 (April 1990), p.165.

Christ, the Liberator and Reconciler

The death and resurrection of Jesus Christ redeemed "all things" from the rebellious powers that have imprisoned them. Jesus' suffering and death on the cross is a power that can truly redeem, heal and sustain creation because it is "power that intimately knows its degradation," be it physical, social or environmental.[38] On the cross, God in Jesus is made poor, abused and scandalized but ironically, it is on the cross that effective power rises extraordinarily to conquer those hellish powers that so imprisoned it.[39] To put it in another way, out of the suffering and death on the cross comes forth resurrection, "a vision of creation restored and renewed."[40]

Therefore, the church bearing the scars of the risen Lord Christ is called to witness the liberating and reconciling work of Christ whose mission is one of self-emptying and humble service. It means that the church is to enter into the pain and suffering of creation just as God in Jesus Christ did, to go to "the places of suffering to find God and God's power there."[41] In so doing, the church moves towards the redemption of the creation, earth and humans.

The dumping of nuclear waste on the earth not only poisons earth but disrupts and displaces the lives of the local communities which in turn affects the region, then the nation and ultimately the whole globe. An example is Taiwan's power company, Taipower which plans to build a nuclear waste plant in Taitung County. News about this project sparked many peaceful demonstrations opposing the disposal of nuclear waste mainly near aboriginal communities. After some discussions on this matter, the Paiwan and East Paiwan presbyteries of the Presbyterian Church in Taiwan called for all churches to unite against Taipower's use of monetary kickbacks as means to seduce aboriginal residents.[42] The use of the power of economics seeks to disunite the aboriginal residents in their resistance to environmental exploitation - this is a form of human exploitation. Accordingly, the Presbyterian Church in Taiwan sees the connection between human exploitation and environmental exploitation and addresses it as part of its missionary task.[43]

The church is also called to undertake the missionary task of reconciliation since it is "the heart of the mission of God and, as a result, the mission of the church."[44] In seeking reconciliation between creation and God, earth and

---

[38] Rassmussen, *ibid.*, p.287.
[39] *Ibid.*
[40] *Ibid.*, p.290.
[41] *Ibid.*
[42] Lydia Ma, "NIMBY: Taitung Residents and Churches Oppose Nuclear Waste Storage Plant," *Taiwan Church News,* 2966 Edition, December 29, 2008- January 4, 2009.
[43] Langmead, "Ecomissiology," *op.cit.*, p.514.
[44] Langmead, *ibid.*, p.512.

humans, humans and humans, the church brings about God's *shalom* to all. God's vision of *shalom* "demands the end to oppression and injustice and commitment to a new life of mutuality, justice and peace."[45]

In the face of the degradation and destruction of earth and humans, the church in its missionary task is challenged to act and affirm God's justice and *shalom* and the integrity of creation. God's vision of *shalom* is *glocal*, connecting "all things" locally as well as globally.

Community: A Call to Eco-Praxis

The church is to live out its missionary task in solidarity with the poor earth as well as the poor and oppressed. On the one hand, the church is to proclaim that Christ is risen and that in his resurrection, God has triumphed over the enemy and on the other hand, "to live the resurrection life in the here and now and to be a sign of contradiction against the forces of death and destruction."[46] With respect to the ecological crisis, it is a call to eco-praxis, to care and tend creation and to building up the lives of the communities for justice and peace. Being a partner in God's mission, the church is committed to be a sign of hope (Rom. 8:18). The following are two strategies which the church could adopt as its missionary task in eco-praxis:[47]

- **Education.** The Sunday school curricula in the church should include the missiological implications of Christ in creation for Christian witness and discipleship, such as raising awareness that poor economies are affected by the mishandling of earth and humans. In an affluent context like Singapore, the inclusion of ecological approaches in the Christian education curricula enables the constituents of the church to understand the privileged affluence Singaporean Christians live in and also to grasp the moral responsibility they have towards people who do not enjoy such privileges.[48] Furthermore, seminaries and mission agencies should include, as part of their training of Christian ministry workers and missionaries, a course on ecological awareness, identifying problems regarding the complex human-made systems as well as eco-biblical studies, eco-theology and eco-praxis.

---

45 Bosch, *Transforming Mission, op. cit.*, p.514.

46 Bosch, *op. cit.*, p.515.

47 Deanne-Drummond, *A Handbook in Theology and Ecology, op. cit.*, pp.165-171. In Appendix 2, Deanne-Drummond gives some practical ideas and suggestions for religious groups who want to embark or working on some environmental projects for a sustainable creation.

48 A note of thanks to Ms. Kimhong Hazra, lecturer at Trinity Theological College, Singapore for this insight.

- **Legislation.** The church must speak out for earth and humans when programmes and initiatives of governments and / or multinational companies might be economically productive but destructive to the eco-systems of earth. For example, the construction of a dam under the Balog-balog Multipurpose Project in the Philippines disrupts the lives of the Aetas of Tarlac who have lived in the mountain ranges of Tarlac-Zambales for centuries. Though the dam will create a huge reservoir, the lives of 500 families will be in disorder because they will be dislocated and uprooted from their land and mountains, upsetting their way of life. Local and foreign corporations have already disrupted the lives of the Aetas through mining, logging, tourism, and agri-business. The Balog-balog Dam project is a further disruption to their already detrimental existence. As such, the Aetas are demanding the preservation of the biodiversity of the mountains in Tarlac and Zambales and also the support of their communal system of irrigation vis-à-vis the Balog-balog dam project.[49] The Balog-balog dam project is a case whereby the church could "press for legislation sensitive to carefully planned sustainability" for earth and humans.[50]

Conclusion

The threat to the life of God's creation is real and grave, as articulated in the words of Rev. Baranite Kirata, "the storms and waves eat away our beaches and as they continue they will some day eat us ..... if we don't end up in the lagoon, we will end up fighting each other over land, food, water."[51] In the face of fragmentation and alienation between earth and humans, humans and humans, rich and poor, the missionary task of the church to proclaim redemption, reconciliation and restoration is ever more urgent. The derelict condition of creation, earth and humans is not the shape God envisions it to be when God first created it. However, sin in its visible and invisible forms has polluted creation, and it is in dire need of liberation and restoration in and for Christ. The death and resurrection of Christ is power over sin in its varied forms. And the church, a redeemed community which is in partnership with God, is constrained in its missionary task to establish justice, peace and the integrity of creation in all aspects of life, including the earth and humans.

---

49 http://www.oikotree.org/issues/viewIssue.aspx?id=18, accessed on 25 March 2009.

50 Kirk, *What is Mission?, op. cit.*, p.181.

51 *World Council of Churches News Release,* 24 November 2008, *op. cit.*

Response by Faustin Mahali

This paper gives a unique definition of the human relationship to creation and adds a critical perspective on the theological understanding regarding human domination over the whole creation. Tan emphasizes that human responsibility "to protect and safeguard earth and all its resources from degradation and destruction" should always be understood from the perspective of God's righteousness and peace. This concept is deeply integrated in the biblical concept of *oikos* as the house of God, making it easy to teach the need to holistically take care of the lives of the people and nature. I pray that in future, the striving of humanity for protection and regeneration of the destroyed and warming world be enriched with such biblical and theological grounds to give basis for a viable eco-theology. This paper can become a corner stone for the new beginning against an irresponsible Christian perspective on environment.

Peacemaking an Essential Element of Church Mission: A United Church of Christ in The Philippines (UCCP) Perspective

Victor R. Aguilan

In the Philippines there are two on-going armed rebellions. One is led by the Communist Party of the Philippines; its united front – the National Democratic Front and its armed wing – the New People's Army (CPP-NDF-NPA).[1] The NDF uses violence to advance its power. During election campaigns, the NPA engages in "revolutionary" taxations, threats and violence to support its candidates and harass opponents. In 2006, the government declared "all-out war" against the communists. The consequence was a wave of extra-judicial killings of left-wing activists.[2] The other one is the Muslim rebellion in Mindanao led by the Moro Islamic Liberation Front (MILF).[3] The recent clashes between government forces and the 12,000-strong MILF have displaced more than 500,000.[4] Amnesty International reported an estimate of a total of 120,000 deaths and a further 2 million displaced from the conflict over a period of 40 years.[5]

The Church recognizes that these armed conflicts between the government forces and rebels continue to pose a significant threat to life, liberty and the development of the nation. The need to end civil strife, uphold human rights and attain peace has become urgent. The United Church of Christ in the

---

[1] Joel Rocamora, *Breaking Through: The Struggle within the Communist Party of the Philippines*, Pasig City: Anvil Publishing, Inc. 1994; Alfredo Saulo, *Communism in the Philippines : Introduction*, Manila: Ateneo de Manila Univ. Press 1990, Kathleen Weekley, *The Communist Party of the Philippines 1968-1993: A Story of Its Theory and Practice*, Quezon City: University of the Philippines Press 2001.

[2] Asian Human Rights Commission , The state of human rights in the Philippines – 2008, Date: 17 Dec 2008, http://www.reliefweb.int/rw/RWFiles2008.nsf/FilesByRWDocUnidFilename/SHIG-7MEGM2-full_report.pdf/$File/full_report.pdf (accessed 10 February 2009).

[3] Hilario. Gomez Jr., *The Moro Rebellion and the Search for Peace: A Study on Christian-Muslim Relations in the Philippines*, Zambonga: Silsila 2001. Salah Jubair, A Nation under Endless Tyranny, 2nd ed., Lahore: Islamic Research Academy 1997.

[4] Asian Human Rights Commission, *ibid.*

[5] Amnesty International, Shattered Peace in Mindanao: The Human Cost of Armed Conflict in the Philippines in http://www.amnesty.org/en/news-and-updates/news/the-human-cost-of-armed-conflict-in-the-philippines-20081029 (accessed 10 Feb 2009).

Philippines (UCCP), a UEM-member church, is one of the Protestant Churches in the Philippines which responded to this call.[6]

The UCCP believes that peacemaking is an essential element of the mission of the Church in the Philippines today. This paper attempts to analyze the peacemaking ministry of the UCCP. Its first part will focus on the concept of peace and the UCCP understanding of peace and peacemaking. It will also highlight human rights issues, the problem of militarization, and church-state relations. The last part will discuss the theological bases of peacemaking.

Peace and peacemaking: a definition

Defining peace is enormously tricky, according to Johan Galtung and Ho-Won Jeong, given the wide range of meanings it has been given by diplomats, scholars, activists and educators.[7] In their studies, they concluded that peace could be defined in two ways, namely: negative and positive peace.[8] Negative peace is the absence of direct violence (physical, verbal, and psychological) between individuals, groups, and governments. The concept of negative peace addresses immediate symptoms, the conditions of war, and the use and effects of weapons.[9]

Positive peace implies reconciliation and restoration through creative transformation of conflict. It is more than the absence of violence or war; it is the presence of social justice through equal opportunity, a fair distribution of power and resources, equal protection and an impartial rule of law. The concept of positive peace involves the elimination of the root causes of war, violence, and injustice and entails the conscious effort to build a society that reflects these commitments.[10]

The National Council of Churches in the Philippines (NCCP) also attempted to define peace.[11] The term *shalom*, a Hebrew word, is used in the NCCP

---

[6] The mainline Protestant denominations in the country are the United Church of Christ (UCCP), the United Methodist Church (UMC), the Iglesia Evangelica Unide de Cristo (UNIDA), the Iglesia Evangelica Metodista en las Islas Filipinas (IEMELIF), Lutheran Church, Salvation Army, and Convention of Philippine Baptist Churches with a total membership of more or less 2 million. Research and Documentation Office (RDO), Church Profiles, National Council of Churches in the Philippine: Quezon City 1989.

[7] Johan Galtung, "Violence, Peace, and Peace Research," *Journal of Peace Research* 6, no. 3 (1969): pp.167-191., and Ho-Won Jeong, *Peace and Conflict Studies: An Introduction*, Aldershot: Ashgate 2000.

[8] Jeong, *op. cit.*, pp.23-30.

[9] *Ibid.*

[10] Galtung, *op. cit.*, pp.167-193.

[11] Feliciano Carino and Liberato C. Bautista, eds., A Vision of Peace, an Agenda for Justice, in: *Tugon: An Ecumenical Journal of Discussion and Opinion*, vol. XI, Quezon City: NCCP 1991.

documents to define peace. To quote from the document "The Effects of Righteousness will be Peace (A Vision of Peace)",

> "Shalom. . . is a state of well-being and wholeness of life that embraces harmony with one's neighbors and social relations, with nature and creation, and with one's self. It's attainment involves a transformation of economic, social and political life so that these begin to embody justice and righteousness, of our relations with nature, and with the whole of creation so that these begin to embody care and respect for God's purposes for them, and of ourselves so that we embody in our lives righteousness, love and human compassion."[12]

Thus, the Biblical understanding of peace is holistic and encompassing. It contains both the negative and positive meanings of peace.

UCCP understanding of peace

In the UCCP perspective on peace and peacemaking both "positive" and "negative" meaning could be found. This notion of peace is reflected in the well-known UCCP statement, "Peacemaking: Our Ministry," which states: [13]

> "Genuine and lasting peace comes when people's needs are served,
> For as long as peasants remain landless,
> For as long as labourers do not receive just wages,
> For as long as we are politically and economically dominated by foreign nations,
> For as long as we channel more money to the military than to basic social services,
> For as long as the causes of social unrest remain untouched,
> There will be no peace."[14]

However, the search for negative peace appeared to be the focus of the peacemaking ministry of the UCCP. Many of the issues or campaigns of the UCCP were conflict de-escalation activities.[15] To address the armed conflict the UCCP has been engaged in and advocated the following:

1. monitoring of, exposing, protesting against, and legal measures to address human rights violations resulting from insurgent and / or counter-insurgency operations;

---

[12] *Ibid.*, pp.9-10.

[13] Council of Bishops, "Peacemaking: Our Ministry, 21 August 1986," in *UCCP Statements and Resolutions (1948-1990)*, Lydia N. Niguidula (ed.), Quezon City: Education and Nurture Desk, United Church of Christ in the Philippines 1990, p.147.

[14] *Ibid.*, p.148.

[15] Lydia Niguidula (ed.), *UCCP Statements and Resolutions* (1948-1990), Quezon City: United Church of Christ in the Philippines 1990; Edna J. Orteza, "The Quest for Lasting Peace: The UCCP Experience," photocopy, 12 December 2005.

2. calling for the resumption of peace talks and the forging of ceasefires;
3. relief and rehabilitation for internal refugees and other victims caught in the crossfire;
4. the establishment of peace zones or sanctuaries to demilitarize the armed conflicts;
5. the campaign to observe international humanitarian law in the conduct of the war; and
6. opposition to militarization and a total war approach in resolving armed conflicts.

The peacemaking ministry of the UCCP could be categorized as a citizen-approach to peacemaking. Several practitioners and scholars have called this approach by various names: conflict transformation,[16] third side,[17] and just peace.[18] Church and religious groups are viewed as "third side" or "third party" to the ongoing conflict between the state and the non-state armed groups. They are in a better position to engage in intermediary peace building basically due to their established neutrality, credibility and non-antagonistic relationship with the state and non-state armed agents. A citizen approach is a strategy that places an emphasis on the role of the community members with regard to steering conflicts away from violence and towards a just and lasting peace. It focuses on what congregations, local churches and individual Christians can do to prevent war or de-escalate conflict. To give three examples from the UCCP experience:

In 1990 the Executive Committee adopted the statement "A Declaration Against Violence," issued by the Council of Bishops.[19] The Bishops became concerned about the alarming increase of violence and senseless killings in society. To address the escalating violence the church recommended concrete actions. To the government, the Bishops recommended the abolition of the para-military units. They also recommended the immediate termination of the U.S. Bases agreement. To the rebels and soldiers, they called to stop all strafing, bombing and ambushes, to respect the rights of civilians and other non-combatants; and to return to the negotiating table to deal with a comprehensive settlement of insurgency. The Bishops admonished the weapons

---

[16] John Paul Lederach, *Building Peace: Sustainable Reconciliation in Divided Societies*, Washington DC: United States Institute of Peace Press 1997, p.24.

[17] William Ury, *Getting to Peace: Transforming Conflict at Home, at Work, and in the World*, New York: Viking 1999.

[18] Glen H. Stassen, *Just Peacemaking: Transforming Initiatives for Justice and Peace*, 1st ed., Louisville Kentucky: Westminster John Knox Press 1992.

[19] Executive Committee, "A Declaration against Violence, 23 February 1990," in *UCCP Statements and Resolutions (1948-1990)*, Lydia N. Niguidula (ed.), Quezon City: United Church of Christ in the Philippines 1990, pp.194-198.

manufacturers to stop making weapons. The Bishops also requested all Christians and people of other faiths to "be true instruments of peace."

Another example is the UCCP statement declaring the "Churches as Sanctuaries and Zones of Peace."[20] The total war strategy of the government had resulted in the displacement of people and communities in conflict-torn areas. The churches saw the influx of internal refugees or internally displaced people (IDP) caught in the crossfire between the government forces and rebels. The UCCP offered its buildings and premises as sanctuaries for the internal refugees. "As sanctuaries, these places and premises are open to all people – regardless of color and creed, sex and status, and of political and religious affiliation – at all times in all circumstances of need." The UCCP welcomed all those needing sanctuary "to use these places for protection, study, reflection, retreat, prayers and meditation, or simply for rest and quiet." As zones of peace, the churches "are to be used for activities that build community and contribute to a deeper understanding of and commitment to peace and justice." Weapons should not be brought to the places and premises designated as zones of peace. The UCCP also asked government soldiers and armed rebels "to respect and support this decision for the sake of Jesus, the Prince of Peace."

During the 8th Quadrennial General Assembly on May 27, 2006 the Assembly adopted a "Resolution and Statement of Great Concern Regarding the Current Explosive Breakout in Human Rights Violations." It was a response to "the increasing number of militants who had been liquidated under circumstances that seemingly point to the military as responsible," which included some church members and leaders of the UCCP. Appealing to the church's prophetic role, the UCCP is called "to strongly decry and denounce the ongoing unmitigated killings of militants and activists in our society, and hereby call upon the military leadership, especially the Commander-in-Chief, President Gloria Macapagal Arroyo, to immediately cause the stopping of these extra-judicial executions, and to employ all means to bring to justice, without delay, all those responsible in the commission of the crimes." The UCCP also urges all local churches "to organize and mobilize so as to address effectively this particular upsurge in human rights violations." And finally the Church encourages and supports "lawyer-members of the Church, in all the jurisdictions" to organize for the purpose of defending those who are victims of human rights violations.

Issues connected with the peacemaking ministry

As seen above, there are three issues which are intertwined in the peacemaking of the church. These are human rights, militarization and church-state relations.

[20] Executive Committee, "A Declaration of UCCP Churches as Sanctuaries and Zones of Peace, 23 February 1990," in *UCCP Statements and Resolutions (1948-1990)*, ed. Lydia Niguidula, Quezon City: United Church of Christ in the Philippines 1990, pp.199-200.

Human rights

The church has consistently emphasized that the protection of human rights is integral to its peacemaking ministry. There is no lasting peace without human rights. The UCCP has made human rights advocacy part of its ministry. The 1993 Constitution and By-Laws incorporated human rights as one of the UCCP's declared principles. The UCCP is the only church in the Philippines to have incorporated human rights instrumentalities and UN declarations as part of its ecclesiology.

Nevertheless, human rights advocacy is controversial in the UCCP. There are those who say that the Bible is silent about human rights; others argue that the church should be concerned with saving souls for heaven rather than protecting and empowering humans for life on earth; a third group insists that Christians should be mediators of reconciliation, rather than conscientizing and agitating people to "fight and claim their human rights," which runs counter to the command of Jesus to love your neighbours and even your enemies; and the fourth criticism is that human rights are "communist propaganda".[21]

The most controversial issue besetting the human rights ministry of the UCCP is the perception that it supports "communist propaganda." It was said that the UCCP statements and resolutions on the alleged human rights violations tend to be biased against the soldiers and police.

These views are mistaken and should be corrected. In fact the UCCP has criticized not only the military but also the rebels. In 1989, the UCCP issued a statement holding the National Democratic Front and the New People's Army accountable for having committed gross human rights violations against civilians who were members of the UCCP in the infamous Rano massacre where more than 40 people, including women and children, were killed by the New People's Army. The UCCP wrote in an open letter:

> We condemn this heinous act, and in the name of the victims, demand justice…As a church committed to a just and lasting peace, we call on the National Democratic Front to acknowledge full responsibility for the massacre and to ensure that such a tragedy will never again occur.[22]

---

[21] Erme Camba, "Interview by Author, Dumaguete City," 5 December 2006. See also "Military Names 25 Red Front Groups," *Pahayagang Malaya*, November 25, 1987.; Christian V. Esguerra, "Government Links Electoral Watchdog to Reds," *Philippine Daily Inquirer*, May 21 2004.

[22] Erme Camba and others, "Justice Not Vengeance: An Open Letter to the National Democratic Front and the Government of the Republic of the Philippines, 3 July 1989," in *UCCP Statements and Resolutions (1948-1990)*, Lydia N. Niguidula (ed.), Quezon City: United Church of Christ in the Philippines 1990.

Militarization

Another issue is the role of the military in society and the danger of militarization or militarism. The UCCP rejects militarization because it will not bring about a just and lasting peace. Militarization has been described as "the process whereby military values, ideology and patterns of behavior achieve a dominating influence on the political, social and economic, and external affairs of the State and as a consequence the structural ideological and behavioral patterns of both society and government are militarized."[23] Militarization is a political process whereby the military plays a dominating role in the formulation and implementation of national policies which undermine civilian society.[24] The church considers this as a major threat to peace. Militarization destroys democracy, civilian rule and violates human rights. It siphons off resources which are needed for social services. It prevents genuine peace talks with rebels and insurgent groups. Militarization thrives on fear, thus it perpetuates wars and conflicts. The militarist solution has in fact fuelled the insurgency. Human rights violations, not ideology, recruit more people to support the armed rebel groups.

Although the Church is critical of militarization it recognizes the legitimacy of the military. The UCCP was the first Protestant church to assign chaplains to the military.[25] For the UCCP, the armed forces exist to protect the people from criminals and the country against aggression. But militarization is a threat to both law enforcement and defence because it undermines the civilian supremacy which is the basis of democratic societies. There can never be peace without upholding human rights. But to protect human rights the people need security.

Church and state relations

The church affirms the necessity and legitimacy of the government in peacemaking. The state is to deter evil and lawlessness in society. Peacemaking theology acknowledges the need for someone, somewhere, sometime to use

---

23 *Ecumenical Movement for Justice and Peace, Iron Hand, Velvet Glove: Studies on Militarization in Five Critical Areas in the Philippines*, Geneva: Commission of the Churches on International Affairs World Council of Churches 1980, p.1.

24 See Mathews George Chunakara, *The Militarisation of Politics and Society: Southeast Asian Experiences*, Hong Kong SAR: DAGA Press Documentation for Action Groups in Asia (DAGA) 1994; Carolina Hernandez, The Role of the Military in Contemporary Philippine Society, *Diliman Review* 32, no. 1 (1984), pp.1-24; Viberto Selochan, Could the Military Govern the Philippines, Quezon City: New Day Publishers. 1989.

25 General Assembly, Resolution Recommending the Assignment of a Protestant Chaplain to Every Major Service of the Armed Forces of the Philippines, GA 21-27 May 1962," in *UCCP Statements and Resolutions (1948-1990)*, Lydia N. Niguidula (ed.), Quezon City: United Church of Christ in the Philippines 1990.

force and coercion to preserve order, maintain public safety and ensure security in a fallen world. In exercising its powers, the state can become dangerous and lethal, thus it should be restrained and regulated. The power of the state is primarily to protect human rights, guarantee human security and execute justice for all people at all times.[26]

For this reason the UCCP asserts that Christians have a twofold duty towards the state, namely 1) the duty to cooperate with lawful authority, and 2) the duty to be prophetic. The notion of cooperation with the state entails a proper understanding of the working of the political system. Before engaging the government, church leaders and members need to be fully informed about social and political issues and how government functions at all levels, what services are available, and how they may best become involved individually and collectively. Intertwined with the Christians' cooperation with the government is the church's prophetic duty.[27] The church must expose human rights violations, lies and deception, cheating and corruption in government. The prophetic witness of Christians can provide the critical dimension which is necessary for the preservation of the state as God's instrument of earthly justice.[28]

The UCCP has recognized that it is essential to maintain a church-state distinction. The church's loyalty belongs only to God. The church must concern itself with the Gospel. The church is not entrusted to wield political power. The church should be suspicious of worldly power because powers are fallen. Thus, the church should be critical of all groups engaged in partisan power struggles, state and non-state agents. This implies that the church should avoid any unqualified form of alignment with political authorities.

But when a government habitually violates human rights and oppresses its people, it loses its legitimacy. Thus the church is no longer morally obliged to obey the government. But the UCCP rejects violent resistance against the government. It rejects "any and all forms of violence and subversion as means of seeking reforms."[29] The church also discourages members', especially church workers' "membership, participation, and involvement in armed groups" because this is contrary to the nonviolent teaching of the gospel and Jesus'

---

[26] Victor Aguilan, Political Authority and the Church: The Challenge of the Reformed Political Tradition, in: *Silliman Journal* Vol 41., no. 1 January-June (2000).

[27] See Hilario Gomez Jr., Appendix 5: Open Letter to the President, 16 December 1994, in *State of the Mission of the United Church of Christ in the Philippines*, ed. Council of Bishops, UCCP Ellinwood Malate, Manila: United Church of Christ in the Philippines 1998, pp.88-89.

[28] Aguilan, *op.cit.*.

[29] General Assembly, A Statement of Social Concern, 1970, in *UCCP Statements and Resolutions (1948-1990)*, Lydia N. Niguidula (ed.), Quezon City: United Church of Christ in the Philippines 1990.

commandment that his disciples are called to be peace-makers.[30] The church should neither legitimize the violence of armed opposition nor endorse state militarism. It is the duty of the Christian to work for justice and for the elimination of all forms of violence.

Theological authorizations of the peacemaking ministry of the UCCP

Furthermore, the UCCP perspective on peace and peacemaking is justified by five theological themes. These are Christology, the nature of the church, doctrine of creation, *imago Dei*, and the kingdom of God.

The foundation for the peacemaking ministry of the UCCP is Christological. Faith in Jesus Christ, the Lord of the church, of life and of history is the ground of peacemaking. He is the Prince of Peace who compels the church to be a peacemaker.[31] The Christological basis of the UCCP peacemaking is rooted in the Gospel that God loves all humanity, including humanity's world, and is concerned about human life in society. The Christological foundation permeates all other theological themes. This is what Bishop Erme Camba was referring to in a speech delivered during the 16th General Synod of the United Church of Christ in the United States in 1987. He asserted that "commitment to the persistent struggle for justice and relentless quest for peace is rooted in this character of the Gospel."[32] Reiterated by Bishop Hilario Gomez, "the Christian mission, being the mission of God in Jesus Christ, is to concretize the *euangelion*, the Gospel of God in the world that God loves so much."[33]

Another theological theme used to authorize the UCCP peacemaking ministry is its understanding of the nature of the church. Ecclesiology is closely intertwined with Christology. Jürgen Moltmann describes this relationship between the church and Christ: "Every statement about the church will be a statement about Christ. Every statement about Christ also implies a statement about the church."[34] It is appropriate for the UCCP to make peacemaking part of the UCCP ecclesial identity.

The UCCP affirms the biblical image of the church as the body of Christ and acknowledges Jesus Christ as the Head of the Church.[35] The image of the

---

30 Executive Committee, Minutes of the Meeting September 19-21,1989 Action 89-178.

31 Council of Bishops, "Neither Shall They Learn War No More, 22 September 2002," *The United Church Letter*, September 2002.

32 Erme R. Camba, Struggle for Justice: Quest for Peace, in: Alice G. Guillermo (ed.), *Religion and Society: Towards a Theology of Struggle*, Philippines: Forum for Interdisciplinary Endeavors and Studies 1988, pp.147-156.

33 Hilario Gomez Jr. , Christian Mission: Church's Timeless Task for God's World, *The United Church Letter*, January-March 1995, p.3.

34 Jürgen Moltmann, *The Church in the Power of the Spirit*, London: SCM Press, Ltd. 1977, p.6.

35 Rom 12:1-21; I Cor 12:1-31; 2Cor 5:16-21; Eph 4:1-16.

church as one body of Christ signifies unity and faithfulness to Christ. As head, Christ governs, commands, and directs his body. Thus, the church as Christ's body is commissioned to continue Christ's ministry until his return.

Hence, when the UCCP Bishops declare that peacemaking is a ministry of the church, the Bishops are announcing that it is Christ's own ministry; and this ministry is entrusted to the church. "As a church, we should actively work for understanding, reconciliation, and unity. We should join hands with peoples of the world in the common quest for peace based on justice. Above all, we should follow Jesus Christ, the Prince of Peace."[36] As Bishop Gomez puts it, "If the church is the church, then the church should follow faithfully the demands of God in Jesus Christ."[37]

The UCCP perspective on peacemaking also finds authorization in the doctrine of creation. God is the Creator and creation is good. This doctrine is based on the biblical creation story. In Article II Section 11 of the Church Constitution, the UCCP declares that "as steward of God's creation, the United Church of Christ in the Philippines shall protect, promote and enhance the ecological balance and the integrity of creation."[38] The church is called "upon to be vigilant to defend God's creation," against mining and logging activities.[39] The UCCP understands that the mandate placed upon humans to assume responsibility for helping to preserve God's creation is a fundamental Christian theme. Since creation which is created good is threatened by violence and abuses, the church is mandated to preserve creation. Peacemaking is a concrete expression of this divine mandate. Thus, it is not surprising for the UCCP to question the policy of allowing the presence of nuclear weapons and foreign (US) military bases or troops in the country.[40]

Another theme that authorizes the UCCP peacemaking is the doctrine of *imago Dei.* The Statement of Faith of the UCCP declares that "persons are created in the image of God, sinful but destined to live in community with God. Entrusted with God's creation and called to participate in the establishment of a meaningful and just social order." The UCCP has made this biblical

---

36 Council of Bishops, Peacemaking: Our Ministry, 21 August 1986.

37 Faith, Human Rights and the Shalom of God, May 11, 1997, UCCP-UEM Fact-Finding Workshop and Consultation, Baguio City, published in The United Church Letter, Vol XL No. 1 January-June 1997, p.25

38 UCCP, Constitution and Bylaws, Quezon City 1996 revised.

39 General Assembly, "Resolution on Environmental Concerns, 21-26 May 1990," in *UCCP Statements and Resolutions (1948-1990)*, Lydia N. Niguidula (ed.),Quezon City: United Church of Christ in the Philippines 1990.

40 General Assembly, "Resolution Urging the Implementation of the Constitutional Declaration of a Nuclear Free Philippines and the Withdrawal of All Military Bases and Facilities in the Country, 21-26 May 1990," in *UCCP Statements and Resolutions (1948-1990)*, Lydia N. Niguidula (ed.), Quezon City: United Church of Christ in the Philippines 1990.

understanding of human beings one of the bases for its peacemaking ministry. The church declares that the root of human rights must be sought in the creation of human beings in the image of God. Human rights are gifts from God.[41]

Hence any violation of human rights is a denial of human dignity and a form of violence. This is emphasized in another document, "A Declaration against Violence," in which the church "affirms that persons are created in the image of God. There is no distinction. All persons have equal worth in the sight of God."[42] The image of God creates value in the human person. And each human being has the same or equal worth. This image of God makes humanity fully human. The church further declares that human life is "a divine gift." Human life is to be regarded not only with dignity but also with sanctity. The concept of human dignity and of the sacredness of human life can be best described as the value of human beings above the market, the state, and ideologies. Hence no human being can rightly take another human life, for human life belongs solely to God.

The image of God in human beings also leads to a creation of a community. The Statement of Faith says "destined to live in community with God." This implies that human beings are created in the image of God for community and not simply as isolated individuals; they are to enjoy and fulfil their human rights in community with other people. Community makes humanity responsible for the welfare of others. In addition this community is an inclusive community. An inclusive community includes Christians and people of other faiths. The UCCP acknowledges that human rights are for everybody. And as God's creatures, Christians are called to live and to serve God in the world, in community.

The final theological theme used by the UCCP in authorizing its peacemaking ministry is the kingdom of God. This signifies the presence of God's rule in the lives of people. This theme is connected with the goal of peacemaking, which is not merely to end deadly conflict but to transform society. The coming of God's kingdom ushers in the transformation of humanity in personal and social, individual and societal ways. "God is at work to make each person a new being in Christ."[43] Although it is God who brings the kingdom, the UCCP believes that human beings are invited to participate in the process. Christians are called to participate in the establishment of a meaningful and just social order.

---

[41] General Assembly, Resolution for the Creation of the Human Rights Desk, 21-26 May 1978, in *UCCP Statements and Resolutions (1948-1990)*, Lydia N. Niguidula (ed.), Quezon City: United Church of Christ in the Philippines 1990.

[42] UCCP Executive Committee, A Declaration against Violence, 23 February 1990, in *UCCP Statements and Resolutions (1948-1990)*, Lydia N. Niguidula (ed.), Quezon City: United Church of Christ in the Philippines 1990.

[43] Statement of Faith of the United Church of Christ in the Philippines, *op. cit.*

Conclusion

In conclusion, this paper has shown that the peacemaking ministry of the UCCP is an essential element of the church mission in the Philippines as well as the rest of the world. It is a response to God's call to proclaim the Gospel in a violent and sinful world. It is a faithful response to Jesus' command to be peacemakers.

From the experience of the UCCP, peacemaking is integral to a human rights ministry. This has led the UCCP to reject militarization to resolve armed conflict. It has been proven in the past that militarization has contributed to worsening human rights violations. But the UCCP recognizes the legitimacy of having soldiers and police in society. This is an important concern which the UCCP has to address. There is an imperative to articulate its theology of peace and security.

In addition the UCCP has recognized that peacemaking requires a democratic government. The role of government is to be an instrument of justice. It is to protect the innocent, the vulnerable and the oppressed from lawlessness and criminality in society. But if it does not do so, it loses its legitimacy, and the church does no longer have to obey it.

And finally the UCCP peacemaking ministry has a solid theological authorization. These theological themes are Christology, the doctrine of creation, *imago Dei,* the Kingdom of God, and the nature of the church. The peacemaking ministry of the UCCP is a response to a violent and sinful world specifically in the Philippine context. These theological warrants continue to challenge UCCP local churches as well as other Christian communities.

Part Five

Mission and Culture (A) In the European Context

The Church and Religious Seekers in a Pluralistic Society: The German Case

Sören Asmus

The situation in the German mainline churches with regard to 'seekers,' people who have an interest in religious matters, is marked by three different general aspects: firstly, the continuing dominance of the churches' role in religious matters; secondly, by a growing – not only religious – pluralism outside the church; and thirdly, by the equally growing awareness of inner-church pluralism. All of this together forms the framework in which the mainline churches try to find an appropriate approaches to reach 'seekers' and to be a welcoming church.

In order to give an impression of the situation, I will initially outline the role of the church in society in religious matters; I will then look at the inner pluralism in the mainline churches; and I will finally offer a brief description of religious pluralism with regard to 'seekers' by focusing on the religious phenomenon of 'esotericism.'

Defining the religious space – still the 'mainline' churches

Though the membership of the mainline churches continues to decrease, both the Roman Catholic and the Protestant churches are the dominant religious institutions in Germany.[1] However, in order to understand the situation in Germany one has to bear in mind that all matters of religion are first and foremost viewed as private matters. While religion is transmitted through families and in congregations, as well as to some degree through the school system, all matters of faith are regarded as individual decisions. German law guards the individual both in their positive and negative religious freedom, German society expects to exclude all social or political pressure or expectations of conformity from the religious realm. Unless one understands the fact that religion is first of all both private and individual matter, it is quite impossible to comprehend the situation in Germany. At the same time the mainline churches remain the dominant religious institution when it comes to the public perception of religion.

[1] For 2007 the EKD found 31.0 % Roman Catholics and 30.2 % Protestants among the population of Germany. *Cf.* Evangelische Kirche in Deutschland: Kirchenmitgliedszahlen am 31.12.2007, November 2008; p.7. http://www.ekd.de/download/kirchenmitglieder_2007.pdf, and: REMID: Religionen in Deutschland: Mitgliedszahlen, http://www.remid.de/remid_info_zahlen.htm, both accessed 16 March 2009.

This also applies with regard to the legal structures: the laws concerning the former state churches form the framework to which the other religious communities must conform.

Similarly, mainline churches continue their dominance over public discussions and awareness. Whenever a public matter calls for religious expression, such as the mourning after catastrophes or remembrance days, the institutions ask for a worship service. While asking the mainline churches to organize them, the public usually demands "inter-religious services" which should include all faiths.[2] This conforms to a general impression: religion is much in the public focus; but while there is little real knowledge of the living religions, there is a tendency to sum up different cultures under religious headlines. For example, there are growing attempts to sum up all the different Turkish, Arabic, African and other migrant groups under the heading of "the Muslim Community", completely ignoring the differences between Sunni, Shiite and, for instance, Alevit and other Islam groupings. Instead, "the Muslim Community" is a token for "the majority of immigrants".[3] While there is a general awareness of religions as a way of coping with crises and major events in one's private life (birth, marriage, death etc.), and of people within the religions who value their faith more then the general mainstream, there is little interest outside the churches or religious communities in their teachings and beliefs. Generally, religion is seen in an enlightenment fashion as a basis for values and a general humanitarian attitude.

While the religious landscape has become more pluralistic in general – publicized through the media and different educational programmes in schools and beyond, as well as by dialogue statements from the churches – most Germans' everyday experience of people of other faiths is quite limited, particularly outside the major migration areas.[4]

On the religious or sociological level, an ongoing debate rages under the heading "religion – yes, churches – no". There is a growing awareness of religious pluralism, and religious groups in the esoteric and neo-pagan fashion

---

[2] Günter Baum, "Ein bisgen Religion" – Über öffentliche Erwartungen *("A Bit of Religion" – About Public Expectations)* in: Walter Klaiber, Sabine Plonz (eds.): Wie viel Glaube darf es sein? – Religion und Mission in unserer Gesellschaft *(How Much Fait his Acceptable? – Religion and Mission in Our Society)*, Stuttgart: Kreuz, 2008, pp.24 – 34.

[3] Levent Tezcan, Interreligiöser Dialog und politische Religionen *(Interreligious Dialogue and Political Religions)*, in: Aus Politik und Zeitgeschichte, 28 – 29 / 2006: Dialog der Kulturen, pp.26 – 32.

[4] Krech, Volkhard: Bewegungen im religiösen Feld: Das Beispiel Nordrhein-Westfalen *(Movements in the Religious Field: The Example of North Rhine-Westphalia)*, in: Markus Hero, Volkhard Krech, Helmut Zander (eds.): Religiöse Vielfalt in Nordrhein-Westfalen – Empirische Befunde und Perspektive der Globalisierung vor Ort *(Religious Plurality in North Rhine-Westphalia – Empirical Data and Perspectives of Localized Globalization)*, Paderborn: Schöningh, 2008; pp.24 – 43.

are booming: new age religion can be found particularly in the big cities and their surroundings, and is being publicized by the media.

While there is a growing awareness of these different religious attitudes, sociological research suggests a dualistic reality: on the one hand – especially in the cities and the eastern part of Germany – there is a high proportion of atheists who do not see any sense in transcendence or spirituality. Usually, those people have no real knowledge or any interest in religion, viewing it as either a lack of knowledge or a reason for social conflict. On the other hand, there is a wide-ranging group of religiously aware people who are mainly linked to the mainline churches and who combine different teachings, views of transcendence and elements of different religions according to their needs and experiences. Those people usually come from the "fringes" of the mainline churches and experiment with different religious worldviews. Those people are the 'seekers' who are mainly addressed by mission activities and who make up, at the same time, the majority of those who participate in esoteric or neo-pagan activities. Sometimes, they are still members of the mainline churches; sometimes they have just recently left the church, but still have contact to the religious views of their grandparents or parents.

Research in church membership in the mainline churches suggests that there are more or less three groups. Firstly, the core parish community which regularly participates in parish activities and services and holds faith tenets which are more or less close to the general church teachings. Secondly, a group of so called "dedicated distanced", who are and will remain members of the church, attend services at the major festivals and celebrate the major events in their lives. They do not feel the need to have more contact, and do not necessarily adhere to all the teachings of the church. The third group is at the "fringes", still religiously interested, but forming views on religion very creatively and freely, and not feeling the need for a community or church. The difference between the second and third group is not really clear cut; rather there is a free-floating from the one to the other in both directions, sometimes also into the first group.[5]

I will now turn to pluralism within the mainline churches, in order to show the main context of church work.

---

[5] For the latest differentiation see Peter Höhmann, Volkhard Krech: *Das weite Feld der Kirchenmitgliedschaft* – Vermessungsversuche nach Typen, soziostruktureller Verortung, alltäglicher Lebensführung und religiöser Indifferenz *(The Wide Field of Church Membership – Measuring Attempts According to Types, Socio-structural Location, Every-day Life and Religious Indifference)*, in: Wolfgang Huber, Johannes Friedrich, Peter Steinacker (eds.), Kirche in der Vielfalt der Lebensbezüge – Die vierte EKD-Erhebung über Kirchenmitgliedschaft *(Church in the Multiplicity of Life Relations – The 4th EKD Membership Survey)*, pp.143 – 195.

Internal pluralism – milieus and patchwork identities

Two approaches to research in church membership have become quite prominent in recent years. On the one hand, churches tend to analyze the different cultural attitudes and life patterns of their members in the model of milieus;[6] on the other hand, the attitudes towards the teaching of the church and the ways of understanding one's own religion are described as 'religious patchwork-identity'. While the first research approach is asking how to communicate the message to different social and cultural groups within the church, the latter challenges the teachings and the message of the church themselves. Therefore the focus lies here.

Religious patchwork identities

Through interviews which centered, at the beginning, on the religious attitudes of young people, the churches found that many of their members hold religious beliefs which are quite different from the churches' teachings. Instead of forming a coherent system they tend to combine religious views *ad hoc*, in order to understand their given situation *en passant*.[7] They do not only combine Christian elements, but also pick up tenets of other religions or esoteric teaching. Believers do not pay much attention to whether these different beliefs relate to each other logically, but rather look for whatever helps them to understand or cope with a given situation.

So, for instance, one person could combine a basic Christian understanding (I am a Christian, Jesus is the "Son of God," God loves all humankind) with the idea of reincarnation (Grandpa's body is now in the earth, but his soul will wait and come again to live – so he will live the life he deserves, since he was a good man and should not have suffered so much.) and a rather Muslim understanding of the "last judgement" (God will judge according to the good and bad deeds, not pardon an evil person). These elements are chosen

---

6 See Eberhard Hauschildt, Claudia Schulz, Eike Kohler: Milieus praktisch – Analyse- und Planungshilfen für Kirche und Gemeinde *(Milieus in Practice – Aids to Analysis and Planning for Church and Congregations)*, Göttingen: Vandenhoeck & Ruprecht, 2008. And: Wolfgang Vögele, Helmut Bremer, Michael Vester (eds.): Soziale Milieus und Kirche *(Social Milieus and Church)*, Religion in der Gesellschaft vol. 11; Würzburg: Ergon, 2002. See also: http://www.bpb.de/publikationen/OZ7GSK,0,0, Soziale_Milieus.html, accessed 16 March 2009. And: MDG/Sinus Sociovision: Milieuhandbuch – Religiöse und kirchliche Orientierungen in den Sinus-Milieus *(Handbook of Milieus – Religious and Church Orientations Among the Sinus Milieus)*; München/Heidelberg: MDG 2005. See as an overview in German: http://www.milieus-kirche.de/index.html, accessed 16 March 2009.

7 See Eberhard Hauschildt, Alltagsseelsorge – Der Alltag der Seelsorge und die Seelsorge im Alltag *(Everyday Counseling – Ordinary Counseling and Counseling in the Ordinary)*, in: Uta Pohl-Patalong, Frank Muchlinsky (eds.): Seelsorge im Plural – Perspektiven für ein neues Jahrhundert *(Counseling in the Plural – Perspectives for a New Century)*, Hamburg: ebv-Verlag, 1999; pp.8 – 16.

according to "what makes sense" at the moment. Their value lies in the way they allow one to live and to manage different situations in life, rather than in keeping one in line with the church's teaching.

The effect of this research in "what the people really believe" was, and is, puzzling to many theologians. For instance, one of the leading mission theologians in Great Britain, Bishop John Finney, was confused to find out that many of those who were reached by the so called "Emmaus" or "Alpha-Courses" did not so much join the church because of their faith in Christ's redeeming action from sin, but rather because of the community and the fellowship of love they experienced in those mission activities. The whole aspect of atonement seems of little interest to many Christians today.[8] Equally puzzled was the German theologian, Klaus-Peter Jörns, who, in finding that certain tenets were no longer held by the majority of church-goers, came to the conclusion that the church has to give up some of its teachings. If people no longer understand Holy Communion as a ritual of being ensured of Christ's forgiveness, but rather as a place to experience community with other Christians – and only in a very limited sense of community with Christ – the church should take this into account in its teaching and preaching.[9]

Such observations assuredly lead to questions: what do parishioners think if we speak of God's unconditional love, or of the life-everlasting or of Christ as the revelation of God?

To understand this better, I will turn now to the example of the sub-conscious religious mainstream.

External religious pluralism – the subconscious religious mainstream

Having noticed the dominance of the mainline churches as representing the understanding of religion in Germany, while at the same time the actual teachings of the churches are not necessarily regarded as the religious truth one holds, the question is: how do these findings fit together in the "religious landscape" and how should churches address those seeking religious faith? I think a key to understanding the situation lies in the realization that communities of faith in the West have developed several ways to deal with the challenge of modernity, enlightenment and pluralism.

---

[8] See John Finney, Emerging Evangelism, London: Darton, Longman & Todd, 2004.

[9] See Klaus-Peter Jörns, Die neuen Gesichter Gottes – Was die Menschen wirklich glauben *(The New Faces of God – What People Really Believe)*, Munich: C.H. Beck 1997. Klaus-Peter Jörns, Notwendige Abschiede – Auf dem Weg zu einem glaubwürdigen Christentum *(Necessary Farewells – Towards a Credible Christianity)*, Gütersloh: GVH, 2004.

Esotericism as a modern religion

Esotericism is one of the four modern models of western religious thought which have developed in the western world since the late 19th and early 20th centuries, the others being atheism, fundamentalism, and liberal theology.[10] Esoteric thinking seems to have reached a kind of hegemony over religious thought in Germany in general, even if few people fully adhere to esotericism.

The basic idea of modernity is that the logic of all matters is potentially open to human knowledge and mastering, if not today then in the future, through the ever-growing progress of knowledge. Esotericism shares this belief in progress and growing perfection, in growing human possibilities and a reality basically open to full understanding, in the realm of this world as well as in the world of the transcendence. Thus, esoteric thinking is a truly modern way of dealing with the challenges of modern times. I will now, therefore, describe some of its core elements, as I believe they are the parameters by which religious seekers judge what is on offer from the religious markets, including Christian thought.

At the basis of esoteric thinking is the idea that within all human beings is a part of the Supreme Being. So, everyone is partly Godly and only has to realize this; everyone needs to become one with everything as everything is part of the Supreme Being. Hence, there is no real difference between the religious and the scientific, as all is part of this one transcendent reality. The idea of 'a Supreme Being' is widely accepted in Germany these days; the idea of a personal God however is disputed.

As the meta-story of esotericism is one of progress and development, reincarnation is an equally central concept. Only if the soul or inner core of a person – that is part of the Supreme Being – is able to achieve perfection, is it possible to achieve this aim. Reincarnation is thereby no longer a way of being trapped in this world – as the traditional religions have it – but a way of becoming better through learning and development through different incarnations. Esotericism talks of a 'life everlasting' but means reincarnation. In some confirmation classes the notion of life-everlasting is no problem, but the idea of a resurrection of the body seems ridiculous, while reincarnation is regarded as quite sensible.

---

10 See Hans-Jürgen Ruppert, Suche nach Erkenntnis und Erleuchtung – moderne esoterische Religiosität *(The Search For Knowledge and Enlightenment – Modern Esoteric Religiosity)*; in: Reinhard Hempelmann et al. (eds.): Panorama der neuen Religiosität – Sinnsuche und Heilsversprechen zu Beginn des 21. Jahrhunderts *(Panorama of New Religiosity – Seeking for Meaning and Promises of Salvation at the Beginning of the 21st Century)*, Gütersloh: GVH, 2001, pp.210 – 309. Jens Schnabel, Das Menschenbild der Esoterik *(The Esoteric View of the Human)*, Neukirchen-Vlyun: Neukirchner, 2007. Kocku von Stuckrad, Was ist Esoterik – Kleine Geschichte des geheimen Wissens *(What is Esotericism – A Short History of Secret Knowledge)*, Munich: C.H.Beck 2004. Werner Thiede, Esoterik und Theologie – Eine gegenseitige Herausforderung *(Esotericism and Theology – A Mutual Challenge)*, Forum Theologische Literaturzeitung 20, Leipzig: Evang.Verlagsanstalt, 2007.

So the aim of all beings is to realize that they are part of the Supreme Being, and to learn about the next necessary step in their own development. Everything can be utilized to gain higher knowledge, which in principle is open to everyone, but only if the respective individual is 'ready' for it. Truth is open and is either understood or not relevant for this incarnation. Thus, every religion is as it were tamed, and cannot pose a real challenge to anyone and so will just be as relevant as it is helpful.

Esotericism agrees to 'God's love' for everyone who draws near in faith – meaning the realization of one's belonging to the Supreme Being. There is, however, no notion of sin or the need for external salvation. Christ can be viewed as 'the Saviour' – thereby indicating that Jesus already knew esoteric teaching and told it to those who could already understand. However, he was neither different from everyone else, nor was the cross in anyway relevant. Rather, the majority of people were not ready, so they killed him – without knowing that the reality within Jesus could not be killed – as it cannot be killed in anyone else. The resurrection was just Jesus' soul returning to the Supreme Being, and all the teachings of the church were distortions of the truth by people who could not yet understand Jesus' words.

One could go on like this. The point, however, is clear: esotericism integrates whatever comes and redefines its meaning. In its basic assumptions it tends to stabilize religious life very much in the way the general awareness supposes religion to be: it is a way to cope with life; it avoids conflicts as it doesn't force any thought onto people and seems to integrate all religions; it is regarded as harmless and does not interfere with other systems of society as it requires no membership or positive public affirmation of its beliefs – it is the 'perfect private religion'. In more critical terms, it could be said that exotericism is the perfect capitalist religion as it affirms the individual pursuit of happiness and the constant struggle for progress and success while offering a way out if one seems to fail in the capitalist struggle. In general, the esoteric scene is organized in the way of the market and is also incapable of developing a critical approach to ethics – you choose your faith and have done so in the process of reincarnation, so what is given is okay.

While there is still acceptance of the mainline churches as representing religion in public, and of ministers as some sort of experts in the religious realm, the final judge on religious matters, however, is the individual and her or his experience. In cases of conflict between one's own thinking and the churches' teaching, the churches are easily portrayed as repressive clerical bureaucracies. Thus, the freedom of the individual is the key to solving religious questions.

The churches facing esotericism

As esoteric thinking is in praxis not a coherent religious worldview, there is little point in systematically arguing against it in an apologetic manner. It would be far more effective to simply make parishioners aware of this thinking, and adapt the preaching and the counselling of the church to the esoteric way of seeking answers.

Ministers and elders play an important role: as the individual is the key for judgment, they need to use their individual testimonies as means to transport the Christian message. On the other hand, in cases of communication about 'life everlasting', the 'meaning of life' or 'Christ as saviour' a clear dogmatic statement is needed.

People in mourning are dealing with the question of what remains of their relationship with the deceased, and 'where the dead are.' Christian faith affirms an ongoing relationship with the deceased as we are all held together in God's love; the church is the community of saints – that is of the baptized – be it here or 'in heaven'. Christ has conquered death, so nothing can come between God's love and us; therefore, nothing can take the living or the dead away from the common space 'before God.' If one holds these beliefs, it would be helpful to present them as one's personal answers to the questions of life and death. The focus should be on supporting and consoling the mourner. By phrasing dogmatic statements in a personal way they become an offer about which the parishioners will decide themselves – how far it will take them. So one should not be too afraid of forcing an alien thought upon parishioners, but rather should be aware of their freedom to decide. Individual experience is the key for that; thus, the church should help the believers to experience Christian faith in their lives.

Similarly, it is a challenge to portray Jesus Christ as both human and God and, thus, different and close to us. While esoteric thinking has few problems in thinking beyond secular reason, it still has difficulties in accepting the non-comprehensible. Here, the notion that faith can rest and flourish without a full explanation but know about the remaining mystery will be both an alternative and a challenge. Again, it would be necessary to show the supportive and helpful aspects in this teaching about Christ which leads to spiritual experience. While Christ, in his human nature, allows us to follow him and trust in his proclamation, Christ in his Godly nature allows us to trust that God has revealed to us his purpose for humanity. So I can assert that God gives us the perspective of closeness to him and that God neglects no aspect of human life in its brokenness, I can also remain truly human and have no need to become Godly myself – God approached humanity, there is no need for humanity to become Godly.

The key to the churches' witness in an esoteric environment is both a genuine faith experience and the development of trusting relationships. The main problem is not that people are not likely to believe anything transcendent, but the lack of experience with the value and the implications of faith in their lives or that of other people. Especially when it comes to suffering, dealing with limitations and with death, there is the need to develop an authentic, individual and helpful Christian witness. The point of reference is: how does this work for me? And to find out how it works, I need personal examples around me. For this, Germans will look to the minister, whom they regard very highly as a person, while not trusting theology or the church as institutions. Thus ministers, elders and other members of the community will have to bear the load of making Christian faith a trustworthy experience. At the same time, they will have few problems in doing so as long as they speak personally and do not refer to "the church". An individual's life and experience are the keys – even the key to rely on the church, if this has helpful implications for an individual's life.

From a Mediaeval and Modern to a Post-Modern Theology

Reiner Knieling

Lesslie Newbigin worked in India for more than 30 years. When he came back to England, he asked what his experience in the inculturation of the Gospel implied in the European context. He remarked that Europe was not simply a Christian continent anymore. Rather, secularisation had more or less succeeded, and the importance of Christian faith for the whole society was declining continuously.

Protestant theology in Europe is mainly shaped by the debates and disputes during the time of Reformation and in the 19th and 20th centuries. But times have changed. People in the 21st century think in other patterns, speak with other words, have other perceptions and images of human beings, the world and God. So the question is: how can the gospel be inculturated in our times?

Thinking about this, we have to regard the following insight by Lesslie Newbigin:

> When you try to be relevant, you can fall into syncretism; when you try to avoid syncretism, you can become irrelevant.[1]

The question which arises out of this is: how can we tell the Gospel and speak about God so that we are involved in daily experiences without being completely absorbed by them?

Jesus as personal and living truth

A main question of the 19th and beginning 20th century was: what is true? Science was booming and took more and more space in the common discourse as well as in daily lives. Engineers constructed skyscrapers, bridges, machines for the growing industries and daily work, based on physical rules. That was real. That was true. Concerning history, people asked: what is true? Archaeology became significant.

The arts, however, lost some of their former influence. Therefore, theologians tried to save their message through arguing in patterns which were generally accepted. Some were looking for the historical Jesus. But they did not really find him. Others began to defend Biblical truth – the truth that they

---

1 Leslie Newbigin, Foolishness to the Greek, Grand Rapids (Michigan), Wm. B. Eerdmans Publishing Company, 1986 (in the German version page 12).

understood as Biblical. That is characteristic of the later Evangelical movement. The Evangelicals are a very modern movement with a very modern question: what is true? And you can belong to it when you accept most of what it defines as truth. The main question for very different Christians was: what is true? And they gave very different answers.

The present main question is not: what is true? but: what is helpful? What is helpful for our lives? What helps us find orientation? What helps us to heal our wounds?

When we realize this, what does it mean to speak about Jesus as the truth? Shall we simply continue to emphasize this and hope that people will accept it? That would be *not* realizing what people feel and think is important. That would express an attitude to people that says: we are not really interested in you, your feelings, your hopes, your questions.

What would an alternative solution be? Shall we give up talking about Jesus as the truth? Some Christians claim that we need to take leave of such idioms.[2] And they are not few, both the people who claim this, and the idioms that should be given up. Some Christians proclaim: "many ways lead to God." You can be a Hindu or a Moslem or believe in Christ. It is important just to believe.

But inculturation does not mean to abandon essential idioms. It rather means to express them in new patterns, new figures, new ways of thinking and feeling. So, from my point of view, the question is not "Jesus alone" *or* "many ways lead to God" but: in which way can we understand "Jesus alone" anew and how can we realize that he will appreciate the people of all nations, who served Jesus - without knowing - by whatever they "did for one of the least of these brothers" for him (Mt 25:40)?

Connecting both questions I understand John 14:6 in the following way. Jesus says: "Everyone who is on the *way* with me will discover the *truth* about him- / herself and about humankind and the world and will become true. So she and he will become *alive*. In no other way can no-one come to the father. "

Some may now think: is this the right truth? Especially someone from an Evangelical background may ask this question. But if we have a look at the Greek term we learn: it primarily means 'true' in a sense of real and truthful. Only secondly it means truth in a sense of something you can find out, understand and have understood, something you can comprehend and conceive.

I think: really, Jesus is the truth. But he is it in another way than Evangelicals suggest. You cannot have understood him. You cannot ever finish understanding him. He is a person and not a doctrine. "The word became flesh" (Jn 1:14) and not letters, books or doctrines. Jesus is alive and on the way. When someone is on the way, he does not know in every detail what is facing him. Jesus met different people and was open to being interrupted in his plans, and for being surprised. His disciples learnt from and with Jesus. They began to

---

[2] *Cf.* Klaus-Peter Jörns, Notwendige Abschiede. Auf dem Weg zu einem glaubwürdigen Christentum, Gütersloh, Gütersloher Verlagshaus, 2004.

get to know themselves in a better, deeper way. Peter recognized that he was a sinner when he met Jesus, not before. And after a long way with Jesus he had to learn that he could not keep his promise: "Even if all fall away on account of you, I never will." Jesus answered: "I tell you the truth ..." (Mt 26: 33f.) Peter had to go the painful way of learning this truth: He denied Jesus. But the truth is as well: it is the same Peter who is the rock Jesus is building his church on (Mt 16: 18). It is the same Peter Jesus came to in Galilee. Jesus asked him three times: "Simon, do you love me? Do you truly love me?" ... (Jn 21, 15-19) And Peter could feel that Jesus had forgiven him; that Jesus accepted, loved and reinstated him.

That happens not only to Peter but to many people on earth, in former times as well as in present and coming times. And my hope is that this also will happen on the way to the last judgement. I ask: could it be true that the last judgement is not irrevocable, but a serious and painful step on the way to heaven – serious and painful for Pentecostals and Evangelicals, for Lutherans and Calvinists, for Catholics and others alike – for people from other religions as well as for people without a religion?

If this is possible, you can understand John 14:6 in the way I described: "Everyone who is on the *way* with me will discover the *truth* about him- / herself and about humankind and the world and will become true. So she and he will become *alive*. In no other way can one come to the father." This can happen here and now as well as in the last judgement.

This is the way from "either or" to "both and": a joint learning from the different Christian teachings.

Sin, salvation and fullness of life

In the age of the Reformation the question was: "how can I find a merciful God?" Luther and his fellows struggled for an answer which was reliable and sustainable for personal faith and strong enough against temptation and doubt. Their discovery was that people are justified by faith alone. How justification was understood was shaped through this central discovery.

But "how can I get a merciful God?" is no major question today as we know since Helsinki 1963 (Assembly of Lutheran World Federation). The questions are: what about God at all? Does he exist? Is there not the same God in different religions? Would believing in him be a help for my daily life? And if I want to believe, shall I join one of the major religions? Do they help me in believing? Or do they hinder me? The situation is very different compared to the age of the Reformation. And last but not least: you cannot assume that sin is something of any importance for most of the people, as I mentioned before.

When we allow these questions to touch us – not only in our mind, but also in our hearts – our own understanding of faith receives a good shaking and becomes mixed up. And maybe for a time we are confused. I think such experiences are healthy in the end. They teach us to remain in powerlessness and to endure because we have no quick answers and no easy solutions. They teach us to wait and to search for new answers together with other Christians from other wings of the church and with people who are not Christians.

For example, one path towards a new understanding of justification was shown by the internationally known German theologian Jürgen Moltmann. He pointed out that justice in this world and righteousness in the relation to God must not be torn apart from one another. They belong together. So what God is giving contains many more aspects than the Reformers could see in their historical situation. The justice and righteousness which God is giving mean: God brings justice and righteousness to the victims and to the perpetrators as well. He will help the victims get justice and healing for their wounds. Justification becomes precise through this. It strikes roots in central human experiences. Justification is not completely absorbed through this. But you cannot have it without consequences in daily life.

Justice for the victims necessarily includes justice for the perpetrators. Otherwise justice for the victims would not be justice. So God will confront the perpetrators with what they have done. They have to bear their pain and punishment. But maybe – as I mentioned before – this pain and punishment does not last for ever. In this way God will give justice, righteousness and salvation together. So: "love and faithfulness meet together; righteousness and peace kiss each other." (Ps 85, 10)

With this priority in what God is doing, in his righteousness and justice we can find a new understanding of sin as well. In this perspective sin is not only what *we* have to overcome, but what God overcomes as well. These two dimensions traditionally belong to the understanding of sin: sin includes what human beings are responsible for and of what they are guilty. This is one aspect. The other aspect which was increasingly forgotten in the theology of the last centuries is what develops, what emerges in a negative way, what we are involved in without having a real responsibility for. In the theological tradition this is called original sin. It is in our world before we act. It cannot be avoided. If we are involved, it does not necessarily result in personal guilt. So from my point of view, war is always sin. It is never lawful and fair. It will never be justified by God. In every war innocent people are put to death. But nevertheless sometimes war may be unavoidable. So people may be involved in a destructive energy without being guilty individually. This is to be distinguished from the other aspect: people can become guilty as individuals in war as well as in other times.

Another example: if people lose their employment, one of the most difficult and pressing questions is: "what is my responsibility in this and what isn't? Could my colleague stay because she is a better worker than me? Or does she just have better connections than I have?" In cases of divorce people often ask: "what was my mistake? What could I have done in a better way? Would this have saved my marriage?" Sometimes you can see specific guilt. Sometimes things have developed over a long time and have destroyed the relationship in an imperceptible way, without someone being guilty in particular. We know the answer to individual guilt. It is to beg for forgiveness and to forgive, which can be very exhausting in some cases. The answer to sin as a tragically destructive energy, as original sin, is not to beg for forgiveness and to forgive.

We cannot take responsibility for what we are not guilty of. As simple as it sounds, this is not a common understanding among Christians. If you feel guilty for something too big, for something no single human being can take the responsibility for individually, then it is easy to feel pressurised and down-hearted.

The answer to sin as a tragic destructive energy, as the original sin, is to mourn. If you lose your job and you do not know if there is any personal responsibility, mourning can help you to get through this difficult situation. It is helpful and healthy to have a room for sadness, for anger and rage, for feeling helpless and powerless. It is good to have people around with open ears and open hearts so you can find the way back to life and energy and power. It is the same after losing your wife or husband through a break-up or a divorce.

The question is not "sin and salvation" *or* "fullness of life" as a main paradigm. We urgently need a third way because the present understanding of "sin and salvation" is shaped by the questions of the 16th century ("how can I find a merciful God?"). But it should not be replaced with the paradigm of "fullness of life". This is an understandable yearning, but the reality of faith is not heaven on earth. The reality of faith includes healing and health in very different ways. The reality of faith includes the power of Christ hidden under its opposite – in our weakness – as well. Sometimes this power cannot be felt. So the paradigm of "sin and salvation" should be replaced with questions like: what is the connection between "sin" and "failure" (both is neither the same nor without any affinities)? Or: how can Christians stay alive or become newly alive while they still fail and remain vulnerable?

Cross and resurrection – the true image of transformation

As a third example for searching for a new, contemporary understanding of the Gospel, I will focus on the cross and resurrection. That is the centre of the Christian faith.

In the Christian tradition the cross stands for atonement, satisfaction and salvation. But if you do not come from a Christian context and you want to understand this, you have to know something about the ancient world and its sacrifices. For many Christians, the main meaning of the cross is: Jesus died for us – and not only for our benefit, but also instead of us. We call it "Jesus' vicarious death on the cross" and the "atonement". One misunderstanding connected with this is that God would need the death of his son to be able to have mercy and to forgive. But it is the other way round: God does not need a sacrifice, but he is the active one. In 2 Corinthians 5:18-20 Paul writes: "All this is from God, who reconciled us to himself through Christ and gave us the ministry of reconciliation. […] We are therefore Christ's ambassadors, as though God were making his appeal through us. We implore you on Christ's behalf: Be reconciled to God." (*cf.* Rom 5:1-11)

I cannot discuss the details of different ways of interpretation of the cross in the New Testament: next to "vicarious death", "atonement" and "reconciliation" we find "redemption" (Rom 3:24, *cf.* Mk 10:45) or "salvation" (e.g. Rom 1:16f.). All these are ways of interpretation which were shaped by the ancient world. My experience is that some of these can hardly be explained to people who are not familiar with the Christian tradition, especially "vicarious death" and the "atonement". People ask: "can't God be merciful without this?" My answer is: "He certainly can. He sent Jesus because He *was* already merciful, not to become merciful." After such an answer I sometimes try to explain what the way of Jesus through the cross to the resurrection could mean. I do it in this way: sending Jesus into this world was a sign of God's really deep love. The great God sent his son into our world, not only for a short visit, but for sharing life with us – and not only the bright side of life but also the shady side. He was not born in a palace but afield, because there was no room for him at the inn. Was there no room for him in this world? (*Cf.* Jn 1: 11: "He came to that which was his own, but his own did not receive him."). When he was grown up, his mission was to go to the needy, poor and sick people to help and heal them. He proclaimed the good news and the kingdom of God. He called people to repent and to believe. He called them to change their lives and some to follow him. All this was an expression of God's love in the midst of our world.

For the sake of God's love, Jesus argued with the Scribes and Pharisees who could not accept his actions and teaching. This eventually led to his death on the cross. In my opinion the deepest reason for this is: people who have their life and their faith, their theology and their health, people who are not really needy, can hardly or not at all accept the love of God which Jesus brought to the poor and sick people and not to them. So they wanted to get rid of him.

Why did Jesus let this be done to him? He could have helped himself at the cross, like the people standing there told him. I am convinced that Jesus walked the way of the passion, the way to the bitter end at the cross, because every other option e.g. the ascension to heaven before suffering so much, would have shown us: whenever he gets into difficulties, he does not face them. Then we could not really trust him and his mercy, grace and love.

You see: you do not need "vicarious death", "atonement", "sacrifice" or the other ways of interpretation to understand and explain God's love in Jesus, in his birth as well as in his actions, preaching and his death on the cross.

Furthermore, there is a second, even more certain reason for his love: the resurrection of Jesus. If I had been God and my son had been murdered, I do not know if I could have been very merciful. So I could understand if God had started the end of the world after his son had been crucified. But he did not.

Rather, he raised Jesus from the dead so that his love could be spread out in this world forever.

For example, when Jesus met Peter, he let him feel God's love. He did not say: "look, I died instead of you." He did not say: "my death was a sacrifice for you. So I can love you now." He laid his fingers in Peter's wounds. Three times Jesus asked Peter whether he loved him (Jn 21:15-17). But Jesus did not nail Peter down to his failure. Rather he gave him a mission - *this* Peter in *this* situation. He did not say: "after another year of discipleship-training and not failing this time, I can use you." Instead he gave him a mission as he was, not as he should be. In this way Jesus showed Peter God's love. Since the resurrection and Pentecost this love of God is spread out all over the world – through Christians filled with the Holy Spirit.

That is what people feel when they come to us: whether we have at least a bit of God's love for them, whether we are really interested in them, whether we are more interested in them and their life and experiences than in defending our dogma.

Finally I ask: what do the previous considerations mean for our hermeneutics?

A new hermeneutic: suspicion and trust concerning the Bible

In a little group of theologians we practised the following exercise for some years: We read a certain text from the Bible and then we first told each other what we would say if we had to preach about this text five minutes later. When doing your job for several years there is a lot which blurts out. Then, as a second step, we checked which parts of what we said were really contained in our Biblical text. Sometimes we were astonished how much was not contained in the text at all. As a third step we looked for all the things we had not noticed during our first reading. Sometimes we were surprised what we could find. Sometimes it seemed that we had never read this particular passage before.

Concerning the Bible we need both: suspicion and trust; suspicion of our own resistance against specific Biblical sentences. For example, some Christians may not like Romans 9:16 if they have an Evangelical or Pentecostal background. Paul refers to Jacob and Esau, to their faith and them being loved by God, and writes: "it does not depend […] on men's desire or effort, but on God's mercy." Others do not like sentences which connect rebirth and baptism. In my judgement we find this in Titus 3:5: "He saved us through the washing of rebirth and renewal by the Holy Spirit." I guess hereafter some of you will teach me that washing in this case has nothing to do with baptism.

Lutheran or Reformed Christians may keep a certain distance from verses about extraordinary gifts or experiences, for example 1 Corinthians 12 where Paul amongst others enumerates "healing by that one spirit", "miraculous powers" or "speaking in different kind of tongues" as a spiritual gift. If you feel any resistance or defence against one of these items then could you imagine developing a bit of sympathy for what you did not like very much until now? Can you even imagine falling in love with certain verses or stories from the Bible which traditionally are closer to another wing of the Christian Church than to your own?

We need a new hermeneutic of agreement and trust in our different experiences with our faith which all together are not sufficient to describe God. But they are sufficient to show what he lets us see: mercy and grace, sometimes in ways we hope for and sometimes against our hopes.

We need a new hermeneutic which is suspicious of our resistance to Biblical predications and stories that we feel not very comfortable with. The other way round: it will enrich us if we become open to things that do not come from our familiar way of thinking and feeling. Some of these things will really touch our heart and soul. And some of these things will remain strange. That is okay. Through such an opening-up we will get enriched not only through new discoveries in the Bible, but also by brothers and sisters from other wings of the church as well. By opening ourselves to these sisters and brothers, our eyes will be opened for unknown areas in the Bible. And maybe, after some time, we can agree with Biblical sentences which we could not agree to before. Maybe they will teach us to trust in God as well as in the familiar sentences.

Local Church Development – An Instrument of Change for Missionary Churches

Jutta Belderman

Comparable situations?

As a pastor working for the German Region of UEM I have long been involved in designing missionary concepts and training for local church development. I am trained in organisational development and have applied my knowledge and skills to the situation of the churches. And I have, for many years, accompanied local churches during their development processes.

For 6 years, a colleague from Indonesia watched me doing so and used to comment that such concepts might be needed in churches affected by the secularized European context, but not in Indonesia. But when he returned home in 2005, he learned that the situation of his church had changed dramatically, and he realized that the concept of local church development might be helpful there as well. In 2008, a group of German and Indonesian pastors had a training course together on how to respond to people seeking for faith without seeking it in the (mainline) churches. The participants realized that they need concepts of church development to enable their churches to meet such challenges.

"You are a letter of Christ" – local churches and their mission

In 2Cor 3:3 Paul describes the mission of the churches: "You are a letter" to the people is how he illustrates the churches' assignment and function. And not a letter that you may compose as you like, but "you are a letter of Christ".

The content of the letter

The church is a letter of Christ, i.e. the churches' message is the message of Christ himself. The style in which the churches deliver the message should also follow the way Jesus approached the people. The content of such a letter may be summarized as follows:[1]

God is already there for each one of his children, he himself wants to be found by anybody searching for him. And even people who do not seek will be

---

[1] *Cf.* Eberhard Jüngel, Keynote address at the EKD Synod, 1999, Reden von Gott in der Welt: Der missionarische Auftrag der Kirche an der Schwelle zum 3. Jahrtausend (*Speaking of God in the world. The missionary task of the church at the threshold of the 3rd millenium*), ed. Kirchenamt der Evangelischen Kirche in Deutschland, Frankfurt/M., 2000.

able to find him. (Is 65:1f.). To accomplish his mission God has sent his son, Jesus Christ. God wants to be with his people (Acts 21:3) and has in Jesus himself become a companion for us.

Once believing in God's compassion and having found God, people will experience God as a God living with them personally. They will find liberation from sin, death and a new life surrounded by God's love and compassion. This will again liberate them from all powers which have had control over their lives. They will experience thankfulness and prayer as a way to be in contact with God, and *diakonia* and struggle for justice and peace as practical ways to share God's love with their neighbours.

In his mission to the world God is pleading with his people, but he is never pressing them. That is his way of mission which Jesus has made visible.

The sender of the letter

The church is already a letter of Christ. That is God's promise and assignment to his church. The church is already shining as a beacon light (Phil 2:15) or as a light on the path (Jn 8:12; 12:46). It is chosen by Christ to proclaim him who has brought the light to them (1Pet 2:9) and to share faith with all people publicly.

In order to enable the church for mission, God has sent his Holy Spirit and will continue to do so. Through the Spirit, Christians will be able to learn from Jesus himself about how to proclaim the Gospel in love and acceptance, not pressing but inviting them, using the right words and images for people of different backgrounds and social groups.

Proclaiming the Gospel, the individual believers are not alone. There are others sharing the same Spirit; together they are members of the Christian church, usually as one denomination. This church again is not alone, but part of an (ecumenical) community of other churches.

They are part of the not yet reconciled world, but together they shall be able to distinguish between the visible church including their own culture, tradition, rules etc. and the invisible church. And they shall be capable of transcending their own boundaries of culture, tradition, nation, and social class in order to proclaim the Gospel to all people.

The recipients of the letter

When writing a letter it is important to reflect on the recipient in order to choose the appropriate style and words. People searching for faith may be regarded as the main recipients of the letter of Christ. In different cultures they may be of different backgrounds. The reasons why they do not seek for faith in the churches may be diverse. Even in one place, recipients of the letter of Christ may live in very different contexts, cultures, and milieus. They may speak different languages, belong to different social groups and practise different lifestyles.

In Germany and Europe many people are sceptical towards the traditional church because it is a big institution with rules and laws which people dislike especially when it comes to faith.[2] They regard faith as something personal and private and reject general rules in connection with religion. They prefer loose networks and flexibility. This may be difficult for those who find that the rules and laws of the church reflect the intention of the churches' rituals and actions and are necessary to secure the life of the church and the fulfilment of its tasks.

Local churches and their mission

Any local church as a sender of the letter of Christ must therefore be ready to

- know the content of the letter well and identify with it in a way that it becomes a living letter of Christ;
- make sure that its message and its 'style of writing' matches the way Jesus himself proclaimed the Gospel to the people;
- explore the culture and lifestyle of the recipients of the letter in order to find the right words and images to communicate the Gospel in an understandable way;
- overcome its boundaries of culture, tradition, nation, social class etc. in order to address people and to be approachable.

From the missionaries of the past centuries any local church can learn that "*convivence*",[3] living together closely with the recipients, may be of great help to write the letter well.

Training for local church development

The current context of German mainline churches

Before I present the concept of local church development, let me describe roughly some major aspects of the current context of the German churches:

- There is great mobility in German society. Many people do not grow old in the place where they were born. This is a challenge for the churches which were used to work with one generation after the other.
- Consumerism has become a new way of finding identity in life, supported by commerce and the media. How does Christian faith fit in?

---

[2] *Cf.* Mission shaped Church: Church Planting and Fresh Expressions of Church in a Changing Context, London: Church House Publishing, 2004.

[3] *Cf.* Theo Sundermeier, Mission – Geschenk der Freiheit: Bausteine für eine Theologie der Mission (*Mission – gift of freedom: Building stones for a theology of mission*), Frankfurt/M., 2005.

- Habits have changed especially in the area of leisure. People tend to choose activities which help them to relax rather than taking over more responsibility. The church usually needs activists.
- German society is highly fragmented. People live in sub-cultures and do not easily cross boundaries. Most of the local churches belong to a certain middle class culture / milieu and are simply not capable of reaching people from other segments of society.
- Most educated people are working long hours and simply do not have the time and energy to add other activities to the many commitments of their lives. In addition, many churches do not respond to the intellectual needs of this group.
- Especially middle-aged and young people have lost their connection to the church, even if they are still church members. For them, the churches' language and rituals are not only old-fashioned but simply incomprehensible.
- There is a wide variety of esoteric approaches, other religions and diverse Christian denominations. Having been the only religion in this country for centuries, the 'mainline' churches are not well prepared to face a multi-religious setting.
- There is a lack of theological knowledge among the churches' staff (church workers, volunteers, elders etc.), and identity of the institution of the church as such is diffuse. Even church activists tend to believe only certain parts of the Christian doctrines and, like society in general, prefer loose networks rather than strong and organised institutions.
- The role of the church in German society has changed. While still a highly recognised institution until the 1950s, its influence and importance have declined dramatically since. Therefore, being active in church is no longer very reputable, and people are often questioned by neighbours and friends why they are involved in the church or why they even believe in Christ.
- This may be a reason for the lack of qualified lay leadership in the church.
- German churches are struggling with decreasing numbers of members and decreasing finances.

German churches in need of change management

Facing this situation, the church in Germany needs to invest personnel, time, energy and money into training for church activists in terms of biblical and theological knowledge, assurance of Christian identity as well as concepts for reshaping church structures.[4] In addition it is necessary to improve the leadership and management skills of (local) church leaders. They need to define clear goals and strategies as well as priorities for their work.

This sounds self-evident, but it is not. Until recently, most of the churches did not work according to clear-cut priorities, but mainly added to their activities without thoroughly checking financial or staff (both employees and volunteers) conditions. It is fairly new for German local churches to decide on priorities and defend them in controversial discussions. Any church development process has to develop ways of how to overcome habits and traditional structures in order to be more flexible and to meet the needs of the 'recipients'.

Below, the concept "Training for Local Church Development" is introduced briefly.[5]

Training for local church development

Local church development is started by a decision by the local church's governing body. It calls a team of approximately 12 people which represents the church in terms of age, gender, and church groups. A pastor, elders and volunteers should be represented. It has proved helpful to invite into the group a neutral person from 'outside', e.g. a member of a neighbouring church.

> Experiences:
> It is usually fairly easy to find enough people willing to be involved in the development process and to become a member of the team. It is even possible to involve people who are not strong church-goers. In many cases people working in banks or companies are especially interested because their skills are needed in the process. Some church boards found it difficult to assign members for the team 'from outside'. But if they had the courage to do so, these people were often very helpful.

The team needs a small leading group (called a trio), mostly: a pastor, one elder, one other team member. The trio is trained together with other trios from other churches of the same region.

---

[4] There are a number of training programmes on the market and more and more churches are making use of them. Many German churches have started to ask their local church boards to develop concepts for their work.

[5] The author has been a member a group of pastors from different German churches and mission organisations who developed the described program and accompanied teams implementing the program in their local church. *Cf.* Gemeindeentwicklungstraining Praxisbuch (*Training for church development. A book for practice*), ed. Arbeitsgemeinschaft Missionarische Dienste im Diakonischen Werk der EKD, Berlin, and Gemeindekolleg der Vereinigten Evangelisch-Lutherischen Kirche Deutschlands, Erfurt/Neudietendorf, Göttingen, 2008.

Elements of the training are:

- Basic knowledge of the theoretical background of church development processes such as theological concepts and sociological views of the church/congregation, methods of organisational development etc.;
- Introduction into the steps of the development process and methods of passing the steps to the team;
- Methods of leading groups, group education and training;
- Participative methods of leading discussions and basic skills in conflict resolution.

Experiences:
There is an interesting side-effect in training trios together. They share experiences and learn from each other. A team from the Western part of Germany learned a lot from a team in the Eastern part. Up to about 10 years ago, the church in D. was still used to full Sunday services and quite a number of active church members. Now, they were somehow taken by surprise that secularisation had reached their church as well. They were shocked and frightened. The team from the East shared its experiences of secularisation with the team from the West and succeeded in sharing their missionary approaches and giving them hope for the future.

Local church development processes follow four steps. The trios are trained to follow the steps together with their teams, but they will have to be aware that the steps are closely linked to each other. Like a triangle with its three corners, the process has three aspects which need to be worked on very carefully. While working on one aspect, teams will at some point of discussion have to come back to another aspect to clarify questions they might not have found relevant when working on the former step.

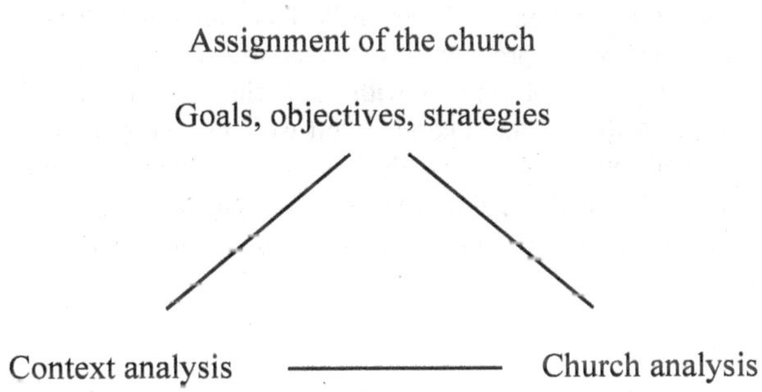

Step 1: Assignment of the church (the content of the letter)

A church as a letter of Christ has to realise which assignment it has. During Bible studies, using the relevant texts[6] the team learns to clarify and identify the tasks of the church.

Experiences:
Defining the assignment of the church was not easy for some teams. Often, they thought this to be the work of the pastor. They had to learn to become self-confident and cooperate with the pastor rather than listening to him or her only.

Secondly, each person had his or her concept of the assignment of the church already. Those concepts were often related to how the church was when the people holding them were young. It was not easy for the team members to step back and listen to the Bible afresh to re-define their concept of what it means to be the church of Christ in a certain context today.

Step 2: Context analysis (the recipients of the letter)

The trio is trained in methods which enable the team to develop an analysis of the context their church lives in. Several methods of analysis are taught, e.g. analysis of the

- structure of the city, town or village where the church is situated;
- living conditions of the people: what are people's needs?
- cultures / milieus people belong to: how do people live? What are their goals in life? What are their questions?

Experiences:
Many teams claim that they know their context well and that an analysis is not necessary. Mostly, the contrary is the case. Because the team itself is part of the context, important information may be so common that people do not realise that it needs special consideration. A church in W. had started a process to draw more children into the churches' programmes for children. The analysis was a surprise to them: figures proved that families with small children had moved out of their respective part of town and those children left went to school in the neighbouring district. It turned out to be very difficult for children to join the church programmes. Having realised this, the church decided to cooperate with their neighbouring church and offer children's programmes together with them – and succeeded.

---

6 For example: Ex 3 and 4; Hebr 8; Is 65:17ff.; Rev 21; Mt 5: 1-16; Lk 6: 20-26; Mk 21:1-12; Lk 16: 11-19; Acts 4: 32ff.; 1Cor 11: 17ff.; Rm 12; 1Cor 12; 1Cor 14; Jn. 4; Acts 10; Acts 16: 6ff; Acts 17:16ff.; Mt 10: 1-15; Mt 28: 18-20; Mt 4: 1-11; Lk 12: 35-48.

Step 3: Church analysis (the sender of the letter)

In order to develop a process of change for the church it is necessary to analyse the local church itself. Not all questions will be relevant for every church. The trio is trained in analytical methods to find answers to questions like:

- Who are the members? Age, gender structures etc. Which members are active, which are not? Are reasons known?
- Where do members live in the town / village?
- What do members / non-active members / non-members want from the church?
- Which programmes does the church offer? Which are lively? Which are 'dying'?
- Which successes / problems does the church have?
- Which resources are available? Finances? Buildings? Which resources are tied (e.g. salaries), which are free for disposition?
- What are the personnel resources (both employees and volunteers)? What are their tasks? What are they trained for, and what are their skills?

Experiences:

One of the most striking results was reached by the analysis of the membership in a church located in the countryside about 30 km. from Cologne. The team found out that almost all villagers worked in Cologne. During the week, they left the village in the morning to return late in the evening after struggling hard with traffic jams. Children went to kindergarten or school in neighbouring villages. In addition, there was no meeting room left in the village because both the local shop and the pub had been closed down. From Mondays to Fridays, only elderly people spent their days in the village. Families and singles were present only during weekends. The church, therefore, decided to offer programmes for families and adults during the weekends only and programmes for children between 4.30 and 6 p.m. (after returning from school and before their parents returned from work). The church also decided to offer their hall as a meeting place for the village community.

Back to Step 1:

The trio is trained to draw conclusions from the analysis: which information is relevant and should be kept in mind for the development of a concept for the church? Now that the team knows better the (potential) recipients as well as the sender of the letter of Christ, it is able to ask the most important question of the process: what does God want from us as his church in this specific context? What is the special assignment we have as his church in the specific situation we are living in? In other words: what special message does he want to give to his people in this place through us as his letter?

Experiences:

The church building in E. is very old. Its history is very much related to the history of the town and people are very proud and fond of the church, even if they do not belong to the congregation. The results of this analysis made the church in E. focus on their ancient church building and develop a vision for their congregation which puts the church building in the centre. They decided to open the church during the week and to invite people to visit the church. They created a prayer corner for visitors. They use the church for almost all church programmes and have created special programmes related to the building, e.g. they started exhibitions with Biblical themes in the church and offer special services and sermons related to the themes of the exhibition.

Step 4: Defining Goals and Objectives

Having found the (special) assignment of the local church the team has to formulate goals, objectives and strategies. The trio is trained to help the team to set goals for a certain period of time ("In three years we will have accomplished the following goal ...") and to define objectives which will finally lead to the fulfilment of the goal ("If we want to accomplish the goal, we will have to do…"). The trio is also trained to plan the steps needed to fulfil the objectives and reach the set goals. They learn how to monitor the process and how to stay in permanent communication with the governing body of the local church during the process, and to evaluate the results.

Experiences:
For many teams it is hard to formulate goals. They are used to vague directions of where to proceed rather than concrete goals. But it has proved helpful to learn to formulate goals. "We want more people to join Sunday services," is what many teams would 'define' as their goal. But it is easier to define the objectives and steps to reach a goal if it is defined clearly: "In two years we want to double the number of Sunday service participants."

The effects of the training

The major effect of this church development programme is that the governing bodies of a local church as well as its employees and volunteers know what they do for which purpose. The church gains a certain profile and becomes more visible in the community. As one pastor put it:

> For our situation, the 'training for church development' was the best thing that could happen to us!

- Some people who used to have only very loose contact to the church have found their place in the church.
- The local church board has been encouraged to take over responsibility for changes in our church.

- Strengths and weaknesses of our church have become clearly visible. Now we start working from the strengths which help us to handle our weaknesses more easily.
- It was very helpful for our local church board to base decisions on the concept agreed upon. Now the decisions lead in the same direction.
- We realise that our church is recognisable by the people outside. We have gained a profile!"[7]

Experiences:
After having been used in about 80 churches, the training for church development programme was evaluated. The most striking results of the evaluation were:

- Teams and trios had gained development skills and were able to use them in similar processes, e.g. in the development of concepts for church groups.
- Almost all team and trio members became self-confident church activists and leaders. They had found out about their gifts and skills and started to make use of them for the church more confidently than before. For many pastors they became true partners in leading the church.

Local church development – a missionary concept for the UEM community?

Many local churches in Germany have benefitted from this or other methods of local church development. The concept described was developed in Germany for German churches. But it is open for adaption in other cultural and structural settings at least in so called 'mainline' churches. A group of Indonesian pastors have already started to adapt a number of analytical steps for the Indonesian context.

As it is the task of the UEM mission community to assist each other in being missionary churches,[8] it might be interesting to develop a training concept for church development which could be used in different cultural settings or could be adapted for different contexts. The UEM community could make use of the existing concepts and transfer them into the international / intercultural setting of UEM. It would certainly need a group of skilled people from Africa, Asia and Germany to develop such a concept for 'common' use and it would need a

---

[7] Sieglinde Repp-Jost: So war es bei uns (*This is how it was in our case*), in: Gemeindekolleg der VELKD (ed.), *Kirche in Bewegung Mai 2004: Gemeinden gestalten Verănderung (Church in movement. Congregations managing change)*, Celle, 2004

[8] UEM Corporate Identity 2008: "To empower each other for mission we share our resources and gifts and exchange co-workers and volunteers.... In working and living together we learn from each other and are willing to be transformed and renewed as we experience that our partaking in God's mission also changes our lives and our work."

phase of tests with churches in Africa, Asia and Germany and a thorough evaluation in order to improve the concept for further usage.

Especially the idea of making use of the 'viewpoint from outside' may be relevant here. The group of German and Indonesian pastors who met in Indonesia in August 2008 have gained a lot of important ideas from their partners for the development of their own churches. Mission has always crossed boundaries and made use of the different contextual and cultural viewpoints of the missionaries from 'outside' for the development of the church. Often it is easier to accept criticism or to listen to 'strange' ideas from outsiders than it is to accept them from colleagues or friends.

> Experiences:
> A church near Koblenz had started the process of change because they had to reduce the number of pastors from two to one for financial reasons. For months they believed this meant to reduce their activities. Their partners from West Papua were surprised to hear this. In their village they do not have any pastor, and the elders and other volunteers have many more responsibilities. From their viewpoint, the church in Germany had become too dependent on pastors. After these discussions the German church found creative ways to involve volunteers and to actually believe them capable of taking over tasks which used to be 'reserved' for the pastor.

Perhaps the field of local church development could be a new area for mission partnerships to share their ideas, to learn from each other and thus become an even closer mission community prepared for the transformation needed in a rapidly changing world.

“Whoever Can Speak Will Always Find Their Way”: Experiences of an African Missionary in Germany

Jean-Gottfried Mutumbo

Introduction

The title of my presentation uses an African proverb: “Whoever can speak, will always find their way.” And, of course, whoever can speak uses their mouth.

My mouth! Yes, that is what I used when I was in Germany to:

- Announce the Gospel of peace and hope;
- Smile and laugh to express the joy of living;
- Sing to inspire life and freedom in worship;
- Learn to know people and to find a place in the church and in the German community;
- And to be a blessing for the people of God established here.

The literal translation of this African proverb would be: “Whoever has a mouth cannot get lost.” Here, I use the word “mouth” to mean the spoken word. I will deal with four aspects of the spoken word and illustrate each of them with my personal experiences as a pastor in Germany.

In choosing this topic, I have two objectives:

a) To speak about my experience of 6 years and 6 months as a missionary in Germany.

b) To explain how the use of my mouth as a missionary tool for:

- Integration,
- Hope,
- Blessing.

To achieve these objectives, my paper will address the following 4 points:

a) The spoken word (language) as part of social integration.

b) The spoken word as a way to share about life, pain, faith, hope, and transformation.

c) The spoken word as a blessing.

d) The spoken word as prayer.

The spoken word (language) as part of social integration, respect and intercultural dialogue

The mastery of the German language was among my greatest challenges as a missionary. How could I do mission work in Germany without speaking and understanding this language very well? I also knew that through this language I could understand Germans better and be understood by the people in this country.

The following fundamental questions were always in my mind: how to proclaim the Gospel to a people with a long Christian tradition? How could I as a young African pastor lead a young German to be a Christian? Do I have anything new to bring to these people who have a culture of criticism? What kind of examples would I use to reach the heart and soul of German people?

In addition to these questions, I had to face the whole question of the purpose of my mission in Germany, my approach and my ability to work as a missionary from a different culture in this new context.

My mouth was a key. In my mother tongue, *Luba*, the proverb I mentioned before is translated literally as, "Who has a mouth cannot get lost." That means, with a mouth, it is possible to find the way, to discover a new environment, to communicate a message and to integrate into the host society.

When, in 1989, I decided to learn German, I could not imagine that I would ever work in Germany as a pastor. But I understood one thing: the German language was a bridge between the German people and me. This was then verified between 2002 and 2008, when I came to Germany as a missionary co-worker of the United Evangelical Mission (UEM). Knowing the language proved to be a bridge to the mission I was to do, and in addition it became a major factor in my cultural integration and my sense of belonging. Language skills helped to break down barriers between the German churches and me, to overcome fear between people, and to create a new respect for differences among people.

For example, when people learned that I spoke German, they did not hesitate to approach me. The enthusiasm with which I was invited and hosted by several parishes in Germany proved how important it had been for me to make the effort to learn the German language and culture, to communicate my experience in faith and to preach the good news of peace in the tongue of Goethe, Friedrich Schiller and others.

The German language is not easy. To speak it well I needed love for the German people, courage to proclaim the Gospel of Jesus Christ and the help of the Holy Spirit. Despite my imperfect German, I was not ashamed to communicate this good news. As Paul said: "I am not ashamed of the gospel of Christ, for it is the power of God for salvation to everyone who believes," (Rom 1:16). My concern was to reach others by this word.

To meet others in the context of their lives – that was another missionary concern. I came as a simple man, without any pretension that I would persuade people with convincing arguments, but with the assurance that I had been sent from God to do his mission among his people living in Germany. I wanted to live and to work together with people in Germany as part of the body of Christ (2Cor. 12). That means I did not want to be considered a foreigner in Germany. I wanted to be called as a pastor of the Church of Westphalia, because the church of Christ, to which I belong, is one. Despite the differences between our cultures and race, we are members of the family of God. The words of Ruth to Naomi inspired me: "Your people shall be my people, and your God, my God" (Ruth 1:16). This decision of Ruth was also mine. When, in April 2001, I was received as a pastor in the Evangelical Church of Westphalia, my first sermon was based on this text.

The experience we had on that day was that we were received as a family. My wife and our children often went with me to do mission work. So we understood ourselves as a Family in Mission. According to the words of Ruth, we tried to live as a part of the church in Germany without losing our identity as Congolese, as Africans.

This was not always easy. My purpose for being in Germany was to do mission work, and I wanted to give all my time to that work. But I had to struggle between my UEM schedule and the agenda of parishes and groups who invited me. I will not forget how people often told me, "You know, Jean, you must learn to say NO sometimes." But a big question still bothered me: how does a servant of Christ say "no" to his master? It was hard to say "no" when there was always work waiting for me and when I felt the master needed me to bring the good news to his people.

Learning about the situation of the people in the church was an element that enabled me to reach the hearts of German people. It was a part of my missionary strategy. In preparing my sermons, I spent much time reading newspapers, listening to the radio and watching television in order to know the problems and the facts of German society. My main question was: how can the Gospel be an answer to the concerns of the people here in Germany? Mission in this context meant "to make the Gospel a response to questions and concerns of men and women of today." I tried to proclaim the Gospel to Germans in the German language with examples from the German context. Even though I came from Africa and sometimes I used my African imagination, each listener was following the message in his or her own language and with examples from their own society. As a result, I hoped that neither the message nor my way of speaking would be strange to the listeners.

I wanted the Gospel to become practical, authentic and real. The fundamental issue was to know: what did the word of God have to do with the daily lives of Christians in Germany? Developed by an African, this approach was attractive in that it made the Bible and the Gospel particularly current and real to people. I did not tell people about stories which happened thousands of years ago, but I spoke about the message of God which transforms the lives of the people who live in a modern and post-modern world. I called people to put their hope in the promises of God, to open their eyes to see injustice and violence, and to be committed as a "letter of Christ" (2Cor. 3:2) to the world. I had many opportunities to talk about the global financial crisis and to share about the link between the wars in many countries of the southern hemisphere and economic injustice. I found among German Christians a spirit of solidarity.

I learned many things, so that the mission came to mean enrichment and a sharing of life experiences.

The spoken word as a way to share about life, pain, faith, hope, transformation

As a missionary, I was sent to work with people of all conditions and all ages. To them, I was carrying a word of hope and solidarity for their lives. Many people now have the sense and courage to live according to the ideas I have been preaching. I remember, for example, a man who, after having heard me preach on the day of Pentecost in 2006 in Münster, said, "I have learned today that the Gospel can take into account the concerns of my life! I am encouraged and I thank you, Mr. Pastor."

I still have a letter from a girl who wrote me about how she was convinced by my preaching in the parish of Bad Oeynhausen. Since then, she and her family are increasingly involved in the parish. On 27th May, 2008, at the ceremony to complete my work in Germany, I was pleasantly surprised to see this girl coming to me to introduce her mother and sister. Thus, a lifetime commitment in the church was possible due to the power of the Gospel, understood as a testimony to life and the sharing of hope.

Speaking of hope, I was often approached by pastors to speak to desperate young Africans and Germans. I remember a German mother who had recommended that her son meet me. The richness of our conversation was enough to open up horizons and a glimmer of hope to the young in searching for direction in his life.

Speaking of life, I remember the answer I gave to a woman who asked whether I had conducted the funeral of someone in my parish in Germany. The spontaneous response was: "I came not to bury the dead in Germany but, through the Gospel, to help those who are alive here." I used the example of Ebed-Melek, an African in the king's palace in Jerusalem, who acted to save the life of Prophet Jeremiah (Jer 38:1-13).

How could I make people more alive in the church? How could young people find their place in the worship service? The worship that I celebrated together with my colleagues was alive and attractive because of its multifaceted liturgy enriched by the African songs that I was able to teach people to sing. My smile and my vivacity both in song and in preaching were contagious because I did not let any part of the worship service become boring. Each person there could celebrate his or her emotions. Many young people who were tired of a "cold" worship service were attracted by this kind of worship. So part of my mission was to transform worship so that it became a time of joy, freedom to glorify God and of sharing the vitality of Christ. Life was understood as something to share through the gestures and words of blessing.

The spoken word as a blessing

In May, 2009, my colleague Remi Nsemi lost his father. Remi received this news while he was with us in the office. Like others, I took time to console him. Remi told us the circumstances of the death of his father. He was very sad about one thing: his father did not speak before dying. The whole family expected that, at the end of his life, their father would speak words of blessing which would serve as elements of a new beginning for them. We know that at the end of a worship service, words of comfort, consolation, support, and blessing are always spoken. Through these words the end becomes an occasion of hope, of experiences of love in community and an opportunity to begin anew at the beginning.

Searching for words that would make possible a new beginning to life, my colleagues and I created a worship service of blessing, a new kind of worship that we introduced and celebrated in several parishes in the Church District of Gütersloh and elsewhere. My concept of a ministry of blessing came from the words which God said to Abraham: "And you shall be a blessing.... And in you all the families of the earth shall be blessed." (Gen 12:2-3).

According to this promise, we wanted to make the worship service a time of blessing for all and through all from God, who is ready to bless and to use his people as tools of blessing. To implement this promise, we took seriously the Protestant principle of "universal priesthood" by involving the laity in the ministry of blessing. This kind of worship was and continues to be open to all people to show solidarity with those who suffer and feel alone. It is a way to show people that God is with them, that they can live abundantly in God. It is a way to lead those who need a new path and the light of God in their lives. It is a way to pray for those who are seeking, to intercede for those who desire help and peace, to pray for the transformation and healing of our world and our church.

This style of worship also had the positive effect of bringing people back to worship who had long ago abandoned the church. In addition, we discovered an enthusiasm among co-workers who came to feel that they are important players in the church. In this context, the mission made everyone an active participant in the church and the world, each one in movement through actions and commitment.

The responsibility to bless makes each person a missionary. Thus, the worship services of blessing became an active place of mission. In addition, they provided an opportunity to share and exchange experiences in faith, and to participate in intense meditation and prayer. Today, this kind of worship continues. It helps to strengthen the initiatives of parishes in order to build the faith of the people and reinforce their witness in society.

The spoken word as prayer

Before I close, let me underline the role of prayer in my missionary experience. Coming to Germany was a voluntary response to the choice and to the call which God addressed to Isaiah: "Whom shall I send?" (Is 6:8) Isaiah's yes was also mine. The context for Isaiah's "yes" was God's presence in the temple. ". . . I saw the Lord sitting on a throne, high and lofty; and the hem of his robe filled the temple. . . One of the seraphs flew to me, holding a live coal . . . The seraph touched my mouth with it and said, 'Now that this has touched your lips, your guilt has departed and your sin is blotted out.'" (Is 6:1b-7).

This text demonstrates both the sovereignty and the presence of God who sends us out, and the preparation and the tools needed by those whom he sends into mission. For the mission remains God's, though it may be accomplished by people in spite of all their weaknesses. Thus, God gives to those whom he sends out the means to accomplish the mission, so that they would neither take it over nor use it for her own glory.

Accomplishing the mission for the glory of God put me in a position of permanent dependence on God through an intense prayer life. Prayer was my instrument of communication with God, through which I was inspired by the Holy Spirit to announce the good news of life.

My conviction remains strong: the work of the Holy Spirit fills the emptiness which exists between those who hear my preaching and myself who preaches the word. It is the Holy Spirit who convinces and transforms lives. That is why it was extremely important to rely on the intervention of the Holy Spirit. The success of the spoken word did not lie in the preaching only, but equally and especially in the activity of the Holy Spirit. Paul affirms this clearly: "My speech and my proclamation were not with plausible words of wisdom, but with a demonstration of the Spirit and of power . . ." (2Cor 2:4).

This conviction which influenced my life was courageously shared with many of my colleagues during spiritual initiatives such as prayer meetings and meditation times. As a result, the mission became a school of prayer. The more the missionary challenges grew, the greater became the intensity of my prayers. Lived out in community, the mission not only helped to reinforce our ties of collaboration and of cooperation with colleagues from different backgrounds, but it also led us to a new understanding of the internal and local mission of the church.

Conclusion

Our missionary work in Germany was a blessing for the UEM, and surely for myself and my family as well. It gave meaning to the South-North Exchange programme and strengthened the belief in the UEM's mission work, which takes into account men and women created in God's image. The Gospel that we taught really did meet people in their social, political, economic and cultural contexts.

We understand "mission" as the proclamation of the Gospel of peace, and sharing of responsibilities for a better world through justice, peace and integrity of creation. Mission is also an invitation to the joy of living in trust and solidarity.

We learned more from the German people and churches in Germany:

- The spirituality of silence and meditation .
- The creative and results-oriented work, transparency in the management of human resources, material and financial resources.
- The emphasis on the social gospel; the mission becomes a socio-economic and political task.

All these shall help me to strengthen the mission of my church in Congo concerning social justice issues, the fight against poverty, violence, corruption and impunity, and the work for transparency and the establishment of the rule of law in Congo.

One area that presents a great opportunity for mission in Germany is to motivate pastors and church members to talk about their faith and to practice their own mission: mission with all and for all. This requires an apprenticeship. How can the Gospel reach people who do not come to church? How can the good news of peace, love and hope be told to those who live on the street, and others who suffer in our communities? How can we break through the shame and fear that many people have when trying to speak about their faith? This requires training. It seems to me that training in how to talk about our faith would help the churches in Germany to get out of the current demographic crisis and to attract young people to them. This training can be reinforced by the diversification of forms of worship, and worship that reflects the needs and tastes of people. That will make the church more alive and its mission very powerful.

MISSION AND CHURCH UNITY: MIGRANT CHURCHES IN GERMANY AS A CHALLENGE TO THE *LANDESKIRCHEN*

Claudia Währisch-Oblau

When the Protestant missionary movement started about 200 years ago, large parts of the world did not have any Christian community at all. The "mission field" was seen as a blank slate onto which Christianity could be inscribed, replacing 'heathen religion'. As more and more mission agencies and missionaries started their work, and as the missionary impulse became caught up in ideas of nationalism and colonialism, competition between mission agencies started to develop.[1] Agencies usually followed after colonial armies (and had to leave when a colony changed hands). But even during these times, situations developed in which several agencies started work in the same country or region. To avoid outright competition, 'comity agreements' were made which assigned each agency a certain region or ethnic group.[2] With the increased migration of people and the end of colonialist rule, these comity agreements eventually broke down. Today, 'mainline' Protestant mission agencies do their work in close relation with existing churches on the ground and usually refrain from planting new churches and ministries without at least consulting existing churches.

Pentecostals and Charismatics never had such compunctions. As Allan Anderson[3] and others[4] have shown, the Pentecostal movement, right from its beginning, used existing missionary networks to spread around the world. In many cases, new Pentecostal churches were started in the same place as existing Protestant churches.

Today, many places in the world have more than one Christian church. In October 2008, I visited a "mission area" of the Christian Protestant Church of

---

1 See Frieder Ludwig, Mission und Kolonialismus *(Mission and Colonialism)*, in: Dahling-Sander, Christoph et. al. (eds.), Leitfaden Ökumenische Missionstheologie *(A Guide to Ecumenical Mission Theology)*, Gütersloh: Chr. Kaiser / Gütersloher Verlagshaus, 2003, pp.79-96.

2 See, for example, Merlyn L. Guillermo and L. p.Verora, Protestant Churches and Missions in the Philippines, vol. 1 (Valenzuela, Metro Manila: Agape Printing Services, 1982), pp.1-3.

3 Spreading Fires. The Missionary Nature of Early Pentecostalism, London: SCM Press, 2007.

4 See e.g. Michael Bergunder, *Constructing Pentecostalism. On Issues of Methodology and Representation* Journal of the European Pentecostal Theological Association. 27,1: 2007, pp.55-73.

Indonesia (GKPI) on the island of Sumatra, in a remote mountain village. In this poor village of about 2,000 inhabitants, four church buildings were lined up: a Roman Catholic one, the GKPI one, one from the HKBP (another UEM member church), and a Pentecostal one. Everywhere, UEM member churches do their mission work in a 'market situation', in a context in which a number of differing (and sometimes very similar!) churches compete with each other for members. In any given German city, there is a number of so-called "free churches" in addition to the Protestant and the Roman Catholic congregations. Mission, other than intended by the first Protestant missionaries, does not seem to lead to church unity, but rather to differentiation and rivalry. Is this something that simply has to be accepted and dealt with pragmatically, or can mission be thought and practiced in such a way that the *unio catholica* of at least the Protestant Church is strengthened?

In the following paper, I want to study this question using one concrete example: the mission of migrant churches in Germany.

German churches: historical background

After the reformation in Germany, church membership was organized along a very simple principle: *Cuius regio, eius religio* – simply stated, the subjects of every state, duchy or principality (and there were many in Germany at that time!) had to follow the religious adherence of their ruler. Each little regional entity was either Catholic or Lutheran or Reformed. Those not willing to accept the faith of their ruler were sometimes allowed to emigrate to another region whose ruler's faith they shared. It took until the 19th century for individual religious freedom to be granted, and only then competing churches started to exist next to each other. Up to the early 19th century, every German was either Roman Catholic or Protestant (Lutheran, Reformed, or United, depending on where one lived). In 1834, the first Baptist Church was founded in Germany,[5] and in the 1850s, the British Methodist Churches sent their first missionary to this country.[6] Immediately, this mission work was seen as competition by the Evangelical and Catholic Churches which understood Germany as 'their' territory – an attitude which can be found up to today.[7]

---

[5] See Günter Balders: Ein Herr - ein Glaube - eine Taufe. 150 Jahre Baptistengemeinden in Deutschland *(One Lord One Faith – One Baptism. 150 Years of Baptist Congregations in Germany)*, Wuppertal und Kassel, 1984.

[6] Karl Steckel, Ernst Sommer (Hrsg.): Geschichte der Evangelisch-methodistischen Kirche. Weg, Wesen und Auftrag des Methodismus unter besonderer Berücksichtigung der deutschsprachigen Länder Europas *(History of the Evangelical Methodist Church. The Methodist Way, Being and Mission, Particularly in German-Speaking Europe)*, 3. Auflage, 2007, Göttingen: Edition Ruprecht.

[7] See, for example, the speech by Methodist Bishop Walter Klaiber in: Ökumenische Zentrale (ed.), Gemeinsam zum Glauben einladen: Aufbruch zu einer missionarischen Ökumene. Ein Impulsheft für Gemeinden und ökumenische Gesprächs- und

Protestant and Pentecostal / Charismatic Christian migrants have come to Germany in substantial numbers since the 1960s. In the beginning, many of them tried to join German Protestant congregations. But the German churches, due to their strongly ethnic character, were often not very welcoming. There were no provisions to provide translations or any other attempts at internationalizing worship services, and immigrants were expected to blend in or leave. Most migrants quickly realized that they needed churches of their own if they wanted to continue to worship on a regular basis. The foundation of such "diaspora churches" was encouraged and supported by the German Protestant churches, and a number of Finnish, Swedish, Danish, Hungarian, Korean, and Japanese congregations were set up with financial and organizational support from the EKD[8] and its member churches. This was not understood as competition, as the migrant, i.e. non-German members of these churches were not *a priori* understood as members of the German Evangelical churches.

Immigrant missionaries: the current situation

Since the mid-1980s, a new wave of immigration has brought Christians from West and Central Africa, from South and South East Asia and from Latin America. Similarly to the earlier migrants, these Christians often tried to join German congregations, without much success, and then started to build their own churches. Contrary to the older churches, though, the leaders of the new churches usually do not describe them as diaspora churches serving an immigrant community, but rather as 'new mission churches' aimed at reviving the church in Germany and evangelizing its society. The targets of their missionary outreach are Germans, and, therefore, the question of competition arises anew.

But is Germany still a Christian country? In 2006, 25.1% of Germans belonged to the Evangelical Churches, 25.7% to the Catholic Church, 1.5% to "free churches", and 1.4% to Eastern and Oriental Orthodox Churches, leaving a non-Christian percentage of 46.3%. Furthermore, projections of membership

---

Arbeitskreise *(Inviting to Faith Together. Towards a Missionary Oikoumene)*, Frankfurt/M., 1999. Klaiber complains that missionary outreach by the 'free churches' is all too often seen as proselytizing, taking away the members of existing churches.

8 *Evangelische Kirche in Deutschland* – Evangelical Church in Germany, the umbrella of the regional Protestant churches in Germany. For an overview of diaspora churches set up in cooperation with the EKD, see Kirchenamt der Evangelischen Kirche in Deutschland (ed.), Kirchen und Gemeinden anderer Sprache und Herkunft *(Churches and Congregations of Other Language and Origin)*, Frankfurt am Main: Gemeinschaftswerk der evangelischen Publizistik, 1997.

for both the Catholic and the Protestant Churches point to a continued downward trend. Very few congregations manage to "grow against the trend."[9]

But the leaders of many Pentecostal / Charismatic 'new mission churches' do not even equate the percentage of church members of the two main churches with the percentage of 'real' Christians, claiming that most of them are simply nominal. Consequently, they see German Christianity as dying and in urgent need of revival. Citing the multitude of church buildings that are almost empty during Sunday services, they insist that divine guidance brought them here to, like Nehemiah, rebuild a ruined Jerusalem. They do not ask permission from German churches to start evangelizing, and often work with little contact with existing churches, even though they often use their buildings. Many of such 'new mission churches', though, would be quite willing to cooperate with existing German churches if such churches were to share their missionary urge and methods.

This mission work collides with the German '*Landeskirchen*' which are the mainline Protestant former state churches. They define themselves as '*Volkskirche*' (people's church, folk church); a term that is often implicitly understood as meaning an ethnic German church, but could also be defined as 'church for all people.'[10] *Volkskirche* definitely has the implication that most or all of the inhabitants of a certain area belong to a certain church. Consequently, both the Catholic and the Evangelical Churches in Germany are organized in geographical parishes. Any Catholic or Protestant basically belongs to the parish which covers the place in which he or she lives. In consequence, the Evangelical Churches, at least in an unspoken way, still understand themselves as 'covering' all of Germany. They engage in evangelism, both to their own nominal members and to those who are unchurched, but feel that at least their nominal members 'belong' to them and should not be 'poached' by other churches. Protestant parish pastors complain if a 'free church' evangelizes their nominal members and causes them to leave the Evangelical Church. As each nominal member is still paying church tax, the Protestant Churches benefit even from those who do not attend church, but lose out financially if a nominal member joins another church.

---

[9] See Wilfried Härle et. al. (eds.), Wachsen gegen den Trend. Analysen von Gemeinden, mit denen es aufwärts geht *(Growing against the Trend. Analysis of Congregations which Develop Upwards)*, Stuttgart: Evangelische Verlagsanstalt, 2008.

[10] Originally, the term '*Volkskirche*' was coined in opposition to the understanding of State Church, denoting a church that belonged to the people rather than to a ruler. The people, though, were understood as an ethnic entity – *Volk* clearly meant the German people.

German Protestant mainline churches and migrants / migrant churches

The German Protestant mainline churches have long been very active in advocacy and counselling for migrants (both Christians and non-Christians). Particularly through their diaconal institutions, immigrants were assisted in many ways, reaching from dormitories for young, female nurses from Korea to counselling offices where migrants can discuss questions of qualification, integration, education of their children etc. Similarly, the Protestant churches have been very outspoken in their advocacy for migrants. It is striking, though, that in all public statements migrants are seen solely as clients of the churches' diaconal work. Almost no thought is given to the religion of migrants, and none to a possible missionary urge of migrant churches.

Protestant migrant Christians are in principle (though often not in practice!) welcomed to become part of a local congregation, but except for the Evangelical Church of Hesse-Nassau, there is no provision in the German UEM member churches for special congregations which would serve migrants from a certain language and / or ethnic group. Neither is there any programmatic encouragement of local congregations to invite and integrate migrant Christians. There is no discussion about the possibility of bi-lingual worship, or of a change in liturgy and style which would accommodate Christians from other nationalities.

As far as Pentecostal / Charismatic migrant churches are concerned, Protestant mainline congregations have been fairly willing to share their premises (though usually for a fee!). Most small migrant congregations meet in Protestant churches and church halls; a growing number of larger churches, though, now rents or even buys their own premises, usually disused factory halls. It is somewhat ironic that at a time when the mainline churches are closing buildings and turning churches into shops and flats, migrant churches are turning shops and factories into churches!

A summary of the situation

What then, do we have in Germany? We have a Protestant church which is in decline but still sees itself as the 'mainline' church which defines what "Evangelical in Germany"[11] means. We have a church that considers migrants as diaconal clients, but has so far no concept of immigrants as members, or of the necessity to change because Germany is becoming an immigration country with a growing number of Protestants with a migratory background. In short, questions of denominational, ethic and cultural identity have implicitly or explicitly been used to exclude migrant Christians from the *Landeskirchen*,

---

[11] See, for example, Kirche der Freiheit. Ein Impulspapier des Rates der EKD *(Church of Freedom. An Impulse Paper of the Council of the Evangelical Church in Germany)*, Hannover, 2006.

both individually and corporately. Finally, we have Protestant churches which insist that their members belong to them and must not be evangelized by a church from the outside, even if they have no contact to their own congregation beyond paying their church tax.

On the other hand, we have two quite different groups of migrant churches. Firstly, there are the long-established Protestant diaspora churches. Their members have been in Germany for most of their lifetime, and a second and even third generation is growing up already. The members are well integrated into German society, but their churches are not integrated into German churches. Many of these congregations find that the second and third generation is not willing to join the diaspora church, often simply because they do not speak their parents' language well enough. At the same time, no German church has any kind of outreach to second-generation Protestant migrants, or joins a diaspora church in reaching out to them. Consequently, many second and third generation migrants whose parents and grandparents were active Protestants have become unchurched.

Secondly, there is a growing number of 'new mission churches.' While their membership is predominantly migrant – this often misleads German Protestants into perceiving them as diaspora churches! – they see themselves as international (and often non-denominational) bridgeheads with a calling to revive and re-evangelize the whole continent of Europe. Their outreach is aimed at anyone and everyone they meet. They hope to be able to also have an impact on the existing churches and begin a revival in them.

From this analysis, three main questions arise:

1. What actually constitutes the unity of a church? Denominational identity alone or also cultural identity? Or can church unity be envisioned beyond such definitions?
2. What is the mission of the German *Landeskirchen* towards migrant Christians? Is it just one of diaconia, or should it also aim at integrating them into a German church? And how could this be done?
3. How should the *Landeskirchen* respond to Pentecostal / Charismatic 'new mission churches' which often use their premises, but at the same time see themselves as revivalists towards a church which they perceive as in dire need of revival? Could the *Landeskirchen* which follow a theology of *missio Dei* develop a concept in which they could understand themselves both as actors and as recipients of mission?

This paper cannot answer these questions, but gives at least some ideas about the direction where answers can be found.

Church unity

Since its inception, Protestant ecclesiology has conceptualized the "real existing" church as a national and / or ethnic unit, while relegating the concept of a worldwide church to the abstract realm of the "believed church." Christian identity is closely linked to one's mother tongue and culture, and an "international Protestant Church" or even a "Protestant Church of Europe" is somehow unthinkable. Rather, Protestant churches proudly bear national labels like the Evangelical Church in Germany, or, in the case of multi-ethnic nations, even ethnic labels like the Batak Christian Protestant Church. Such labels implicate that Christianity in a given area belongs to the 'indigenous' people and not to people who are immigrants in that area. That such nationalist ecclesiologies were a necessary antidote against colonialism does not need to be discussed here, but the question remains whether national and / or ethnic churches can be a true expression of the church of Christ in a globalizing environment. If the church universal is concretized solely in terms of 'ecumenical cooperation' between different ethnic incarnations of this church, the relationship between indigenous and migrant churches in any given area remains asymmetrical, with the indigenous churches holding a position of power and the migrant churches more or less marginalized. The problem about such ethnic definitions of churches is that they are inclined to assume that cultures are static, and consequently become backward-looking and conservative. In Indonesia, a country which is faced with growing internal migration, Protestant churches tend to jealously guard their respective ethnic identities against newcomers rather than welcome them into their fold. In Europe, while the presence of migrant churches may have pluralized the church landscape, their Christianity is not (and cannot easily become) "European," as such 'cultural change' is associated with 'losing one's identity.'[12] The recent statement of the outgoing Secretary General of the Protestant Church in the Netherlands, Bas Plaisier, that his church is "far too white"[13] and no longer representing world-Christianity as it is present in the multi-cultural composition of Dutch society, does not look likely to be taken up any time soon by other Protestant church leaders.

---

[12] For a discussion of static and dynamic images of culture and their influence on the understanding of 'religious identity,' see Michael Bergunder, Pfingstbewegung, Globalität und Migration *(The Pentecostal Movement, Globality and Migration)*, in: Michael Bergunder and Jörg Haustein (eds.), Migration und Identität. Pfingstlich-charismatische Migrationsgemeinden in Deutschland *(Migration and Identity. Pentecostal-Charismatic Migrant Churches in Germany)*. Beiheft der Zeitschrift für Mission 8. Frankfurt am Main: Otto Lembeck, 2006, pp.153-169.

[13] D. Visser, 'Ds. Bas Plaisier: "Onze Kerk is Veel Te Wit,"' *(Our Church is Far too White)* Kerkinformatie, no. 160 (2008), p.4.

The mission towards migrant Christians

Protestant churches have so far negotiated their identities in relation to their respective national contexts. Consequently, they could only understand their mission towards migrant churches in the framework of diaconia and advocacy which might even include helping migrants set up their own 'diaspora' churches. But a real opening-up towards migrant Christians would mean a process of radical re-definition of their own heritages and identities. If a church starts to incorporate migrants, it cannot just assimilate them into the existing structure – integration means that both the integrators and the integrated have to change.

Such a change could draw its inspiration from a biblical-theological perspective which does not only look at migrants from a sedentary viewpoint in which the (indigenous) church is called to protect the stranger. The Bible, both in the Old and the New Testament, abounds with 'migrant theology:' "At the beginning of the history of the People of God stands the call to migration. [...] This [i.e. Abraham's] emigration is not just an accidental event at the beginning of the story of Israel. It is the characterization of the People of God in Old and New Testament. They are people who have been called out of this world *(ekklesia!)* and are travelling to a new land. They are migrants who have not found it in this world and who persist in their search for a new homeland."[14] From Abraham who left his home in faith to become a nomad in Israel moving out of slavery in Egypt, and later into exile and back, from Jesus who had "nowhere to lay his head"[15] to the travels of Paul, faith is understood as setting people in motion and making them homeless in the sense that they no longer simply belong to the place and the culture around them: "for here we have no lasting city, but we seek the city which is to come."[16] If even indigenous Christians saw themselves as essentially 'homeless' and 'expatriate,' their relationship to actual migrants would be one of equality rather than of benevolent largesse.

It is quite striking that the European Protestant churches which are so aware of the processes of economic globalization and have had so much to say on this[17] find it so difficult to accept that the deterritorialized transnationalism of migrant churches is a form of ecclesial postmodernity that challenges their territorial identities. If they could recognize this, rather than considering the international identities of migrant churches as a lack of integration, they could

---

14 P.de Jong, Migration in Biblical Perspective, in: *In A Strange Land. A Report of a World Conference on Problems of International Migration and the Responsibility of the Churches, Held at Leysin, Switzerland, June 11-16, 1961,* Division of Inter-Church Aid and Service to Refugees, World Council of Churches, p.24.

15 Matthew 8:20.

16 Hebrews 13.14.

17 See, for example, the list of documents on www.wcc-coe.org/wcc/what/jpc/globalization.html, accessed on 7 October 2008.

understand them as models for the future from which they as white, indigenous churches could learn.[18]

In Europe, this seems to be somewhat easier for small minority Protestants like the Waldensian Church in Italy: this church which was originally ethnic Italian but now has a majority of immigrant members, most of them from West Africa. The style and even the language of worship have changed dramatically, as have organizational patterns. Waldensian pastors talk about the enormous difficulties this has brought, and not all of them are optimistic that the unity between the Africans and the Italians will work out in the long term. Nevertheless, the Waldensian experiment is a true beacon for other churches, as it shows how a church has to act and change if it sees its mission towards migrants as a holistic one. Protestant churches in northwestern Europe, in the meantime, have seen the presence of migrant Christians not as a challenge to their essence and towards a holistic mission, but at most a challenge to their ethical (i.e. diaconal) behaviour.

For the Evangelical churches in Germany, a holistic mission towards migrant Christians and churches would mean a reform of their church orders to allow migrants to set up foreign language congregations within the framework of a German church. Once such congregations have been set up, models of cooperation and community need to be found which help such congregations to negotiate the difficult process of integration. Once a church allows special congregations for migrants, it also needs to look into its training for pastors. Migrant congregations, particularly in the beginning, need a pastor from their own background – which means that churches which allow such congregations also have to recognize pastoral training of other churches! –, but when considering a long-term perspective, it would be good to start as early as possible with a pastoral team composed of both migrants and indigenous pastors. This would also be helpful for the second generation. In reverse, migrant pastors could also take pastoral duties in German congregations, thereby helping the church as a whole to become more multicultural.

Missio Dei: becoming a receiving church

One of the most important paradigm shifts in the mission theology of the 20th century was the move from an understanding of mission as the task of the (Northern Atlantic) churches to a definition of mission as "*missio Dei,*" a movement in which God engages with the world and in which the church may play a part if it is faithful to him. The concept of *missio Dei* is important as it allows us to discern God's Spirit as active in the world outside and independent

---

[18] See also Hijme Stoffels, A Coat of Many Colours, in: Mechteld Jansen and Hijme Stoffels (eds.), *A Moving God. Immigrant Churches in the Netherlands,* Zürich / Berlin: LIT-Verlag, 2008, p.26.

of the churches. The mission does not belong to the church, it belongs to God. "Mission means recognizing what God is doing and joining in."[19]

Thinking mission as God's mission means that any church is not only an actor in this process, but also its addressee. Indigenous churches in Germany should look at the migrant 'new mission churches' and seriously ask whether these churches are an expression of the *missio Dei* and, therefore, have something to say to them. So far, the German churches clearly see themselves still as the givers and the strong ones who need to help others, rather than as those who need help and could be enriched by the migrants.

But if, despite all of what they might find questionable about the migrants' theology, European Protestant Christians were to read the blossoming of migrant churches on European ground as a movement of the Holy Spirit, and the mission of the New Mission Churches as one filament of the *missio Dei*, then their relationship would have to be taken out of the diaconal helper – client realm and to be defined in missiological terms: how does their mission relate to ours, and ours to theirs? And how does their being in Europe shape the face of Christianity in this continent?

Such questioning does not mean that European Protestant churches have to accept uncritically what the migrant Pentecostals and Charismatics are preaching and teaching. After all, the Holy Spirit, throughout history, has relied on human beings with all their faults and failures. Being part of the movement of the Spirit does not make anybody perfect; accepting the mission of the migrant churches as part of such a Spirit movement does not mean that their theology and practice may not be questioned or criticized. But a dialogue based on the recognition that the Spirit moves in the churches of the other as it moves in my own church leads to an attitude of respect and humility – the only attitude that will make a dialogue successful. This, of course, holds equally true for migrant churches: Where migrant pastors, with only a superficial knowledge of the Protestant churches, claim to know that they are spiritually dead and what needs to be done to revive them, they will not evangelize, but antagonize.

The crucial question is undeniably whether a 'theology of receiving' is possible. Do European Protestants have the humility and the humor to accept that they need correction and assistance from Pentecostal / Charismatic migrants? Indeed, if the European Protestant churches, in their encounters with migrant Pentecostals and Charismatics, allow themselves to be reminded that they, too, are strangers in this world and citizens first and foremost of the Kingdom of God, a real dialogue and learning process may ensue.

---

19 Quote taken from a lecture by Bishop Graham Cray, Iserlohn, 6 September 2007.

Response by Abednego Keshomshahara

This paper shows that mission and unity among churches in Germany are affected by cultural and denominational differences. For example, in the 1960's, migrant Christians who went to Germany wanted to join the German established churches but they were not integrated because of ethnicity and language barriers in the German churches. As a result, migrant Christians formed 'churches in diaspora' to address their spiritual needs. It is very interesting to see that the German Protestant Churches and other foreign churches supported these 'churches in diaspora' and viewed them not as competitors.

However, since the 1980's another wave of migrant Christians has come from Africa and Asia to Germany. These Christians are of the opinion that the Germans ought to be evangelised, a situation that creates competition between the migrant and the German churches. Although one may think that Germany is a predominantly Christian country, Währisch-Oblau puts it very clearly that 46.3% of Germans are non-Christians, a point that justifies the claim of the migrant churches that Germany is now a "mission field". Moreover, in the eyes of many Pentecostal / Charismatic church leaders, even those who are Christians in Germany are not 'real' Christians unless they are revived.

In the midst of these challenges, Währisch-Oblau argues that churches should not take culture as static but rather as dynamic while creating a room for changes and development resulting from inter-cultural relations that change both the integrators and the integrated. Biblical theology reveals that emigration is not an accidental event, but rather a plan of God that sets people in motion to seek something beyond this world, a conviction that makes every believer like a migrant who should relate well to the actual migrants. The churches in Germany should see the migrant Christians as a challenge and an opportunity for enrichment rather than viewing them as needy and passive. Of course, as the author comments, migrant theology should not be accepted without criticism bearing in mind that the Holy Spirit uses people who have weaknesses. The same applies to the migrant Christians who are challenged to avoid prejudices and generalisation about the German Christians whom they think are all dead spiritually. The author aims at the enhancement of dialogue among Christians of different cultures and denominations for the sake of unity in doing mission in a multi-cultural, denominational and global context. The ideas that are presented in this paper can be helpful to many churches worldwide since the problem of ethnicity, cultural differences and denominationalism affects mission and church unity in many places of the world. While differences are unavoidable, the essence of Christianity which is the salvation we receive from Jesus Christ should always unite and guide us in our discipleship and mission.

PART FIVE

MISSION AND CULTURE
(B) IN ASIA

Crossing the Boundaries
Retelling the Story of my Journey into Christianity

Anwar Tjen

In the beginning was curiosity...

I was born and brought up in a Chinese Indonesian family following our traditional Chinese religion which is a blend of Confucianism, Daoism and Buddhism. It never occurred to me that all the familiar things I had experienced would have to be given up someday. Out of curiosity I borrowed a strange thick book from my classmate in high school. Its title was 'Alkitab'. Its appearance was very humble, not appealing at all. But I remember the experience of reading it for the first time: "*Bahwa pada mula pertama dijadikan Allah akan langit dan bumi*" ('That in the beginning heavens and the earth were created by God').[1] That first line sent me back into an unknown past. Immediately it caught my imagination. So, I thought, this is a book about the beginning of our universe as taught by Christians.

Prompted by my initial curiosity I read on without much prejudice. In fact, I treated it just like other story books I liked. After the first two chapters, I quickly learnt that it was not simply a story of creation. It was a story of humans' disobedience towards God, and his harsh punishments against them as well as, strangely, other 'innocent' creatures. The themes of evil, destruction and renewal recurred one after another, narrowing down to stories of a group of people favoured by their God.

One of the highlights was the story of Joseph and his brothers. The key theme looked universally appealing. Others might hurt us, but we should never forget that even a bad experience could be a blessing in disguise. I read on until I reached the boring point somewhere in the middle of the book of Exodus. The boundary is clearly there! All the ritual stuff and detailed instructions about the Tabernacle were so foreign that I found it hard to chew. I decided right away to return the book to the owner.

The familiar and the unfamiliar observed

Before doing so, however, a distant memory from my childhood suddenly came to the surface. It was Christmas, and a church bus came to pick kids up from our neighbourhood to a candlelight celebration. The most interesting incentive

---

[1] Cited from Alkitab Terjemahan Lama (Indonesian Old Translation; Lembaga Alkitab Indonesia, 1965).

was, of course, the promise of sweets and gifts! The church was crowded by people who were clapping their hands while singing joyfully. And then there was a birthday story about someone called "Jesus". That was all I remembered about the joyful celebration. It was hard to imagine that someday such a frail memory would visit me after the first attempt to read the book. "Could I find the story about Christmas and Jesus in this book?" I wondered. Later my Christian friend told me to skip through most of the book, jumping almost to the end.

Bearing with the boring genealogy for a while, I was soon captivated by the opening line of the story: "Now the birth of Jesus Christ took place in this way" (Mt 1:18). Here is the story I might have heard! There was nothing really earthshaking. The birth was miraculous, but it should come as no surprise for anyone still believing in spirits and supernatural phenomena. Though I had little idea who Jesus was, I read it with much interest. When it came to the Sermon on the Mount (Mt 5-7), I began to hear familiar voices among the unfamiliar. In Jesus' teachings about love, forgiveness and integrity I could hear echoes of the ancient wisdom I learnt from my grandmother, as she often told us, "We should never hurt others in this transient life if we don't want to be hurt and reborn in the next circle of life as a miserable creature." Through stories and conversations, she would pass on to her grandchildren noble virtues such as compassion, responsibility and honesty.

My initial image about Jesus was, therefore, that of a semi-divine sage, a teacher of compassion and obedience to the gracious Father of all. "Love your enemies and pray for those who persecute you, so that you may be children of your Father in heaven; for he makes his sun rise on the evil and on the good, and sends rain on the righteous and on the unrighteous." (Mt 5:44-45). My admiration of this wise teacher was growing gradually, and so was the process of identification with the protagonist on the way to his tragic death. When the climax was reached on the cross, his cry "My God, my God, why have you forsaken me?" (Mt 26:46) went deeply into my pre-Christian heart. Not knowing how to respond exactly, I stopped to reflect on the injustices that often took place under the sun. How could such a compassionate miracle worker end up that way? The seed of the theology of the cross – to borrow a concept I learnt later - was already sown in my inner soil, waiting for its season to grow and blossom.

Troubled conscience

But he came back to life! The gloomy tone in the long narrative of passion was suddenly turned into a joyful cry. Was it really hard to believe this miracle? It may well be, but I did not bother to ask skeptical questions about its historicity. Since I read it like other profane stories, it was there for me to enjoy. There was joy and hope beyond the teacher's death. Noticeably, amidst the chaotic circumstances, the disciples experienced a sudden burst of energy after the resurrection. And the new energy inspired fresh activities that reached out beyond their inner circles. I noticed Judas' tragic death but also Peter's transformation of life. From then on, the disciples were driven by the desire to share the story with others. Indeed, they had to suffer insults and persecutions on behalf of the Risen One even to the point of death. The stoning of Stephen (Acts 8:54-60) and the conversion of Paul (9:1-31) were powerful stories about the unshakable conviction of these men and also the price they had to pay. I began to see the connection between Jesus' fate and his disciples'.

The stories of Paul's encounter with other religious adherents were of special importance to me. They were more directly related to my religious convictions. Before I had not been aware of Jesus' or his disciples' response towards other belief systems. Some passages in the book of Acts (e.g. 14:11-17; 17:16-34; 19:26), most notably Paul's message to the Athenians, gave a clear response to polytheism. While in Athens, Paul was saddened by the presence of many idols in the city. Interestingly, he found an altar dedicated to "an unknown god". His message had a universal tone that underscored the unity of mankind under the one Creator: "In him we live and move and have our being" (Acts 17:28). The Creator of all does not live in shrines made by hands nor does he need anything. Human beings everywhere have been searching for him, groping to find him. Moreover, "being God's offspring, we ought not to think that the Deity is like gold, or silver, or stone, a representation by the art and imagination of man" (17:29). The message was clear. It was followed by a call to repentance.

Thinking about it, I started questioning my religious convictions and practices. I had learnt from my childhood that there was a Deity who resided in heaven. This highest God was transcendent, almost unapproachable. But he had many intermediaries, the lesser gods who would care for us, and help us in our troubles. In a world full of evil spirits and all sorts of dangers, we human beings had to rely on them for protection. My parents regularly offered sacrifices to the gods of their choice as well as to our ancestral spirits to pray for their blessings and protection. "Is it wrong to worship these gods?" I wondered

The painful break

As the process of identification with the shaping story of Christianity gradually deepened, there was an inner struggle I had to overcome. Not knowing yet how to resolve it, I asked my classmate if I could join him in church. I would like to know what sort of people read the book, and how they put its teaching into practice. So I went to his church that happened to be a congregation of GKPI (Christian Protestant Church in Indonesia). It was another journey into the unfamiliar.

Being a church whose members were mostly Batak, the language and culture were 'Greek' to me. Luckily, some of them were willing to explain to me in our national language, Indonesian, what was said in their ethnic language. I highly appreciated this welcoming gesture. However, my long list of questions regarding Christian faith found only few satisfactory answers. I soon learnt that very few knew the content of their Bible. Most of the time the answer would be to ask some else, especially the pastor who visited the congregation only once or twice a month.[2]

A more radical break took place later. It was not easy and not completely comprehensible to me. Initially, I had a divided commitment, going to nearby temples regularly, while attending church services from time to time. The painful journey had to be made, however, prompted by some radical statements about leaving everything to follow Jesus (e.g. Mt 19:29; Lk 14:27). I did not know when I had crossed the boundary until my grandma asked me one day to join her at a nearby temple. Spontaneously, I replied: "No, grandma. I'm sorry. I can no longer join you to go to the temple." I remember how surprised she was at my refusal. When she asked me why, I told her honestly I had read the Bible, and would follow Christ. To my surprise, she was curious but did not become angry. This is a quality I cherished in her. A charming personality, we all loved her and highly respected her as a wise grandma who taught us through her life how human and kind-hearted we should be despite all our differences.

My father, in contrast, warned me not to let myself be baptized. Apparently, he regarded baptism as a kind of oath taken by anyone to be initiated into Christianity. "You've to stop reading that poisonous book!" he insisted, pointing to the Bible I had been reading. Appealing to the virtue of filial piety, he reminded me of my duty as the eldest son in the family to take care of him and my mother once they had become elderly people. Indeed, this duty must go beyond their death. I was obliged to venerate their deceased spirits once they breathed their last. Interestingly, my father seemed to understand that Christians were not permitted to do so. Any children raised in a traditional Chinese family knew they had to fulfil this filial duty if they did not want to bear the *anathema* of being a disloyal child. So I did not answer back. I was very sorry I had to hurt them, but did I misinterpret what Jesus said in the Gospel (e.g. Mt 10:34-39)?

Uprooted and replanted

To whom should one turn for guidance in such a transition? I remember that hardly anyone at church could give me a helpful orientation in this process of crossing the boundaries. In the absence of a clear direction, I relied on my personal reading of some biblical texts (e.g. Mt 15:3; Phil 3:8; 1Pet 1:18). For instance, in his letter to the Philippians (3:8), the Apostle Paul said he counted everything as loss because of the surpassing value of knowing Christ Jesus. Whatever gains he had previously, he regarded as "rubbish", in order that he

[2] Indeed, until now within GKPI, due to limited human and financial resources, most pastors still serve several congregations.

might gain Christ. Reading them out of context, I was misguided to interpret their message as a call to do away completely with my former background.

In the process of redefining my identity, I began to wrestle with discrepancies between what Jesus taught and what Christians did. Particularly discouraging were internal conflicts I saw among church members. Often the conflicts turned quite nasty. When the community bearing Christ's name was driven by mutual hatred, it was very hard to believe that Christians really practiced what Jesus taught about forgiveness and reconciliation, let alone love towards enemies (Mt 5:43-44). I am convinced more and more that it is our faith bearing fruits in real life that speaks most clearly to the outside world.

In this respect, I should note as well that I may have suffered from some culture shock in my initial encounter with the Batak culture. The Batak are known to have strong characters and be very outspoken. It was not easy to get used to "vigorous" discussions that are very common in the decision-making processes. Only later, having immersed myself in the predominantly Batak environment at the Theological Seminary of HKBP in Pematangsiantar, I learnt to appreciate more and more the Bataks' frankness and outspokenness.

It may be of interest to observe some reactions from our Muslim neighbors about my changing religious allegiance. Before, they showed little interest, if at all, in my religious identity. Once they learnt that I started going to church, all of a sudden they made the efforts to approach me. Some of my friends offered me literature about Islam. Others invited me to see their religious leaders for personal dialogues about Islam and Christianity. I still remember vividly how they were trying hard to convince me that the Bible had been falsified, presumably, by the Jews. A long list of contradictory passages was presented to prove it.

Most disturbing of all were their objections against the doctrine of the Trinity. Does it stand to reason that the creator of all became part of the creation itself? Is it logical to believe that God became a human being who could be crucified and who died? Thus, right from the outset, I was alerted to the rivalry between the two competing Abrahamic faiths, a situation that has not changed much to this day in our society. Unfortunately, when I turned to our church people for help, little could they offer as an intelligent explanation of the much-debated doctrine.

Later I was asked to join a catechetical group at church as part of the preparation for baptism and confirmation. The curricula were very basic, mostly consisting of Knowledge of the Bible. On a number of occasions I tried to raise questions related to biblical texts as well as other doctrinal issues such as the "Trinity", but the answers given were often very basic and even simplistic. Often it sounded as if I had to have faith first before really understanding!

Eager to study the Bible more, I then joined a Bible study group at school. It was an ecumenical group whose members came from various denominational and ethnic backgrounds. As far as I know, the group was not directed by any particular church body or parachurch organization. It grew out of the simple desire of some young people to discern and obey the word of God. As a matter of fact, the Bible study group became a support group for me, offering a more personal and deeper fellowship in the unsettling period of my journey in faith.

The approach adopted in studying the Bible itself was very practical. It was oriented, above all, towards applying the principles observed in biblical texts to our daily lives. Occasionally theoretical questions were raised by some members of my group but the practical application of God's word was never missed. All the members encouraged each other not only to learn and pray together but also to share what had been learnt with others. Consciously or not, it became a mission-oriented group. Admittedly, our horizon about the complexity of biblical texts and their interpretation was rather narrow. But our enthusiasm for outreach was quite high. I remember inviting a schoolmate to such a group. Showing a growing interest in God's word, he later accepted the call to be Christ's follower while attending a Bible youth camp.

Interestingly, when reading biblical texts together with others, I became more aware of their communal aspects. The tendency to individualistic interpretation was reduced significantly. The message was not only addressed to "me" personally but also to "us" collectively. It was in our Bible study group that I appreciated more and more what Jesus prayed for concerning his disciples and the world: "I am not asking you to take them out of the world, but I ask you to protect them from the evil one" (Jn 17:15). We learnt to be more realistic about the imperfect world and our involvement in it. Indeed, I remember one session when we discussed the parable of weeds among the wheat (Mt 13:24-30). Our discussion centered on the distinction between "wheat" and "weeds". Who could judge whether one was wheat or weed? The discussion not only helped change my view about the world but also reshape my view about our church. So it was not my business, I concluded, to separate weeds from the wheat! Being wheat was much more important than policing others.

I was baptized and confirmed at our church without my parents' knowledge. Meanwhile my father had observed a familiar routine in my activities. I would not be at home on every Sunday from morning till noon. From an ethical point of view, however, my Christian faith did not transform my behaviour drastically. Noble virtues such as love, kindness, compassion, generosity and honesty, of course, do not belong uniquely to Christianity. More importantly, I continued to respect and listen to my parents. One Sunday when I was still at home, my father surprisingly asked me why I did not go to church. I took it as a clear sign of his approval of my new identity.

After my confirmation I got more actively involved in youth activities in our church, including our regional youth meetings. My horizon was broadened by my encounter with many young people from other congregations. Later I met Dr. Ira Vaughn Collins†, a missionary who was our mentor in regional youth meetings. He became a confidant with whom I could discuss many things, theological and personal alike. The boundaries seemed to have been crossed safely over some "troubling waters" in my initial search. Having been uprooted quite abruptly from my former ground, eventually I was replanted and settled in a new soil of faith.

Concluding reflection

Over twenty years have passed since my first journey into "the Way". A lot has happened since then. In my seminary years, I came to see more clearly a missing link in my crossing of the boundaries. My former backgrounds, cultural, religious or other, have never been taken seriously. As it were, I had been replanted in a "foreign" soil, both religiously and culturally. No doubt, part of its foreigness is the message of the cross which will continue to be "a stumbling block" to any worldview and belief-system (1Cor 1:17). It would be naive to deny this side of the story. But even in its "foreigness", the Word has become "flesh" and lived among us (Jn 1:14).

When I revisited some of the traditions that formed the earliest layer of my religious consciousness, I rediscovered treasures of our ancient wisdom. To mention a classic example: in the Golden Rule (Mt 7:12), I heard similar echoes in Buddha's voice ("Consider others as yourself"), as well as Confucius' ("Do not to do others what you would not like yourself"). Jesus' compassion towards the poor, the outcasts, the sick, and his call to be compassionate (Lk 6:36) would sound familiar to anyone raised in Buddhist traditions.

I realized more and more that symbolic worlds of different faiths may diverge, but their ethical expressions tend to converge. For the point of view of divergence, my spontaneous reaction when reading the ritual laws in the Pentateuch was pretty understandable. I remember having a similar reaction in reading Paul's letters, the contents of which look pretty much like an internal religious controversy, quite foreign and irrelevant to non-Christians. In fact, I wonder where the journey might have ended up if I never came across passages like the Sermon on the Mount (Mt 5-7). No wonder this famous sermon has been one of the biblical passages most highly regarded even by non-Christians because of its down-to-earth and universal message of love and compassion.

That is not to say, of course, that ethics are all that matters in witnessing to the world. To use traditional language, the starting point is God's gracious initiative to heal his creation broken by sin. But how are we to share this 'foreign' story with others outside Christianity? Should we not start from a genuine appreciation of what we have in common? Often there is the impression that witnessing means convincing others of the supremacy of Christ and the urgency of responding to his way of salvation within the framework of a purely Christian belief-system, while assuming the inadequacy and deficiency of the others' framework. Thus, it is about talking rather than listening, replacing and discarding rather than transforming. If that is the case, what will one encounter in the process of crossing the boundaries? An enriching transformation of one's authentic roots? Or an unimaginative transplantation of one's newly acquired identity into a new soil that has little to do with one's cultural and theological heritage? With such questions in mind, I would end this retelling of my journey into Christianity. Hopefully, it may also stimulate further reflections and discussions on doing mission today.

Response by Jutta Beldermann

In "Crossing the Boundaries" Tjen has retold the story of his journey to Christianity and has at the same time (unintentionally?) written a 'manual' for mission. His story is private, but the lessons it teaches may be helpful not only for churches in a multi-religious situation like Indonesia but also for the missionary approaches of churches in a "post-Christian" situation like Germany.

1. The Bible should be the centre of any missionary approach. It is the good news itself which speaks to people and convinces them of the truth.
2. The biblical stories are there for people to enjoy. Missionary approaches should start with these stories followed by 'down-to-earth-stories' which connect people's lives with the message of Christian faith.
3. Christian faith is always connected and interwoven with culture, whether in Indonesia or a certain middle-class milieu in Germany. Churches' in-groups speak their own languages ('Greek') and share their social symbolism. Newcomers need time and accompaniment to get acquainted with the new culture and to distinguish between what is Christian and what is cultural.
4. People exploring a new understanding of life need anchor-points. Their childhood stories (Christmas traditions very likely) may function as such. These anchor-points are important 'homes' for those to whom Christianity is attractive but still feels like a strange land on the other side of a border.
5. At first those interested in Christianity may encounter Jesus as a 'semi-divine sage' or a 'wise teacher'. For many people, the established theological Christology is difficult to understand. A relationship to a newly encountered 'teacher' may be a seed which will, under the accompaniment of experienced Christians, eventually develop into full understanding.
6. Those who try their first steps on their way to faith need mentors to guide them during this period of transition. Church members should be ready and capable of answering basic questions and explaining

their beliefs. Special questions will need intelligent answers by competent discussion partners (not pastors only).

7. Seekers are interested in the way believers put the teaching of the Bible and their faith into praxis. For Christian doctrine the fruit is second (CA VI), but for outsiders it is "our faith bearing fruit in real life that speaks most clearly to the outside world."
8. Those who want to learn more about Christianity need informal peer groups to discuss their newly gained understanding. The communal aspect of those groups offers comfort for those who may in the course of their way have to give up friends.
9. Those who seek to understand the Christian faith are already part of a certain belief system which should be respected even if the 'call to repentance' is inevitable at the end.
10. Therefore, should mission not be more about listening than about talking, more about transforming than about replacing or discarding?

Part Five

Mission and Culture (C) In Africa

Health and Healing: The Maasai Prophet Isaia Orishi Ole Ndokote and His Evangelistic Mission in Kenya and Tanzania

Christel Kiel

Introduction

When my husband and I were working in Tanzania as UEM missionaries in the North Eastern Diocese of the Evangelical Lutheran Church in Tanzania from 1986-1992, we got to know the evangelist and freelance prophet Isaia Ole Ndokote. He went with us and our fellow Tanzanian pastors on several evangelistic tours and slept in our houses. In reverse we, the white missionaries, visited him several times in Olasiti, his village in Kenya.

His personality seems to be most unusual, at least for Europeans. In his call to conversion Isaia uses till today an evangelistic method following Maasai tradition and customs, which is highly successful among an ethnic group which withstood social change and the conversion to the Christian religion till the end of the last century. Part of his success was the combination of the call to conversion with an extensive healing and pastoral mission among a people facing the threat of extinction due to the progress of the modern global society. I want to structure my paper along the following five aspects: ethnic background and biography of Isaia, his evangelistic method, his theology, his success and an evaluation.

The ethnic background and biography of Isaia[1]

Isaia was born as Leiraroi[2] Ole Molonkó around 1940 in Kenya. He belongs to the so-called Plain Nilotes, a group of semi-pastoralists who live both in Kenya and Tanzania. They number around a million people all speaking the "Maa" language. For reasons hitherto unknown, the Maasai have a monotheistic religion. They pray to Enkai and are led in spiritual matters by the so-called IlOibonok, who are found in family clans of prophets and lawyers. On some rare occasions these clans are controlled and eventually contradicted by single charismatic prophets who are sent and driven by the Spirit of Enkai in times of

---

[1] Until now only two books exist referring to Isaia Ole Ndokote: The Dissertations of C.Kiel, Christians in Maasailand, Makumira. Makumira Publication Nine 1997, pp.260-272 and M.Fischer, Maasai gestalten Christsein, Erlangen: Erlanger Verlag für Mission und Ökumene 2001, pp.302-364.

[2] Personal communication, received during one of our visits to his Kenyan homestead.

special need.[3] According to Isaia's own preaching, his grandfather on his mother's side, Ndokote, belonged to an ancient charismatic group, the so-called "binders": therefore, he calls himself Ole Ndokote. His grandfather could do all kinds of miracles: people stumbled over their own feet, stolen meat got stuck to the mouth of the thief, threatening lions became motionless as if they were frozen etc.[4] Isaia's charismatic gifts seem to be rooted in the genes and tradition of his family.

When he still was a young elder, the spirit of Enkai called Leiraroi in 1968 into the service of his people. Every time he heard Enkai's loud voice, his ear was extended towards her / him or vice versa: God reached down and extended Isaia's ear. Isaia let his hair grow, wore a black cloth, prayed and offered sacrifices to Enkai.[5] The main scope of his service was to make peace among the rival Maa-speaking groups of the Purko, Loita, Kekonyokie, Kisongo, Parakuyu, Arusha etc. He soon got the byname "Orishi" = mediator, peace - maker.[6] He met heavy opposition among the elders of his neighbourhood. They pointed to the fact that Leiraroi was young and not rich. How then could he be called by Enkai, whose blessing was evident if a person owned large numbers of cattle? The young man reacted to the elders' doubts by charging fees in the form of goats and cattle for his counselling sessions. He married two more wives as soon as his herd had been enlarged. Because his prophecies came true most of the time, he had many clients. Since 1973 the government of Kenya has acknowledged his efforts and called him to peace missions as soon as minor or major troubles broke out among the Maasai[7].

Orishi first opposed Christianity, but when in 1979 the Christian elders of his community prayed for him intensely, he had a vision of Christ himself standing under a rainbow. Christ told him to call his people into the church and to Christian baptism.[8] Orishi left the traditional practice of sheep and cattle offerings behind, no longer took money for his service, shaved off his hair and for six months he became a catechumen in the Bible School of the African Inland Church (A.I.C) in Siyapei, Kenya. Because of his extraordinary memory as a member of an oral culture he memorized large parts of the New Testament and can tell even the book, chapter and verse of his quotations during his

---

3 For further information about the Maasai refer to T.Ole Saitoti, C. Beckwith: Maasai, New York: Harry N. Abram, 1980. – T.Ole Saitoti is a Maasai himself.

4 Personal communication received during Isaia's visit to the Theological College and Bible School at Mwika-Moshi in 1997.

5 Fischer, *op. cit.*, pp.307ff. - The article „en" points to female entities or to beings larger than human understanding: enkop = earth, EnKukuu =a monster lurking in the bush, EnKai = Goddess, God.

6 According to my understanding, differing from M. Fischer, Isaia said the name was given him by the Kenyan Government in acknowledgement of his peace-making work.

7 Fisher, *op. cit.*, pp.348ff.

8 *Ibid.* pp.320ff.

sermons. The church elders of the A.I.C. were sceptical because he continued to refer to his visions and was not willing to separate from his three legal wives. They delayed his baptism. In his vision, Christ had ordered him to become baptized. So in 1980, Orishi turned to a Baptist Church,[9] got baptized and immediately returned to his home church, the A.I.C. He chose the name of the prophet to the nations, Isaia, as his baptismal name because he was convinced that his message was important not only for the Maasai but for all the nations.[10] Unfortunately, Isaia and his fellow evangelists are not fluent in Swahili or English. They speak the Maa language only. Therefore, until now their service has been restricted to the Maa-speaking communities. Isaia explained in 1996, that from the time of his baptism onwards, the voice of Enkai no longer made itself audible by extending his ear as before but that the Holy Spirit told his heart what Isaia needed to know.

At the beginning of 1988, Isaia was evangelizing in the Arusha region with the full support of the Arusha Diocese. We were able to meet with him and with his team and plan an evangelistic journey together with all of them a month later. Several journeys followed. Our missionary colleague in South Tanzania, Rev. Muck, invited Isaia and his team, too. In 1995, when we came back to Tanzania from a three years' home leave in Germany, it was a common practice among all the Maasai missionaries to go with Isaia on evangelistic excursions. Meanwhile, in an official ceremony in December 1993, the Arusha Diocese had made him its special Maasai evangelist.[11] Until today he is evangelizing among the Maa-speaking tribes in Tanzania with great success.

Isaia's evangelistic methods

The team

No Maasai elder of any important social status goes around alone. He is always in the company of some of his friends and age-group mates. During the first years of his evangelisation Isaia's uncle Noah Kandonyo went with him because he had played an important part during Isaia's conversion to Christianity. From 1989 onwards, Noah stayed at home because the extensive travelling put too much stress on the elderly man. Isaia travelled together with his age-group mate Yoshua and his nephew Isaka. Both of them are living in Isaia's home area, in Olasiti, Kenya. Yoshua is a singer and Isaka leads the prayers.[12] Isaia does the preaching which can go on for more than an hour, depending on the listeners' willingness to agree with Isaia's message. His preaching is never boring since it is interspersed with songs and sketches by the

---

[9] *Ibid.* p.341.

[10] Personal communication, received in Lushoto, March 1988.

[11] Fischer, *op. cit.*, p.343.

[12] Fischer, *op. cit.*, pp.336ff.

three men. People from the audience are called upon to read from the New Testament, and there is much laughing in between, standing up and sitting down. A listener never knows what will come next. Isaia leaves the organization of the meetings and the administration of the sacraments to the accompanying pastors.

His message[13]

Isaia's evangelistic message can easily be summarized:

> Listen regularly to the word of God in the Old and New Testaments – or learn to read it yourselves! Repent and leave your old sins behind so that you will become joyous children of Enkai.
>
> By baptism turn to Jesus Christ, the Child of Enkai = Enkerai Enkai! He will help you to adapt to the new and difficult present times.
>
> Try to till part of the land and send your children to school.

Isaia himself is a good example of his message: he and his team wear European clothes during their evangelistic journeys. By their dress they signalize two important things: 1. A change is necessary! 2. We are of equal rank to the European missionaries. Our message is by no means less important. Isaia sent his children to school. He has a large field of maize near his home.

The peace-maker

From 1993 onwards Isaia put an additional element into the liturgy of his evangelistic preaching:[14] a ritual to reconcile the often bitter feuds between parents and children, elders and their wives, between the several wives of a polygamous household and between rival families and sub-groups of the Maa communities. The public feuds are mostly centred on water and herding grounds for cattle or cattle-thieving. In order to initiate the peace process Isaia used symbolic actions. He, Yoshua and Isaka called the congregation to stand in a large circle. Then the three of them placed adversaries together, asked them to join hands as soon as they were ready for reconciliation, talked to them and prayed with them individually, giving them God's blessing. After the peace-making sinners and the sick were called into the circle to pray. Then Isaia drew a large cross in the soil in the middle of the meeting ground. Four accompanying pastors were called to the four ends of this cross. Isaia remained standing in the middle of this cross. The African and white pastors had to say

[13] Kiel, *op. cit.*, pp.261ff.

[14] Fischer, *op. cit.*, pp.358ff, following a description of services held in August and September 1997 in the North Eastern and Northern Lutheran Dioceses of Tanzania. – Rev. M. Geißner sent an e-mail in Jan. 2009 which confirms that Isaia continues this peace-making ritual till today.

different prayers in their mother tongues: one prayed for the faith and the conversion of the congregation which was a mixture of baptized and non-baptized people, Maasai and Bantu, another at the other end of the cross asked God for peace and reconciliation, a third prayed for the healing of the sick, the fourth for sufficient food for the people. A combined meal of an animal which had been slaughtered ended the gathering. Isaia met with bitter opposition to this last action, the killing and eating an animal according to the Maasai tradition as soon as enemies had been reconciled. The A.I.C excluded him from his work as a church elder and a Maasai student in 1994 wrote his certificate thesis at the theological college in Makumira attacking Isaia for not having clearly abandoned heathen customs.[15] This ritual, according to him, was too close to the ritual of Holy Communion.

Charismatic gifts

Rarely mentioned by Isaia himself but clearly recognizable for everyone meeting him are Isaia's charismatic gifts. By the power of the Spirit of Enkai he can foretell incidents in the near future and divine events in the past history of his clients, and he has the gift of healing. Telepathy is so much part of his inner conviction that he seems to take it for granted in everybody else, too. All these are gifts the Maasai expect in a man or woman who claims to be a person sent by the Deity. For 40 years now, Isaia has proven that he is driven by the Holy Spirit. His fame among the Maa-speaking ethnic groups is enormous. At the beginning of the 1990s we experienced how he was respected as a spiritual authority not only by ordinary people, men and women, but by the highest IlOibonok, too, the official Maa spiritual leaders. What astonishes us more and more today, as retired pastors ourselves, is the health and vigour with which Isaia continues to live his mission among his people. As soon as he is travelling he has almost no time to himself. As early as seven o'clock clients want to have private counselling with him. The extensive preaching and rites of reconciliation follow. In the afternoon, eventually follow the transfer to another locality or visits in a nearby village. After that, extensive evening prayers are followed by private counselling till midnight. Even twenty years ago it was my duty to see to it that Isaia got enough food and sleep. Till today, his capacity for self-regeneration seems to be unlimited.

Although Isaia has the gift of healing he mostly leaves this service to his team worker Isaka. Isaia's peace mission has taken priority in his preaching. The reason for this slowly upcoming development is Isaia's theology. This brings us to our next point.

---

[15] J.Mameo Ole Paulo, Moreto: Historia fupi ya Isaya Ole Ndokoti na Mchango wake ktk. KKKT, unpublished.

Isaia's theology

It has been mentioned already that Isaia's theology sometimes caused nervousness, animosity and even open contradiction. The cause of this trouble is Isaia's conviction that the God who called him into his service and talked to him since 1968 in auditions and visions by his Spirit is also the father of Jesus Christ. Generally speaking this conviction is shared by all Maasai theologians. The complete Bible, released in Namanga in 1992, calls God Enkai from the first to the last page. Nevertheless, traditional missionary theology is highly sceptical of charismatic gifts, especially auditions and visions. People who claim to be inspired by the Spirit can easily be charlatans, deceiving the faithful. These doubts can be found in the Bible already. But where is the radical conversion to be seen in Isaia's life? Too numerous are the continuing elements like polygamy, - an unsolved problem in most of the African churches - his talk of angels and visions and, since the nineties, the slaughter of animals after the peace sessions. The general problem underlying these doubts is the problem of continuity and discontinuity between non-Christian and Christian religion and the relationship between ethnic tradition and the Christian faith in its traditional western habit.

When Isaia himself explains this problem, he is absolutely sure that the God who called him in 1968 is the one who revealed the existence of Jesus Christ to him 11 years later. The same God who first spoke to him in auditions is now putting the truth into his heart by his Holy Spirit, and told him to turn to the churches for further instruction and for baptism. Through incessant prayer and his ongoing visions, the Risen Christ is so real and luminous for him that it is radiating from Isaia's person in constant waves of warmth and laughter and convincing people by the force of Isaia's personality. Jesus Christ by his life, death and resurrection is the one who removes all the sin and difficulties which stand between Enkai and his people. He is the potent mediator between the Maasai and their present difficulties of adaptation and he alone is able to open up the future for the Maasai. Isaia's theology is fundamentally Christ-centred. The healing of ailments in individual persons and their health are of minor importance compared with the all-embracing message of adaptation to the future. Enkai wants her people to live, not to die. As during the times of the life of God's child, Jesus Christ, healing and personal health are accompanying signs, not the target of Isaia's ministry.

The common meal of a freshly slaughtered animal belongs to the Maasai peace-making tradition. The closeness and eventual rivalry of this "eating peace" with the sacrament of Holy Communion cannot be felt by Isaia who has no feeling for the exclusivity of the Protestant Lutheran understanding of sacraments. He insisted on his baptism because Christ had ordered him to become baptized. He participates in Holy Communion when it is distributed by the pastors who are present during his evangelisations – but his inspiration, his vitality, his aura of spiritual strength and joy in the presence of God depend on his intense and incessant prayer life.

Like the Old Testament prophets and Jesus Christ, Isaia's clearly stated conviction is that sin stands between God and his blessings for the Maasai. Sin holds up the rain. Without rain there is no grass for the cattle, without grass there is no milk, without milk there is no health among the Maasai. His understanding of health is a holistic one, therefore, from the beginning his preaching admonished his listeners to separate from their sins and make a renewed connection with God.[16] His preaching about sin has nothing to do with scrupulous self-destruction. It is a kind of laughing conviction: "this burden is unnecessary in your life." Using his prophetic insight during individual counselling he is ready to put his finger on the dark areas which separate his clients from God. During the peace sessions after his preaching he shows them the way to repent and begin a new life.

Sometimes during his sermons he may mention Satan and his dark powers. During our travelling with him and his team we ourselves experienced the forces which were interested in keeping Isaia away from the people he came to help. Totally unruffled by extreme thunderstorms, broken-down cars, glaring Loibons and similar nuisances he sat and prayed and the difficulties got solved somehow. Even if he had to lie down hungry on the floor of a cold church he remained at peace. Dark forces exist but, unlike in other revivalist theologies, they are no match for Isaia's omnipotent triune God.

His success

Isaia's team and his charismatic gifts combined with natural eloquence, following traditional Maasai lines, are one side of his great success. The other side is his never-tiring readiness to serve God and the Maasai people under the shelter of God's blessing.

Let me clarify what I mean by the example of one of the most difficult and least successful parts of Isaia's work – his mission to his fellow prophets, the IlOibonok. In their area behind the Usambara Mountains our work stagnated. 70 women together with their children attended our services but men were more than rare. Under these circumstances evangelisation by Isaia and his team was extremely necessary. But at the end of 1988 the village of the leading area Loibon Kopera, was not accessible by car although his young men tried hard to open up a path with their bush knives. Isaia stepped out of our car and told the youngsters: "You see we cannot come to you. You must come to us. Tell your father that I expect him and all the members of your family tomorrow morning at eleven here at the roadside." The following morning my husband and I did

[16] One outward sign of this conviction was his insisting on the stripping off of all weapons before unbaptized men entered any church. The baptized knew this custom anyway.

not believe that any man would be there. The Usambaras were too far from Kenya. How could a completely foreign prophet order a leading Loibon and his entourage to meet him at the roadside! When our Land Rover came to a halt the usual number of women was sitting under the trees of the meeting point – together with forty men! We couldn't believe our eyes. Two years later the leading Loibon Kopera was baptized. Six years later, half of the men in his large family were Christians. The other half had decided to remain members of the traditional religion and had lost a large part of their cattle in a money-making deal with a charlatan.[17] From the length of time between Isaia's evangelization and the final conversion of half the family to Christianity one can guess at the resistance of the IlOibonok towards the Christian religion.

Less successful was the mission to the Head Loibon, Loibon Kitok, of all the Parakuyu, Mtare OleMoreto, near Morogoro in 1992.[18] We arrived in the afternoon together with Isaia, Isaka and Yoshua in the Loibon's large village, which to our surprise included a huge school. The Loibon's brother Paulo, a younger son of the former Head Loibon Moreto, had been sent to school, was converted to Christianity and previously had been killed on a peace mission in 1991, when he was trying to pacify a feud between the quarrelling groups of agriculturists and cattle herders of the region.[19] When we arrived, Mtare was in a counselling session from which he returned inebriated. Isaia did not talk to him until the next morning when Mtare was sober. The aging Loibon was obviously a sick person. The alcohol, used as a starter for prophesying by lesser charismatic persons than Isaia, had done its work and made the Loibon half blind. Isaia, in his public preaching, fervently called for repentance and a change of lifestyle. Mtare humbly knelt before Isaia when he called for the prayer with the sick. The Head Loibon died, not baptized, two years later.

The IlOibonok feel responsible for their people, their well-being and their tradition. Therefore, they may build schools on their compounds. They tolerate Christian wives and children in their villages, but they keep themselves and the sons, who might become their successors, away from Christianity. Isaia, on the other hand, feels responsible for his people, too. He is deeply convinced that the old ways of life will not help his people any more and that salvation lies in conversion to Jesus Christ. He is well aware of the great influence the Loibon have on the Maasai and how they hinder the progress of Christianity because they stick to the continuation of Maasai tradition. He does not give up his evangelistic efforts among his fellow prophets. He is well received in their villages and with astonishing humility attentively listened to, but they seldom follow his call to be baptized.

---

[17] Interview with Mattaio Ole Kairanga, Dec. 1995.

[18] 17-18th February 1992, described in C.Kiel: Maasai Diviners, unpublished.

[19] His son Yacobo Paulo Ole Moreto is the present Bishop of Morogoro Diocese.

In summarizing it can be said that the enormous success of Isaia's evangelistic input is lessened by the restraint of the group he originally and foremost felt called to evangelize – the Loibon.

Evaluation

The Bible has a holistic concept concerning health and healing: When a person is in harmony with God's creation, with the creator and with him / herself as well as with his or her neighbour, then *shalom* reigns, the heavenly peace which in its realm harbours health and the healing of illness and sins. Fortunately, the indigenous Maasai religion has the same all-embracing worldview. So Isaia, when his visions demanded the incorporation of the idea of the "Enkerai Enkai", the Child of God, expanded his concept of God, but his worldview remained the same. He had already originally been the peace-maker, Orishi. Through his conversion he got a holy book and a mighty helper, the power of the risen Jesus Christ, to fulfil his mission. He could become a Christian and fulfil his mission more effectively than before.

Isaia did not lose his identity and, therefore, he has remained credible and convincing to his non-Christian fellow Maasai. Moreover, he became a largely encouraging model of hope for his contemporaries. All of them are aware that change has to come in a changing world. But nobody knew how to put this change into practice. Isaia, by his own convincing personality, has shown them that you can change and through this change still remain economically successful. You can become a Christian and yet remain faithful to the Maasai tradition. You can send your children, even the girls, to school without uprooting your Maasai identity. This man did not preach by mere words, as many missionaries did, he preached with his whole vibrant personality. That this man was highly gifted with charismatic power helped to underline his convincing sermons and peace missions but is not the most essential aspect. What is essential is that by his personal example and by the symbolic actions during his peace missions he brought his audience back into the harmony with Enkai, with their neighbours and with themselves. His peace rituals enable them to make a new start in life which gives them new faith and new hope and yet does not uproot them but empowers them to evaluate their previous life and to make the decisions which are necessary in order to adjust to the challenge of the present time. During this general re-setting of life, many a physical healing process among parents, children and their neighbours is started and gives courage and energy to make the steps necessary for further adjustments.

Response by Ferdinand Anno

Contextual theology and ministry mean many things. Within the rubrics of both academic and pastoral theology, the phraseology becomes even more interesting. Even the seminaries' / divinity schools' curricula are a little convulsed on the different schools of understanding of contextualization in relation to the old business of doing theology. Contemporary missiology, however, prompts us into examining the contextuality of faith expressions (from doing theology to doing mission) through the prism of mission work, outside of the ivory towers of academic theology. This paper issues a call to understanding missiology and mission work, literally from the wilderness, in the life and work of a Maasai tribal leader-turned evangelist.

Kiel tried to sum up the message of Isaia as that of calling people to turn toward the good life, to till the land and send children to school, to become joyous children of *Enkai,* who helps believers to adapt to new and difficult times. She also highlighted the peace-making and healing aspects of the Masaai evangelist emphasizing these as central to Isaia's work of evangelization.

Calling and moving people toward the good life, following the path marked by the ancestors, is truly an amazing feat in missions and / or missionary work. Traditional mission work normally required following the 'different path', necessitating a radical cultural break that, at most times, resulted in the cultural and spiritual colonization of peoples and communities. The good life according to Isaia, and as presented in the paper, has more to do with the embracing of a culture of peace than the value systems, images, symbols, and rituals of Western culture. Even the case of Isaia's wearing European clothing, as suggested by Kiel, was the evangelist's way of elevating native mission personnel to positions of respectability.

Also, markedly important in the work of Isaia, was his way of demonstrating that peace-making is realizable within indigenous, social, political and cultural processes. The employment of indigenous rites of mediation / peace-making and healing is an innovation that stresses the importance and efficacy of the indigene. More importantly, it also serves to affirm and celebrate in practical ways, the catholicity of the *imago Dei.* Moreover, the paper described the peace-making ritual devised by Isaia as illustrative, in a very concrete way, of how 'laws' are being 'fulfilled', in the tradition of Jesus who affirmed and innovated from tradition to reveal the new in old forms, as well as the old in new forms. The issue of continuity and discontinuity (between non-Christian and Christian religion), an age-old theme in missions that was also partly raised in the paper, should be understood paradoxically within this Christo-praxis of traditioning.

Historically, Protestant missionary enterprise was conversionist, colonial and negative of non-Western culture. It had been more of a Westernization process that only aggravated the cracks in civilizational faultlines. Kiel correctly addressed Isaia as a prophet since prophecy is basically an exercise in indigenity. This is one aspect of prophecy that has been neglected in colonial interpretations of biblical religious 'offices'. The fact of the matter is that the prophet-missionary calls people to remember the desert, the covenant – which is the very 'textual' foundation of the Judaeo-Christian ways of *shalom /*

salaam. The prophet also brings healing to peoples and communities through efficacious ritualizations in and through the ritual-culture that evolved out of narratives of redemption in the desert. That, at the least, is biblical. In the faith tradition of Christianity, the contemporary included, prophecy is about being spatially rooted and radically immersed in societal conditions, whence prophecy, in the full sense, is also about indigenity, about touching ground and taking root.

The Edinburgh World Missionary Conference of 1910 was an event populated by perspectives that were yet to fully appreciate indigenizing methods in doing missions and the theology of mission. What Kiel achieved in this short essay is a re-surfacing of one of those methodologies in mission that should serve as a corrective to our hitherto colonial-neocolonial paradigms.

Reconciliation and Avenging Spirits

Reinhard Veller

This essay is the result of a working group with African pastors from Zimbabwe's mainline churches (Methodists, Presbyterian, UCCSA, and Lutherans). While I taught systematic theology and ethics at United Theological College (UTC) in Harare, my students regularly drew the attention to the fact that there are situations where African Christians are forced to seek healing and peace in rituals outside their churches.

The phenomenon of avenging spirits in Africa

This is especially true with regard to the fear of avenging spirits and in order to cope with the wrath of the ancestors:

> In Shona [Bantu peoples of Zimbabwe and southern Mozambique] religion, in addition to the guarding characteristics of the *vadzimu* [deceased ancestors], there are also avenging or evil spirits, *ngozi*, and witches who communicate with them. The *ngozi* are, briefly, the spirits of deceased individuals who were greatly wronged, neglected by a spouse, murdered, or otherwise neglected, and they attack through sudden death of several members of the same family, or through ill people who fail to respond to treatment.[1]

It is obvious that the *ngozi* are surrounded by fear, contrary to the *vadzimu* who have a guarding role for the family. The pastors maintained that neither the Christian churches nor the Christian faith provide help in cases involving avenging spirits. But performing certain rituals of African Religion and making respective payments can alleviate fear and restore peace. Apparently, in Zimbabwe, Christians and practitioners of African Religion (AR) share the fear of avenging spirits in the same way.

Are there avenging spirits in European culture?

The phenomenon of avenging spirits is not restricted to African culture and belief. Dreams and nightmares in which victims haunt those who caused their deaths are universally known and literature is full of examples. Let me give two

---

[1] Hilde Arntsen in: *www.unhcr.org/refworld/docid/3df4bece1c.html*, accessed 11 November 2009.

of them: in his novel, The Reader,[2] Bernhard Schlink tells the story of Hanna, a female concentration camp warden, who is haunted by such nightmares. Time and again she sees the women for whose deaths she is responsible, hears their cries and witnesses them die. She tries to cope by making the concentration camps the object of her studies while serving a life sentence. Before she is finally released she commits suicide. According to the African worldview, this is a typical story about the wrath of the ancestors who have unleashed avenging spirits against the person who caused death.

In order to reach a common understanding with the students about the phenomenology of avenging spirits we discussed another example from the European cultural context. It is found in Mark Cocker's, "Richard Meinertzhagen, Soldier, Scientist & Spy.[3] Meinertzhagen, born into a British-German business-family and later chief of the military intelligence in two British campaigns in World War I (East Africa and Palestine) can hardly be suspected of being particularly open to the spirit world. It is all the more surprising then to read about the following episode during Meinertzhagen's early years:

> According to his autobiography, shortly after Christmas of 1897, he and his elder brother Dan were returning home from hunting. Suddenly, the brother spotted somebody walk across the lawn and then jump into the sunken ditch. Richard never saw the figure, and although they chased after him they were unable to catch up. He claimed that in the morning they searched for footprints where the person had crossed the sodden ground, but failed to find any. A curse, of which both boys were aware, had reputedly been passed on the house by the last prior at the time of the abbey's dissolution, which foretold that the eldest son of the owner would die in his prime, and a ghost would appear to him as a sign of his impending death. Apparently, the two boys agreed not to tell their parents, since two previous tenants, both eldest sons, had died unexpectedly at a young age, and a story of inexplicable figures ghosting across the lawn at dusk might alarm them. Six weeks later Dan was dead.[4]

When confronted with this episode, the students at UTC did not hesitate for a moment with their analysis: *Ngozi*! Avenging spirit! For them, the story of the Dan's death was proof that Europeans might understand what Africans mean with that spirit experience. I did have to admit that occurrences as presented by Meinertzhagen are rare in the Western world while being rather common in Africa. In fact, they are so common and so frightening that it is, for instance, difficult to understand life in Zimbabwe without them. It is the fear of avenging spirits that causes people to be so particular when it comes to death and funeral

---

[2] Bernhard Schlink, *Der Vorleser,* (Diogenes: Zürich, 1995), p.207.

[3] Mark Cocker, *Richard Meinertzhagen, Soldier, Scientist & Spy*, Martin Secker & Warburg: London, 1989.

[4] *Ibid.*, p.35.

rites. The deceased's will must be respected under all circumstances in order to avoid misfortune sent by the deceased; even public life has to reckon with those powers. If before Hero's Day the government of Zimbabwe decides to repatriate the remains of fighters who died in the liberation war in one of the neighboring countries it would first seek the counsel and advice of spirit mediums. Any mistake or oversight regarding the appropriate rituals could anger the ancestors and unleash the avenging spirits. The fear of being punished by the ancestors is so great that it may even be used in political battles or to settle old scores. For example, on 5th March, 2003, the *Harare Daily News* published a lengthy letter to the editor in which the floods in the Zambezi valley were interpreted as being a punishment for President Mugabe and his closest supporters:

> […] now that the avenging spirits (*ngozi*) are visiting Mugabe for all the souls that he destroyed, his offspring must not cry foul if they are caught in the crossfire. This is how the *ngozi* operates. It does not start with the offender, no. It first afflicts other people who are close to the offender. First to be afflicted by the curse was Leo Mugabe (a relative to the president). Now *ngozi* has invaded a whole area to wipe out all his descendents […]. Yes, they are going to die and they have to die because their father killed as well […].[5]

Since such messages of doom are taken seriously in Zimbabwe, it is essential for the people to know the counter strategies against *ngozi* and to have ways and means by which fear of those spirits can be alleviated or overcome. In a nutshell: the avenging spirit is usually the spirit of someone you have killed or whose death you have caused, either intentionally or inadvertently. The spirit of the deceased will return to you, even years after the event, and will cause all sorts of misfortune (e.g. sickness in the family, loss of work). While the churches seem unable to help, representatives African Religion do. People know that you better consult a diviner, *n'anga*, who will perform rituals and advise on the payment of compensation to the family of the dead person. If you follow his advice, the avenging spirits will leave you and misfortunes disappear. If not, the misfortune will continue and might even get worse. In her study, "Witchcraft, Sorcery and Spirit Possession–Pastoral Responses in Africa,[6] Leny Lagerwerf cites a case where misfortune was not dealt with in the traditional way and the worst happened.

She tells us of a Protestant pastor whose son was seriously ill. On the quiet, his wife consulted a diviner who prescribed that a sacrifice be offered on the tomb of the child's grandfather. She then urged her husband that they act on the

---

[5] The Harare Daily News, (5 March 2003), p.9.

[6] Leny Lagerwerf, *Witchcraft, Sorcery and Spirit Possession – Pastoral Responses in Africa*, Mambo Press: Gweru, 1987.

diviner's advice. He refused angrily and left the healing of their child to God's will. The boy died.

Lagerwerf's example shows the dilemma in which African Christians often find themselves. Should they do what culture suggests, consult a diviner and thereby turn to African Religion again? Or can they trust the powers of the risen Lord and the whole armour of God against the spiritual forces of evil (*cf.* Eph 6:10-12)?

The students are aware of the dilemma Christians face if they seek help in African Religion. The Gospel is good news against all fear (Lk. 2:10; Jn. 14:26), and when being baptized in the name of all names, Christians have renounced all other powers. So, if the claim of the Gospel is true and baptism places believers under the Lord of all Lords, why is it that there is no Christian way (and no Christian ritual) to attain freedom from the wrath of the ancestors? After all, the power of Christ to bring peace and salvation is not limited to any one culture. If disquieted souls can find rest and a terrified conscience can be comforted in Jesus' name why should there be no Christian ritual to overcome the fear of avenging spirits?

Ancesters, avenging spirits: a taboo area

Ancestor veneration, ancestor worship are officially taboo. The whole area belongs to traditional religion and is, therefore, at best, part of people's culture. Contrary to West Africa, there are no theological discussions about it. Students might just encounter it when the "phenomenology of religion" is taught. Nevertheless the topic remains on the agenda. This is all too obvious when it comes to death and funeral rites. The latter are of utmost importance because of the respect and fear of the ancestors. This is very clear at funerals. As a pastor of a predominantly African congregation, I was on and off cemeteries due to the AIDS pandemic. While officiating at a funeral, I sometimes got a little hint after the blessing, indicating that for further rites and procedures my presence was no longer necessary and I was free to leave. So I do not know what happened thereafter. But surely the deceased was supplied with everything needed on the great journey. On all graves you would later see pots and bowls, all with holes in it, in order to be worthless to thieves but nevertheless useful for the departed.

Another way to link elements of ancestor veneration with Christian ritual is the "unveiling of the tombstone". This memorial service takes place a year after the funeral, at exactly the time when the family traditionally welcomes the deceased ancestor back into the family. This ritual is very popular in Zimbabwe. To lead it has become a genuine pastoral duty.

Because the whole topic is a taboo and banned, people are very often left alone between the old family traditions and Christian belief and practice. The extended family, especially the older generation, expects that everyone takes part in traditional feasts and rituals. They are, at the same time, all too ready to blame those not participating for any misfortune that might occur in the family. Therefore, there is a lot of pressure on all those whose conscience does not allow them to participate. They live in a real dilemma.

Various ways of relating to the ancestors

A dilemma ignored: the mainline churches of Zimbabwe

From the above we can conclude that for African Christians the avenging spirits pose an embarrassing dilemma. The truth is that the embarrassment includes the relationship to the ancestors in general. Christians and churches in Zimbabwe are not at ease when it comes to the ancestors for the following reasons:

(1) In the Shona religion, the ancestors seem to compete with the Christian perception of God. They are sacred; they guide and protect and they are consulted at all major family events.[7]

(2) Although the "Shona religion is not a 'theistic' single God centered religion,"[8] people pray to *Mwari* (God) by way of the ancestors.

(3) In certain instances, such as a drought, a spirit medium "might suggest that the community brew beer for the *varipasi* (buried ones) because they are 'thirsty'."[9]

(4) The ancestors might make unethical demands, such as demanding that a virgin girl be given to another family as a payment for a homicide.

(5) Scripture seems to be clearly against consulting the ancestors. "Now if people say to you, 'Consult the ghosts and the familiar spirits'[…] should not a people consult their gods […]?" (Is. 8:19).

(6) In addition, the departed seem to be easily offended, unforgiving and always ready to punish. So the fear of the ancestors appears to be quite justified. As already mentioned the relationship with the ancestors is rarely discussed in the churches. Consequently, people receive little or no helpful advice and are torn apart between the demands of the extended family to participate in traditional rituals and the official "no" by the mainline churches.

"Christians must give up their ancestors" – the Pentecostal churches

Pentecostal churches offer a radical response. They suggest severing the ties to one's own family to accept the fellowship of the church and certain church members as their new family. People would then give up their family names, their totem and any other connection to the extended family and the ancestors. They stop taking part in any ancestor-related rituals. The Lord is their ancestor.

7 Jameson Kurasha, *Shona Religion – a metaphysical statement and dialogue with Christianity* (1998), pp.1-2.

8 *Ibid.*, p.5.

9 *Ibid.*, p.3.

This radical step apparently yields freedom from attacks by avenging spirits and freedom from fear of the ancestors. There is, however, a price to be paid in the form of a loss of cultural identity and a loss of natural family ties. In case of a serious conflict with their church and possible excommunication, they have no social backing whatsoever.

Christians may have dealings with the ancestors – West African voices

There is a third way of relating to the ancestors. For years, theologians in West Africa (Ghana) have tried to contextualize the Christian faith and relate it to traditional ancestrology. According to Kwame Bediako[10] and others, Christians may have dealings with the ancestors for a variety of reasons. They are part of the living community and like anyone else in the community they cannot be worshipped.[11] The reverence of and respect for the ancestors is nothing more than an expression of family and tribal solidarity and continuity.[12] Like in the Shona religion (*kurovaguva*), it is the living community that establishes the departed as a family ancestor in the first place.[13] The Akan in Ghana welcome the ancestor at family functions with libations. Bediako presumes that in these libations, water was originally used to clean the dusty feet of the arriving ancestors. After the ancestor is welcomed by the family already gathered, any prayer made is not to the ancestor but in the presence of the ancestor and on their behalf to God or Christ.[14] African theology proceeds further with a theology of ancestors: applying Hebrews 1:1, it draws the consequences of the fact that God spoke to the African forefathers as well, who in word and deed prepared the people for a Christian future of Africa.[15] African theology would give the faithful ancestors their rightful place in the communion of saints and the cloud of witnesses with whom we pray and in whose footsteps we walk.[16] It is enlightening to see that there is no need to shy away from discussing the issue of ancestors openly, seriously and theologically and to advise and consult with the congregations accordingly. Jesus' promise that the truth will set you free (Jn. 8:32), certainly applies.

---

[10] Kwame Bediako, *Christianity in Africa: The Renewal of a Non-Western Religion*, New York: Orbis, 1995.

[11] *Ibid.*, p.219.

[12] *Ibid.*, p.223.

[13] *Ibid.*, p.218.

[14] *Ibid.*, p.221.

[15] *Ibid.*, p.225.

[16] *Ibid.*, p.22.

Towards a ritual of reconciliation

In our classroom discussions about the apparent inability of the mainline churches to respond to the challenge of the avenging spirits, there came a day when a student made a stunning contribution. He told us that his congregation in Eastern Zimbabwe had recently responded in a case of avenging spirits. We were stunned because his report implied that deliverance from attacks by avenging spirits was possible without turning to African Religion, and that Christian counselling could play a role. Perhaps an effective ritual of reconciliation already existed in a church, and we just did not know. This is what he told us:

> A man was converted to Christianity in our church. In 1999, he stood up in the church and confessed: "I have killed a person in Mozambique. I want to be a born-again Christian. Now the Spirit of the Lord is telling me to go and pay for what I have done." After this confession, he was accompanied by the pastors of our church on his journey to Mozambique. When they returned he witnessed that payments to the family of the killed person were done and "I am now cleansed."

The response of the student's church was apparently appropriate to the cultural setting and led indeed to forgiveness, peace and freedom. The church had responded through a ritual of reconciliation that involved two pastors. Together with the victim of the attacks, they had travelled to Mozambique and performed what needed to be done to have the two parties reconciled.

Inspired by this example, we worked towards an effective Christian ritual of reconciliation and deliverance. Group work played in important role. Always two pastors were to design a ritual. Their proposals were then discussed, accepted or rejected by the working group. Two important elements had already been mentioned in the report of the journey to Mozambique: payment of compensation and the facilitating role of counsellors / pastors. There was agreement on other vital elements: an identification of the cause of the problem had to occur at the beginning of the process. From there, an idea of what could be done should emerge (I have killed…now the spirit of the Lord is telling me to go and pay…). In order to be effective, the ritual was to involve both families because the avenging spirit acts on behalf of the wronged family. The ritual must, of course, include an admission of guilt.

The challenge was: could those elements (analysis, meeting of families, admission of guilt, payment) have their rightful place in a Christian ritual and cater effectively for the African spiritual need? As we have seen, certain Christian communities in Africa are already responding effectively to those needs. They do so in the power of the Spirit according to African culture and worldview.[17] In the end the UTC working group agreed that for an effective

---

[17] The demand for an appropriate ritual is actually not new. R. Bowen (*So I Send You*, SPCK, London 1996, p.149) names W.V.Lucas in Southern Tanzania who saw already

ritual of reconciliation, altogether six steps should be taken. All of them seem to be compatible with the mandate "to go and heal" (Mk. 6: 7). For none of them a diviner or a spirit medium is needed, not even for the first one:

1. Identifying the cause of the problem and devising a way towards a solution. Most Christians are quite clear about the underlying causes of a certain problem; on the whole, people know where they have failed. In the church, the confession of sins together with counselling establishes clearly where the problem lies. Even in an individualistic society, the admission of guilt may be followed by acts of repayment and restitution following the biblical example of Luke 19: 8. The communion of believers has genuine ways to get clarity. In the Christian church, the Holy Spirit speaks quite clearly and directly, providing wisdom and knowledge and enlightenment through the gift of prophecy (1Cor 12:4-11). In the past, the problem might have been that Christians in the mainline churches did not emphasize the distinctive gifts of the Holy Spirit. But that has changed over the past ten or twenty years. Most mainline churches are now considerably more open to the moving of the Holy Spirit than they were before. They conduct revivals on a regular basis and practise certain gifts of the Spirit, especially the ministry of healing. In Tanzania, people have come to know "that even Lutherans have the Holy Spirit." Consequently, the need to turn to diviners and spirit mediums has been greatly reduced since the mid 1980s. In 1988, the principal (T. Jeni) of a Lutheran Bible School in southern Tanzania reported that:

> We used to have many Christians in the Matema area go to Malawi to consult diviners for their healing. In the meantime, we take pains to elaborate to them the Gospel truth concerning healing by the power of the Holy Spirit through prayer only. We do not use any paraphernalia, herbs, or medicines, but simply prayers of faith. And thank God, many sick Christians are coming to pray instead of consulting diviners and medicine men. Many have received healing from God, this includes those who are demonically possessed [...]. When we come across a hard case, we voluntarily decide to pray and fast [...].[18]

---

in 1913 that the Mission Churches did not meet the needs which people felt most severely. "He felt that (1) the Church should supply Christian rituals for any need felt by society; (2) the Church should preserve African tradition as far as possible, e.g. the blessing of fields, exorcism, initiation ceremonies and bride price; (3) local Christian should decide what traditional elements be 'baptized' and what had to be cut out; (4) the church should take the people's beliefs seriously, not dismiss them. "

[18] Reinhard Veller, *Der Heilige Geist und die Kirchen*, VEM Mitarbeiterbrief, Wuppertal 5 (1991), p.27.

2. Meeting of the two families – facilitated by one or two counsellors (pastors)
The aim of this meeting is, first of all, to go back to the past and establish what happened. It is important that both sides agree on the facts. The next step to follow is:

3. Admission of guilt and plea for forgiveness
In African culture, a ritual has to be a community ritual. It is in the gathered community that the admission of guilt and the assurance of forgiveness have to take place. Perhaps this could happen as at meetings of the East African Revival (since the 1930s) to which many Lutheran bishops belong. In their fellowship meetings, public confessions take place against the background of the ongoing praise of Jesus' blood that cleanses completely. In addition, those confessions are followed by practical acts of restitution.[19] In order to make an act of restitution and to pay compensation there need to be:

4. Negotiations about payment of compensation
When it comes to the avenging spirits, practical steps are also needed. Besides the admission of guilt payment is essential. Without it, there can be no peace between the families involved and, therefore, no peace of mind for the individual either. The details of the payment are to be negotiated between the parties concerned. The negotiations will be very similar to those about a bride price (*lobola*) or when payments are negotiated after a fatal road accident. But, as numerous examples especially from the Hebrew Scriptures show, to negotiate a settlement and peace between families is very biblical indeed (*cf.* Gen. 13, Abraham and Lot; Gen 30, Jacob and Laban). There is nothing exclusively African about those negotiations, except that such a settlement will include the ancestral spirit who is part of the community.

5. Payment
It is of utmost importance that what was agreed upon in the negotiations is then paid. Otherwise, the attacks by the avenging spirits will continue. For Western minds payment of compensation is very uncommon to say the least. Human life cannot be measured in financial terms. However, for African and Asian communities such payments are completely normal as they assist a family that has to make up for a severe loss. Without such payment the issue is not solved.

6. Meal of reconciliation
It is important that the ritual of reconciliation ends with a festive meal. It is there where the agreement between the two families (including the avenging spirits) is confirmed and peace is celebrated.

---

[19] Roger Bowen, *So I Send You. Study Guide to Mission*, SPCK: London, 1996, p.143.

Summary

We can conclude that local churches in Zimbabwe are able to rise to the challenge that avenging spirits are posing. Moreover, it seems clear why the ritual followed was effective. It was both inspired and culturally based. It appears that African Christianity does not need to go back to the "old religion": Faithfulness and a contextual response are sufficient. In addition, the example confirms yet another instance that there is no African problem to which an African solution cannot be found. This means for the churches: increased communication, more visits, and more sharing, less with partners from overseas, but with sister churches on the continent.[20] They share the same problems, and one might have found an answer already. In this context, the affirmation of the 1997 United Church of Christ in Southern Africa (UCCSA) Assembly, admittedly regarding another problem, applies:

> We affirm our tradition that "the Lord has yet more light and truth to break forth from God′ s word."[21]

Well stated, if we remain conscious that God's light and truth may have broken forth with neighbouring churches already.

Response by Victor Aguilan

During the consultation, I interjected with a statement that the belief in the spirits (good, malevolent and avenging) is part of the Filipino religiosity. This is an opportunity for me to share my thoughts on this paper. The Filipino religious worldview includes the belief that there are spirits (*anito, diwata*) everywhere. They co-exist with human beings. This belief challenges the Philippine church to meet not only the members' ultimate concerns (salvation, sanctification) but also their everyday concerns (sickness, well-being, fortune, marriage, love, etc.) This paper urges us - Christian theologians, pastors, missiologists, missionaries and leaders - to include the belief in various spirits in the scope of our ministries and mission. I was not surprised to learn that in Europe and in Western-influenced theological seminaries and churches (Africa and Asia) this spirit world belief system, especially of the ordinary members, is

---

[20] Sometimes it looks as if the African churches fail in the same areas as the missions. According to Roger Bowen (note 19), "They did not listen to Africans. Therefore they often failed to relate the Good News to African issues such as witchcraft, spirits, ancestors, land and community. They also failed to bring the holistic deliverance from evil which Africans longed for. Most missionaries were not sure how to deal with African spirit-powers, and they were nervous of calling on the Holy Spirit to conquer evil powers."

[21] Minutes of the 1997 UCCSA Assembly, p.1.

largely ignored. As a consequence, members who are confronted by these 'spirits' are compelled to return to their pre-Christian religious practices or folk-Christianity. They seek out shamans, local faith healers, diviners, mediums etc. rather than pastors for pastoral care and counselling. This paper is a challenge which should not be ignored by those engaged in mission today.

Response by Christel Kiel

When the protestant missionaries arrived in East Africa at the end of the 19th century, they brought the Gospel, filled the hunger for better education and health, but had no sufficient explanation for the irrational but continuing reality of bad luck. In the long run this deficit led to the double strategy of going to churches on Sunday and visiting the traditional healers in times of sorrow and need as soon as African Christians felt threatened by the curses of the living or the wrath of the avenging ancestor spirits. The reaction of the Asian participants during the VEM Consultation on Mission in May, 2009 shows that the same problem exists in Asian countries too. In Tanzania, this problem was rarely mentioned officially since one of the few efforts to integrate ancestor worship into the traditional teaching of the Lutheran Church ended with the loss of the mental health of the first President and Bishop of the former South Synod, Judah B. M. Kiwovele. This paper opens the possibility to verbalize the problem of dubious Christian behaviour in an open discussion by looking into a distant and, therefore, less threatening reality in a different country. In addition, Veller gives a Christian example of how to deal with threatening events in a Christian way without becoming alienated from the teaching of the official churches. Therefore, the paper should be accessible to a larger public.

Part Six

Mission and Other Religions

STRAIGHTWAY CHAPEL – A CHARISMATIC THEOLOGY OF MISSION TO MUSLIMS IN GHANA?

Andreas Heuser

Introduction

In the euphoria about the upsurge of Pentecostal-type churches in many parts of Africa, Charismatic and neo-Pentecostal alike, one feature remained rather unnoticed. In the mid-1980s the phenomenon of churches founded by former Muslims surfaced. With their fundamental criterion to convert Muslims to Christianity, these churches differ immensely in their theological design from the rest of the movement. One of the pioneering churches of converted Muslims in West Africa is Straightway Chapel, based in Ghana. Its most innovative aspects are the style, method and strategy of evangelism that is rooted in a still experiential or implicit theology of mission.

Straightway Chapel's founder, Ahmad Aygei, was brought up in a prominent Sunni Muslim family. As a consequence of his conversion to Christianity in 1983, he was banned from his family.[1]

In a post-conversion process, he realised that churches of whatever kind completely lacked a support structure for Muslim converts. His experiences of both rejection and indifference convinced Aygei to initiate an organisational set-up to assist other converts. He experimented with several church structures before he founded Straightway Chapel, in Kumasi, in 1988.[2] It attracts converts by a system of mutual assistance to strengthen the converted Muslims' faith, and by political demands of religious freedom. The name resonates the *Surat-al-Fatiha*, the first Sura (1:6-7) that is recited in the five Muslim daily prayers:

> Guide us in the straight path, the path of those whom you have blessed, not those against whom there is displeasure not those who go astray.

Aygei reinterprets the Qur'anic meaning to identify Jesus Christ as the straight path. In other words, he presents a reading of the Qur'an that points to

---

[1] *Cf.* Ahmad Aygei, *Sharing the love of Christ with your Muslim Neighbour*, Kumasi: UGC Publishing House Breman 2002, p.24. His father acted as a spokesperson of the Ghana Muslim Mission that aims at an autonomous expression of Islam in Ghana independent from immigrant Hausa muslims. On Islam in Ghana, see Nathan I. Samwini, *The Muslim Resurgence in Ghana since 1950. Its Effects upon Muslims and Muslim-Christian Relations*, Berlin: LIT Verlag 2006.

[2] Elom Dovlo and Alfred Ofosu Asante, Reinterpreting the straight path: Ghanaian Muslim converts in mission to Muslims, in: *Exchange* 32/3, 2003, pp.214-238.

Christianity as the revealed true religion; he offers a Qur'anic hermeneutics of conversion to Christianity.

Conversion experience

Aygei's vintage point is his conversion experience. He describes it as an individual process of rational choice and theological reasoning.[3] According to Aygei, his conversion resulted from a critical reading of the Qur'an. Quoting two passages in the Qur'an (Sura 3:55 and Sura 57:27), he concludes that the authority of Jesus Christ and his followers had not ended and were not superseded by a Muslim era. A comparative reading of the holy scriptures, both the Qur'an and the Bible, substantiated his findings. He discovered an inner Qur'anic logic to point to Christianity as the chosen path to God.[4] Aygei leaves the impression of relying on the Word alone as the cornerstone of his conversion.

However, a next stage in the distancing process from Islam is characterised by non-scriptural bodily experiences. His textual analysis was repeatedly backed by visions and auditions of prophets that urged him to convert. In a state of confusion, he resorted to a period of fasting and prayer. When visions reoccurred, he suffered from severe physical trouble. Finally, he accepted Christianity and had to leave his father's house with a curse.[5]

Aygei's conversion narrative contains two sets of arguments. One points to discursive elements i.e. scriptural analysis, systematic comparison, and rational reasoning. The other circumscribes a complex of non-discursive arguments such as visions, auditions and physical emotions. Embodied experiences are seen in African worldview in general as revelations from the spiritual world. They reveal a manifest reality of invisible powers that cannot be manipulated. As in Aygei's case, visions and dreams can be an avenue for religious conversion.[6] In Aygei's theology of mission, however, the rational set of arguments is over-represented. This contradicts sharply with the ordinary range of Charismatic and neo-Pentecostal theologies in Ghana. Here, essentially non-

---

[3] Contrarily Hollenweger found that in Africa "people usually become converted either because of a healing (…), because of a dream or vision, or because they have a friend who is Christian. We have found not one single instance where somebody was saved on the basis of arguments (...)." Walter J. Hollenweger, *Pentecostalism. Origins and Developments Worldwide*, Peabody: Hendrickson Publishers 1997, p.255.

[4] *Cf.* Aygei, Sharing *op.cit.*, pp.21-25, and Ahmad Aygei, *Ishmael shall be blessed*, Kumasi: UGC Publishing House Breman 2002, pp.109-110.

[5] *Cf.* Aygei, Sharing *op.cit.*, pp.21-26.

[6] Following Humphrey Fisher, dreams are a point of contact between African world-views and Islam: "the very dream … may be an avenue for the acceptance of new ideas or objects, or even of religious beliefs, being thus in itself a channel of conversion." Quoted in Peter B. Clarke, *West Africa and Islam. A Study of Religious Developments from the 8th to the 20th Century*, London: Edward Arnold 1984, p.260.

discursive arguments are used to articulate theology, so that visions or dream images, or bodily reactions describe an identity as born-again Christians. Furthermore, churches cope with such bodily experiences by initiating ritual innovations. And finally, the ritual frame serves to effect a "complete break with the past".[7] Compared with the surrounding Charismatic and Pentecostal discourse, Aygei marginalises the status of bodily phenomena. Although his conversion process entails elements of vision, dream, and of curse, they do not play a major role to unfold neither his theology nor his ministry. He basically presents a hermeneutics of inter-religious encounter, and he does not urge for a radical break with the past.

Inter-religious hermeneutics

An important fragment in Aygei's conversion narrative relates to the question, who interprets the Holy Scripture(s) correctly? Thus, he favours an explicit hermeneutical approach in the context of Christian-Muslim relations. This is, once more, strikingly different compared to other African Pentecostal-type churches. Here you find ritual strategies of the denial of Islam, often seen as a power-encounter situation, in which the 'powers of darkness' are expelled in the name of Jesus.[8] Aygei's interpretation of Islam is more dialectical in nature.

As mentioned, Aygei's conversion process was supported by scriptural evidence and a comparative analysis, for an intense reading of the Qur'an accompanied his Bible studies. By insisting on an in-depth study of the Qur'an, he respects Islamic claims to possess the final revelation, believed to be preserved in the Qur'an. Consequently, a thorough understanding of the Qur'an and Islamic theology became a presupposition in Aygei's theological quest. Instead of ritual practices, Aygei initiated several theological training programmes as identity markers of his church. The curricula introduce the logic of theological arguments as well as inter-religious comparison.[9]

The comparative approach advocates a careful study of the Qur'an and sensitizes believers for the interrelatedness of both religions. However, it leaves space for dissonance. Aygei inverses the Islamic exegesis, according to which Christianity is an incomplete earlier phase in the chronicle of salvation history that ends with Islam. While examining the revelatory content of the Qur'an, he insists that the scriptural evidence unmistakably points to the Messiahship of

---

[7] See Birgit Meyer, "'Make a Complete Break with the Past': Memory and Postcolonial Modernity in Ghanaian Pentecostal Discourse", in: Richard Werbner (ed.), *Memory and the Postcolony. African anthropology and the critique of power*, London: Zed Books 1998, pp.182-208.

[8] *Cf.* Emmanuel Kingsley Larbi, *Pentecostalism. The Eddies of Ghanaian Christianity*, Accra: Blessed Publications 2001, pp.388-398.

[9] Theological training is provided in weekly workshops that treat foundations and doctrines of Christianity, and comment the Qur'an from a biblical viewpoint.

Jesus. Considering the Sonship of Jesus Christ, and reflecting the status of prophets, he refutes Islamic assertions that the Qur'an contains the genuine and correct meaning of the Bible. For him, the Qur'an "aims at abrogating the Bible."[10] From a discussion of the Qur'anic titles of Jesus, Aygei draws heavy-weight conclusions. Instead of Muhammad who bears the title of a 'Messenger of Allah', it is Jesus, the 'Spirit of Allah' who needs to be considered as the greatest of all prophets. In Aygei's mind, this title of Jesus is even proof of his divine nature:

> As 'His Spirit', he is brought very close to the very being of Allah. Do we not recognise that by identifying Jesus so closely with Himself, Allah is revealing the deity of Jesus Christ, which Muslims vehemently object to?[11]

Aygei's inter-religious hermeneutics uses the methods of exegesis and scriptural comparison. His debate of diverse modes of theological interpretation is controversial as it challenges the Islamic language of faith in its most sensitive layers.

Moralistic anti-memory

Aygei stretches this method of comparison to a re-reading of Islamic history. He raises questions of doubt about the life of the prophet Muhammad and his era. In his re-reading of Islamic history, Aygei applies a moral discourse as a tool to discern 'true' prophets from questionable claimants of truth. The recurrent argument in his repertoire to judge the beginnings of the Islamic era is Muhammad's marriage policy. "He surrendered himself to the cares and discord of polygamy and the unity of his family was broken, never again to be restored."[12] The description of the beginnings of Islamic history follows a path of moral failure. The prophet could only settle a series of family disputes caused by his polygamous way of life, according to Aygei, by his imagination of revelatory conflict solving. Thus, Aygei withdraws the prophetic claim from Muhammad to having received divine revelations. Commenting on the marriage intentions of the Prophet, Aygei states, that "nothing short of a divine revelation could settle the matter." The Qur'anic verses "produced" by "the Prophet (in the name of Allah and His Apostle)" served "to sanction his heart's desire."[13] Quite obviously, Aygei aims at the dethroning of the founding prophet by interpreting his personality in terms that derive from present-day Pentecostal-type catalogues of moral behaviour. The moralising re-reading of

---

10 Aygei, Ishmael, *op. cit.*, p.29.

11 Aygei, Ishmael, *op. cit.*, p.111.

12 Aygei, Sharing, *op. cit.*, p.64.

13 Aygei, Sharing, *op. cit.*, p.67.

Muhammad's era is biassed in its strong emphasis on sexual ethics and the nuclear family as a God-given institution.[14]

The moralising politics of memory does not only serve to de-construct early Islamic history. The act of reading aims at establishing difference. Yet, African Pentecostal-type Christianity usually conceptualises difference by means of ritual cleansing and protection. Bodily reactions are seen as part of the permanent spiritual fight between God and Satan. Because the forces of 'evil', emanating from the spiritual world of African religions, are believed to intrude in the life of the saved ones, African Pentecostal-type discourse applies the key category of a 'rupture with the past' in order to distance the new belief from the former other. The notion of rupture enables converts to draw a line between 'them' and 'us', between 'then' and 'now'. This discourse of 'othering' does not rely on rational arguments but on a ritual praxis oriented towards the individual. One popular ritual to break bonds with the Satanic is 'deliverance', in which the powers of darkness manifest themselves to be exorcised by especially gifted members of a congregation.[15]

Such ritual means to control the influence of demonic bondage are significantly missing in the congregational life of Straightway Chapel. In the liturgical and theological context of Straightway Chapel, the progress in Christian life-style also demands a critique of one's past. But the type and the practice of memorialising differ from the mainline African Pentecostal ways. Rather than defining a dualism, Aygei favours a dialectical approach of appropriation and rejection of his Muslim past. And instead of a ritually manifest break with the past, he opts for a practice of remembrance by reading the revealed scriptures.

In conclusion, African Pentecostal-type churches perform ritual acts of individual deliverance from demonic bonds primarily identified with the African religious heritage. Straightway Chapel, with a membership of converted Muslims, chooses a different memory praxis. It arranges a collective anti-memory against the mainstream interpretation of the Qur'an and the life of the Prophet Muhammad, canonised in Islamic scriptural memory. The divine revelation in a holy book finds an adequate response in a new community of the 'text'. In other words, in a setting of Muslim converts, textual coherence, infused with moral standards of Pentecostal identity, replaces ritual coherence.[16]

---

[14] Neo-Pentecostal literature sees the family as a daily warzone against demonic powers. *Cf.* Leonhard Soku, *The Spiritual Warfare in the Warzone*, Accra: Tonia Press 2003, pp.37-38.

[15] Allan Anderson, "Exorcism and Conversion to African Pentecostalism, In: *Exchange* 35/1, 2006, pp.116-133.

[16] The shift from ritual to textual coherence has been interpreted as a paradigmatic step in the history of religions, *cf.* Jan Assmann, *Religion und kulturelles Gedächtnis*, Beck: München 2000, pp.148-152.

Theology of suffering

A similar change in the use of key notions in Pentecostal-type churches takes place in connection with the meaning of curses. In the spiritual mindset of many Pentecostal believers afflictions caused by curses play a prominent part. Curses are directly addressed towards an individual but they have a basic social significance. In many instances individual problems are attributed to influences from existing social relations. Especially family circles are considered potentially dangerous for keeping a born-again life-style.[17] Pentecostal-type churches promise solutions to the difficulties caused by curses, and again offer deliverance services. Here, social networks are scrutinised and individuals are asked to separate from them. Thus, born-again consciousness presents an image to be in control of such destinies, propagating an independent individual who deliberately chooses to loosen ties with the past. In contrast, in Aygei's case, being cursed meant the expulsion from his family, and his break with the past was a forced one. His conversion narrative does not mention any ritual support to disengage from social relationships. Instead, he copes with the curse resting on him by a theology of suffering.

For Aygei, being rejected by his family points at an essential dimension in his belief. Circumscribing the consequences of his conversion, he generalises that "Christian faith is about suffering."[18] Aygei unfolds his theology of suffering by distinguishing between trials and temptations. He defines temptations as "strategies and plans designed and purported by Satan to cause us to sin and thus separate us from God." Trials, on the other hand, "help us to know God better" and "to become stronger in our faith."[19] Aygei equates the curse of his father with the destiny of the Christian martyrs, and all Muslim converts may face such trials. On an existential level, his theology of suffering implies self-control and discipline to endure in the new faith. In his view, his biography as a Muslim turned into a successful church leader, encouraged other Muslims to convert "because they were no longer afraid of the power of curses in their lives." Aygei comments:

> I was being maltreated, but now I can testify that the training I had has made me a better person. God was disciplining me as the son He loves. ... A positive attitude towards trials and suffering is the key to the triumphant Christian life.[20]

By insisting on the reality of suffering, Aygei complains about converts who downplay the seriousness of trials to look for easy solutions. He advises churches to:

---

[17] African theology classifies curses in detail, *cf.* Kwaku Dua-Agyeman, Deliverance from Ungodly Soul-Ties, Accra: UGC Publishing House 2001.

[18] Personal communication, 30 January 2006.

[19] Aygei, Sharing, *op. cit.*, p.27.

[20] Aygei, Sharing, *op. cit.*, pp.26 and 34.

> stop pampering new converts. The most common mistake in the Christian circles is that we shower gifts, money etc. on this new convert. Before long, they become greedy. That is why many of them go from church to church sharing their testimonies with the intention of being paid for.[21]

With this intervention, Aygei contrasts the politics of conversion in other churches.[22] He disengages from a distinctive form of Pentecostal-type theology of prosperity that focusses on the material side of celebrating a born-again identity. The prosperity gospel combines material expectations to improve one's personal situation here and now with a spiritual emphasis on individual salvation in the hereafter.[23] Whereas many people are motivated to join Pentecostal-type churches by such promises, Aygei disqualifies those conversion motives. His theology of suffering is far from an enthusiastic approach in mission to Muslims. He rather advocates a self-reflective approach.

Self-reflexion

According to Emmanuel Larbi, African Pentecostal-type Christianity considers people of the Muslim faith as mere objects of evangelisation:

> The Pentecostals do not see any common ground between themselves and non-Christian religious groups such as Muslims or the priests of the primal religion. The only expectation of the Pentecostals of such groups is that of outright conversion to Christianity.[24]

The imagery invoked is of a complex spiritual battleground. In this picture, Islam is painted as a pillar in the realm of Satan. Remarkably enough, Aygei's writings on Islam dispense with such antagonistic rhetoric. Despite his moralist interpretation of early Islamic history, he portrays Islamic theology in an almost neutral or descriptive style. He clearly aims at facilitating Christian-Muslim encounters in the proximity of daily life. Aygei wants "to encourage Christians to share the love of God with their Muslim neighbour."[25]

Aygei's theology of suffering prohibits a triumphant style of encounter between Christians and Muslims. Outlining the contemporary global religious landscape in terms of a "Muslim-Christian polarisation", he advocates a self-

---

[21] Aygei, Sharing, *op. cit.*, p.33.

[22] Incorrectly addressing Aygei, John Azumah accuses him of "parading" Muslim converts to give "testimonies" about their conversion, "most of it involve exaggerations and blatant distortions." John Azumah,"Interfaith Relations in Ghana: Faith and Citizenship", http://nifcon.anglicancommunion.org, accessed 10 January 2008.

[23] *Cf.* Paul Gifford, *Ghana's New Christianity. Pentecostalism in a Globalizing African Economy*, Bloomington/Indianapolis: Indiana University Press 2004, pp.90-101.

[24] Larbi, Pentecostalism, *op. cit.*, p.,435.

[25] Aygei, Sharing, *op.cit.*, p.1.

reflexive attitude. Aygei laments the stance of repulsion toward Islam. The vocabulary chosen to describe the current state of affairs is drastic. It ranges from religious "prejudice" to a common "stereotype mentality", all rooted in "ignorance" of the Muslim world. Aygei criticises the polemics to expose Islam as "fallacious and an orchestrated lie by the Evil One". He ends his ideological criticism of Christian misinterpretations of Islam:

> What is even more disturbing is the fact that many Christians have fallen victim of this lie and have become partakers in deepening the gulf between the Christian and the Muslim worlds.[26]

Aygei is well aware of one's own bias in the perception of the religious other. The self-reflexive starting point of his approach uncovers projections on the other that are vital specifically within his own Christian tradition. What is important here, is the change of perspective in comparison with current opinions on Islam in African Pentecostal-type Christianity. He does not locate Islam as an entity in the realm of Satan, but identifies the prevailing Christian ignorance on Islam as an element in the Satanic strategy in contemporary society. The missionary answer he opts for is based on interpersonal relationships. Starting from the level of neighbourhood networks, Aygei seeks to bridge those two worlds.

Discourse of difference

Aygei's request for inter-religious dialogue is incomplete without a defined agenda of his own. The people of the Muslim faith are his target group. Though, even with this zeal in mind, Aygei abstains from objectifying Muslim believers. His esteem for Islam, as claiming divine revelation, is too high. Since his early life, he was convinced that both Islam and Christianity were just similar paths leading to God: "When I was in Islam, I thought that both Christians and Muslims served the same God, but with differences in approach."[27] This statement resonates with the basic convictions of a pluralist theology of religion, essential in order to accept the sovereignty of God. But with his conversion, Aygei accentuates differences between the religions. He now dismisses the pluralist categories in inter-religious dialogue, for they declare any evangelising practice obsolete. He states that some Christians:

> are afraid to cause offence because our modern world teaches that everyone has the right to his own belief and that there are different ways to worship the same

---

26 Aygei, Sharing, *op.cit.*, pp.2-3.
27 Aygei, Sharing, *op.cit.*, p.21.

> God. All these are further lies from Satan to keep Muslims from hearing the truth of the gospel.[28]

Aygei insists on difference in the understanding of God in Christianity and Islam. The "straight path" is reserved for the biblical revelation, from where the evangelising motive follows. However, Aygei does not remain with dogmatic orthodoxy. He seeks to engage individual Christians and churches in public debates on religious difference. Claiming difference must be proven in transparent theological discourses. An imperative debate about God belongs to Aygei's concept of mission. The discourse about God is a systematic part in his interpretation of the Great Commission "to reach all people with the gospel." This command is sacrosanct for Aygei. It is an incontestable element in Christian identity and an axiomatic principle in any Christian initiative of an inter-religious nature. As a consequence, it affects the Christian-Muslim dialogue directly. "Muslims should therefore welcome Christians for peaceful religious discussion." But also from a Muslim viewpoint, Aygei reckons, there is an incentive for a dialogue with Christians, who are identified by Aygei as the people of the Book. Quoting Sura 10:94, he asserts that Muslims should "seek clarification from the people of the Book when any doubt arises in the course of reading the Qur'an."[29]

To sum up, Aygei argues in two directions. Based on the Qur'anic advice, Aygei diagnoses an inner need on the Muslim side to enter into a dialogue with Christians. Moreover, Aygei struggles to harmonise mission and dialogue. He tries to show that the Christian missionary impulse and the insistence on an inter-religious dialogue based on difference can converge.

Concluding remarks

Aygei's theology of mission in the context of a Christian-Muslim neighbourhood is exceptional for African Pentecostal-type churches. He unfolds a hermeneutic circle according to which the reading of the Qur'an points at the biblical revelation of God. His method of comparison and scriptural interpretation has, in the worst case, a potential to create inter-religious tension.[30] Too drastic appear his inversions of Islamic traditions of knowledge i.e. his perception of the Qur'an that disarms salient features of Islamic exegesis, or his pleading for a re-orientation of Muslim spiritual life. Nonetheless, Aygei insists on the right to articulate theological difference which is his precondition for any responsible Christian-Muslim dialogue.

---

[28] Aygei, Sharing, *op.cit.*, p.19.

[29] Aygei, Ishmael, *op. cit.*, pp.105-106.

[30] Clashes occurred in the mid 1990s in Kumasi, when Straightway Chapel operated "crusades" in sections with a dominant Muslim population.

His position ranges between two poles of conceptualising Christian-Muslim encounters in Africa.[31] One pole instrumentalises inter-religious dialogue for evangelism. In this respect, a key strategy is to postulate religious difference and to define Muslims as a mere target group of evangelism. Any inter-religious contact is legitimised by the ultimate end of converting Muslims as fast as possible. The method applied is confrontational and the time frame makes neighbourhood relations unnecessary. This objectifying understanding of inter-religious dialogue is well articulated within Pentecostal-type African Christianity. Aygei, however, withdraws from this church heritage. For him, inter-religious dialogue contains a self-critique of stereotypes on the religious other. He seeks to explore the self-understanding of the partner in dialogue and to dismantle prejudices about their counterparts by way of self-reflection. The other pole of Christian-Muslim dialogue in Africa makes use of a romanticising stereotype of Islam. This is an effort to clear the atmosphere of a long-standing antagonism between the cross and the crescent. The vision is to shift the agenda towards a policy of mutual understanding. Aygei is far from any romanticising promotion of Islam. He imagines a scenario of inter-religious communication that balances competing claims of truth. It is at the same time dialogical and self-critical in nature. In a pose of unveiling deficiencies in his own religious tradition, Aygei urges for a direct and sometimes confrontational exchange of primarily theological arguments.

31 Lamin Sanneh, *Piety and Power. Muslims and Christians in West Africa*, New York: Maryknoll 1996, p.80.

MISSIONARY OUTREACH IN ZANZIBAR: AN ALL-NIGHT TOIL WITHOUT A CATCH?

Chediel E. Sendoro

Introduction

When one engages in a business, that person expects to reap the fruits of the toil corresponding to the labour engaged. Missionary outreach, in this case in Zanzibar, is not an exception to this general statement. The first Lutheran missionaries to the Tanzania mainland (then Tanganyika), particularly in Dar es Salaam, arrived in July, 1887 from Zanzibar led by Johann Jakob Greiner (1842-1905).[1] This gives a clue that Zanzibar was reached by missionaries earlier than 1887.

However, there is a feeling among Christians that the achievement of the missionary outreach in Zanzibar does not correspond with the time taken, when we look at the quantitative growth of Christianity on the islands. According to Elinaza Sendoro, the retired bishop of the Evangelical Lutheran Church in Tanzania, Eastern and Coastal Diocese (ELCT-ECD), church growth in Zanzibar is not so encouraging, and the majority of the Christians in the islands are those who have moved to Zanzibar because of employment or business. The indigenous[2] Christians are very few if not negligible in number.[3] This situation renders Christianity a religion of the foreigners in Zanzibar.

The Biblical depiction of Peter's fruitless fishing as found in Luke 5, an 'all night toil without a catch', continues to shape the critical assessment of Christian missionary strategic approaches in Zanzibar, where the majority of the population are not only adhering to the Islamic faith, but are also reluctant to respond positively to the Christian message and be converted to Christianity.

The 2002 census shows the population of Zanzibar to be about 984,625 people with an annual growth rate of 3.1%.[4] This growth rate predicts the current population of Zanzibar to be about 1,147,000. The ELCT Mission and

---

1 S. Von Sicard, The Lutheran Church on the Coast of Tanzania 1887-1914: With Special Reference to the Evangelical Lutheran Church In Tanzania Synod of Uzaramo-Uluguru, Uppsala: Almquist&Wiksells 1970, pp.52-59.

2 I understand that the terms "indigenous" and "natives" sometimes give a negative connotation, which is not my intention, but I did not find a better alternative to use.

3 Interview with retired Bishop Elinaza E. Sendoro of the ELCT-Eastern and Coastal Diocese, 11/11/2006, Dar es Salaam. This view is also shared by retired Bishop John Ramadhani of the Anglican Church in Zanzibar, 21/7/2007, Zanzibar.

4 http://www.tanzania.go.tz/census/figures.htm, accessed 4/1/2008.

Evangelism Department estimates the Lutheran members to be between 650 and 800, a number that happens to be less than 0.1% of the population.[5] It is also estimated that all Christians put together are less than 2% of the population in the area. Sheikh Shibli, the Personnel Officer and Coordinator of HIV/AIDS in the Ministry of State, President's Office, Constitution and Good Governance, states that Muslims are between 97 – 98% of the population.[6] There are also a few people belonging to Hinduism, traditional religions, and even secular ones.

This situation incited an interest in me to study the missionary outreach in Zanzibar with several questions in my mind. These include: is there any notable achievement with the missionary outreach in Zanzibar? Is the church using the right missionary approach according to the context? What kind of challenges does the church face in Zanzibar? Being a pastor in the diocese that cares for Zanzibar as a mission area of the ELCT, these questions challenged me to embark on writing a paper with the intention of contributing something in terms of suggestions so as to improve the situation.

The aim of the paper, therefore, is to study the missionary outreach in Zanzibar, particularly by the Lutherans, Anglicans, and Catholics. The objective is, firstly, to describe the missionary methods used in Zanzibar. Secondly, the paper identifies challenges facing the church in the course of doing mission in Zanzibar, and finally suggests strategies that could improve the situation.

Religious background of Zanzibar

Religiously, Zanzibar is one of the areas in East Africa mainly dominated by Islam.[7] It is said that shortly after its rise in Arabia, Ali Ummar Zaddiya, a relative of Ali, the cousin of Mohammad the Prophet, introduced Islam in Zanzibar when he arrived shortly after the death of the Prophet.[8] The rise of Islam in the Middle East in the 7th century caused some of the Arabs to flee from their countries to escape persecution, and eventually some of them came to East Africa. The Oman Arabs are particularly remembered to have

[5] Paper presented by Rev. Ambele Mwaipop, Deputy Secretary General for Mission and Evangelism in the ELCT, titled "ELCT Missionary Regions and Programs" in the Missiology class at Makumira University College, 14/11/2006.

[6] Interview with Sheikh Shibli Makame, Personnel Officer and Coordinator of HIV/AIDS in the Ministry of State, President's Office, Constitution and Good Governance in the Government of Zanzibar, 21/7/2007, Zanzibar.

[7] Bengt Sundkler & Christopher Steed, *A History of the Church in Africa,* Cambridge: Cambridge University Press 2000, p.510.

[8] Douglas M. Toto, "Women in Islam", Research paper for diploma of theology, St. Marks Theological College, Dar es Salaam, 1998, p.2.

contributed to the deepening of the roots of Islam in Zanzibar.[9] Douglas Toto is convinced that the natives were converted to Islam through intermarriages between young Arabs and the natives, and through observation of the foreigners' worship that impressed the natives who thus decided to be Islamised.[10]

The fact that the first foreign visitors to Zanzibar were Muslims gives a clue to the reasons for the strength of Islam in the islands. This might also have been due to the absence of an established majority religion among the indigenous people on the arrival of the Arabs. This situation was very much to the advantage of the Arabs and Islam.

The first effect of Christianity was felt in Zanzibar as far back as 1498 through the Portuguese. The Portuguese were few in number and were more interested in trade and plunder. As a result, they were not successful in other spheres, including the local culture and religion.[11] They managed to baptise the king of Pemba by the name of Dom Filipe, although he did not remain a Christian.[12] This first attempt of Christianity came to an end around 1652 when the Portuguese were ousted by the Oman soldiers.[13] It was not until the middle of the 19th century that Lutherans, Anglicans and Catholics, came to Zanzibar to re-establish missionary work.

Missionary outreach in Zanzibar

The arrival of the early missionaries and mission societies in Zanzibar marked the beginning of the missionary outreach in the island. This chapter will look into the methodology of the Anglicans, Catholics, and Lutherans.

Anglican missionary outreach

In pursuing their missionary goal, the Anglicans had three basic settlements. Mkunazini, with the Christ Church Cathedral, that was opened in 1879 on the site of the former slave market, became the headquarters of the mission staff. A hospital, an industrial home, and a boys' school were later added to this settlement. Kiungani was the second settlement where a training centre for

---

[9] Amir A.Mohammed, *A Guide to a History of Zanzibar*, Good Luck Publishers 1991, p.3f.

[10] Toto, *op. cit.*, p.2.

[11] Mohammed, *op. cit.*, p.18f.

[12] Carl-Erick Sahlberg, *From Krapf to Rugambwa: A Church History of Tanzania*, Nairobi: Evangelical Publishing House 1986, p.12.

[13] Sundkler & Steed, *op. cit.*, p.517. See also Mohammed, *op. cit.*, *p.*9.

ordinands was located. Mbweni was the third settlement regarded as a Christian village, where adult freed slaves were settled and a girls' school was located.[14]

The Anglican missionaries mainly used three methods. These were, firstly, fighting against slave trade; secondly, spreading Christianity and strengthening those already Christians; and thirdly, the provision of social services.[15]

The result of their work is that Anglicans are currently about 2,000[16] in Zanzibar, which is about 0.17% of the population. It should also be noted that even the few converts originate from the mainland.[17] The Anglicans' growth is mainly through people's movement from the mainland, and other parts of the world.

Catholic missionary outreach

The Catholics too embarked on social services as their major means of missionary outreach. The Spiritans began offering health services in August 1884 at a place called Gulioni. It is noted in the archives of the diocese that by May 1st, 1885, 2,196 people had come to attend the hospital.[18] They also started another hospital at a place called Malagasy in Zanzibar.[19] Again, in collaboration with the government of Zanzibar, the Spiritans cared for the lepers and controlled a home for the sick and infirm at Welezo.[20] Sisters also contributed in this service by visiting the sick.[21]

The French Mission was essentially practical in character. Among other things, they ransomed 200 slaves. All these ex-slaves originated from the mainland. The plan was to educate and convert them to Christianity.[22] Concerning education, three different schools were started for three different groups i.e. Catholics, Muslims, and Asians.[23] The response was somewhat better compared to the other two mainline denominations.

---

[14] Sundkler & Steed, *op. cit.,* p.526. See also Halmashauri ya Kanisa Kuu Zanzibar, Kutimiza Miaka Mia Moja 24.8.1980, Kanisa Kuu la Kristo Mkunazini-Zanziba, Dar es Salaam: University of Dar es Salaam 1980, pp.2f & 12f.

[15] *Ibid.*, p.9.

[16] Interview with John Ramadhani, retired Bishop of the Anglican Church in Zanzibar, 21/7/2007, Zanzibar.

[17] Interview with Emmanuel Masoud, Director of the Department of Christian Education, Information, Apostleship and Evangelism in the Anglican Diocese of Zanzibar, 21/7/2007, Zanzibar.

[18] http://www.dioceseofzanzibar.org, accessed 5/1/2008.

[19] Sundkler & Steed, *op. cit.,* p.524.

[20] Robert N. Lyne, *Zanzibar in Contemporary Times: A Short History of the Southern East Africa in the Nineteenth Century,* Zanzibar: Gallery Publications 2001, pp.184f.

[21] http://www.dioceseofzanzibar.org, accessed 5/1/2008.

[22] Sundkler & Steed, *op. cit.,* p.524. See also the website of the Catholic Diocese of Zanzibar, http://www.dioceseofzanzibar.org, accessed 5/1/2008.

[23] *Ibid.,* p.524.

Of late, the number of Catholics has been increasing mainly through the baptism of children. Between the years 1991 and 2007, 3,036 children have been baptised.[24] This gives an average of 178 children being baptised annually. This trend allows us to conclude that the growth of the Catholic Church in Zanzibar is mainly from within. The number of Catholic members has now risen to approximately 10,000, about 0.87% of the population but there are absolutely no indigenous Christians.[25]

Lutheran missionary outreach under foreign missionaries

Johann Ludwig Krapf was the first Lutheran to visit Zanzibar in 1844 as a German missionary, but sent by the Church Missionary Society (C.M.S.) in England.[26] Nothing much is said about Krapf in Zanzibar as he later proceeded to Cape Delgado in Mozambique.

Another Lutheran missionary, Johann Jakob Greiner, arrived in Zanzibar on June 16th, 1887. Von Sicard considers the first Lutheran service, led by Johann Jakob Greiner at the Usagara House on June 26th, 1887, to be the beginning of missionary work in Zanzibar under the E.M.S.[27] Greiner had a conviction that the practical approach to evangelism was the method *par excellence* to manifest the message.[28]

The E.M.S mainly used a single methodology in Zanzibar i.e. the provision of social services, especially health services. The idea of the E.M.S was that Zanzibar was already served evangelistically by the U.M.C.A and the Holy Ghost Fathers.[29]

A hospital was started in 1887, which performed very well to the extent that it attracted some patients from the mainland. The Helgoland Treaty of July 1st, 1890 between Germany and England interfered. In this treaty, Germany acquired Helgoland Island in exchange for Zanzibar. Kaiser William, the then Germany ruler, valued Helgoland, which is in the north-west off the German coast, more than Zanzibar because he needed to establish a naval base there.[30] Zanzibar became a British sphere of influence. The Mission Board in Germany ordered the transfer of the hospital and all personnel from Zanzibar to Dar es Salaam in January 1891.[31]

---

[24] Information collected from baptismal register in the St.Joseph Cathedral Archives, 5/1/2008, Zanzibar.

[25] Interview with John Mfoy, Vicar General of the Catholic Diocese of Zanzibar, 20/7/2007, Zanzibar.

[26] Von Sicard, *op. cit.*, p.52.

[27] Von Sicard, *op. cit.*, p.58.

[28] *Ibid.*, p.151.

[29] *Ibid.*, p.57f.

[30] *Ibid.*, p.67. See also S.G. Ayany, *A History of Zanzibar*, Nairobi: Kenya Literatures Bureau 1970, p.14.

[31] *Ibid.*, p.73.

This marked the end of the first chapter of the Lutheran missionary outreach in Zanzibar. It is unfortunate that there are no statistics showing how much they achieved number-wise.[32] Since then, about seven decades elapsed before the reappearance of Zanzibar in the Lutheran records.

Lutheran missionary outreach under local missionaries

After the union of Tanganyika and Zanzibar in 1964, some government workers from the mainland were transferred to assume responsibilities in the isles. Some of them were Christians. This is when the Lutheran missionaries reappeared in Zanzibar, as Africans from the Lutheran Church of Uzaramo-Uluguru in the mainland.[33]

This second beginning was in response to the request for a minister made by Lutherans who were residing in Zanzibar. Dr. Mhagama recalls that they were only four when they started in 1963.[34] Between 1963 and 1969, the Lutheran Church only aimed at providing pastoral services to Lutherans living in the isles. The Lutheran Church in Zanzibar grew only through the movement of Christians from the mainland.

In September 1993, a big open air meeting was prepared in collaboration with an organisation called "New Life Crusade[35] on the Kidongo Chekundu grounds in Kariakoo area of Zanzibar. It was during and after this open air meeting that Christians in Zanzibar experienced an open confrontation from the Muslims.[36] Open air meetings were the first missionary method by the local Lutheran missionaries in Zanzibar and are still in use.

The second method used by the local Lutheran missionaries is that of the provision of social services. When a church building was erected in the Mwanakwerekwe parish, a building for a dispensary was also erected. This dispensary started operating in the year 2002. The dispensary is attended by thirty patients daily, on average. Out of these, 95% are non-Christians, especially Muslims.[37] In this way, non-Christians feel that the church is a friend to them because it cares for their needs.

Recently, in cooperation with foreign partners, two more methods have been added i.e. dialogue and vocational training.

With dialogue, leaders of the different religions, especially Christians and Muslims, are brought together in a body called the Inter-Faith Committee that

---

32 *Ibid.*, p.230.

33 *Ibid.*, p.73.

34 Interview with Gabriel Mhagama, retired Medical Officer, 22/7/2007, Zanzibar.

35 Currently the organization has changed its name to New Life in Christ.

36 Interview with Joel Nzota, Evangelist in Ubungo parish of the ELCT-Eastern and Coastal Diocese and a member of the Diocesan Evangelism Committee, 8/1/2008, Dar es Salaam.

37 Interview with Cliff Ndossa, Clinical Officer at the Mwanakwerekwe Lutheran Dispensary, 5/1/2008, Zanzibar.

was formed in August 2005.[38] The main aim of this dialogue is to create an atmosphere where people of both sides will live together peacefully and in respect of one another.

With vocational training, *Danmission* has supported the church to initiate a tailoring project for women with an intention of empowering women through education and work. The name of this project is '*Upendo*', which means 'love'. The project is admitting a new sewing class each year composed of 50% Christians and 50% Muslims.[39]

Currently Lutherans number about 1,200[40] in Zanzibar, which is about 0.10% of the population. Growth is still mainly dependent on the movement of Christians from the mainland.

Challenges facing the church in doing mission work in Zanzibar

The church has been facing a number of challenges. The list below is not exhaustive, but covers the most important categories of the challenges facing the church in Zanzibar.

Islam

One of the major challenges is that Islam has its roots deep in the history of the islands and that the people have adapted its doctrines to their habit of thought and life in general. The religion also had a large number of teachers in that every educated Arab acted as a priest of Islam and an exponent / interpreter of his religion.[41] This situation prevails and has given Islam a very strong position in the isles.

Citing the parable of the sower (Mt 13:1-9), Kane shows that the deciding factor was neither the sower nor the seed, but the soil. Kane goes further to equating the soil with the hearts of individuals exposed to the Gospel or the different kinds of cultural and religious soils found in various regions of the world where the Gospel has been taken by Christian missionaries.[42]

Islam has made Zanzibar to be a rocky ground for the different mission fields. Rev. Canon Emmanuel Masoud asserts that there has never been a problem between Muslims and other religions apart from Christianity in

[38] Interview with Arngeir Langas, Pastor and Missionary from Denmark through *Danmission*, mainly dealing with dialogue, 4/1/2008, Zanzibar.

[39] Personal observation in the *Upendo* Project, 4.1.2008, Zanzibar. *Cf.* www.upendo meanslove.com, accessed 4/1/2008.

[40] Figure provided by the District Secretary of the Zanzibar Lutheran Mission.

[41] Robert N. Lyne, *Zanzibar in Contemporary Times: A Short History of the Southern East Africa in the Nineteenth Century*, Zanzibar: Gallery Publications 2001, pp.183f.

[42] J.H. Kane, *Understanding Christian Missions,* Grand Rapids: Baker Book House 1978, p.185.

Zanzibar.[43] This suggests that there are some common reasons for the situation arising from the nature of the religion. To mention a few, these may include the age of Islam as compared to Christianity, the denial of the deity of Jesus Christ, the harsh treatment of defectors of Islam, and the public practice of the religion.

Being a Christian community in a Muslim society

Christianity is viewed as a religion of foreigners in Zanzibar. The website of the Catholic Diocese of Zanzibar contains a statement that says, "During this time, i.e. between the independence of Zanzibar and 1980s, the church was tolerated in a culture that continues to be Arabic in nature and Islamic in religion."[44] This statement shows that the church, in a way, is not an acceptable institution in the society, but for some reason the society tolerates its presence. The church then has to be clever if it wishes to continue being present and work in Zanzibar. That is a very big challenge to the church because the situation is not expected to change in the near future as with time, Christianity becomes even less tolerated as a religion.[45] Choices will have to be made regarding the way in which the Christian community wants to be present and active in the Muslim society of Zanzibar.

Politics

The political situation has not been so encouraging for missionary outreach in Zanzibar. Thanks to the union with Tanganyika that prompted the adoption of the national constitution that gives freedom of religion, there is freedom of worship,[46] otherwise the situation would have been different.

On several occasions, churches have been losing their properties to the government in a manner that is not well understood, although attitudes against Christianity can be sensed. The first occasion was a result of the nationalisation policy of Tanzania that was introduced in 1967. However, for the case of Zanzibar there have been more events after the Revolution, not only concerned with the confiscation of church property, but also on other matters like the difficulty in land acquisition for the church and problems with the education system that includes the Arabic language in the average pass-mark.

Vandalism against church property

Church properties have been subjected to vandalism and destruction on several occasions. Referring to an incidence that occurred at the Mwanakwerekwe

---

[43] Interview with Emmanuel Masoud, 21/7/2007, Zanzibar.

[44] http://www.dioceseofzanzibar.org, accessed 5/1/2008.

[45] Compare with the website of the Catholic Diocese of Zanzibar, http://www.dioceseofzanzibar.org, accessed 5/1/2008.

[46] The Constitution of the United Republic of Tanzania of 1977, Dar es Salaam: M.P.P., Article 19. Compare with the website of the Catholic Diocese of Zanzibar, http://www.dioceseofzanzibar.org, accessed 5/1/2008.

parish of the Lutheran Church, Dr. Gabriel Mhagama says that there have been some terrorist acts against the Church and its property.

In the late 1990s, a bomb was found close to the altar of the Mwanakwerekwe Lutheran parish.[47] The Catholic worship building at Legezamwendo was burnt down twice.[48]

Such events are so discouraging and may even inflict fear among Christians and the church in the islands of Zanzibar. Even plans of the church for further development may be affected because of fear of material loss resulting from such vandalism and destructive acts.

Suggested strategies

Having discussed the different challenges facing the church in carrying out the missionary task, we are now in a better position to suggest strategies that might work better in Zanzibar. I have categorised the suggested strategies into two major groups i.e. social and missiological strategies.

Social strategies

The first social strategy is equipping the clergy. Due to the uniqueness of Zanzibar and the make-up of its population in terms of religion, the competence of the clergy is so important if the church is to make an impact on the islands. The church has to have a strategy of recruiting and developing the clergy, expected to be sent to, or already working in Zanzibar, to a level competent enough for them to master their working environment. This may include equipping them with some knowledge of Islam and the Qur'an.

The second social strategy is to involve the laity more in the missionary work. The laity should not only be asked to participate in the implementation of the decisions made by the church leadership, but also they should be involved in all the stages of decision making. They will obviously have a contribution because they know the situation better as they live, work, and trade with the native people. This will motivate the laity to participate more in the missionary outreach, and the entire church will work as a unity to achieve the desired goals.

The third social strategy is the involvement of the church in the development of the society. The church has to get to the roots of the problems that affect human life. It is the opinion of Bauer that Christian mission should deal with difficult issues facing the society such as social justice, self reliance and economic development.[49] Surely, a faith expressed in the midst of the affairs of the people stands a great chance of taking root in the people.

---

47 Interview with Gabriel Mhagama, 22/7/2007, Zanzibar.

48 Interview with John Mfoy, 20/7/2007, Zanzibar.

49 Arthur O.F. Bauer, *Making Mission Happen,* New York: Friendship Press, Inc., 1974, p.32.

Missiological strategy

As it is with the social strategies, there might be a good number of approaches that could be applied missiologically. However, having thought carefully of the context in Zanzibar and the possibility to prosper in missionary outreach, I came to conclude that the incarnational approach would work better than the conversional approach.

The incarnation of Jesus Christ offers a holistic mission approach because through it God enters into the totality of human existence and identifies himself with people. If the church is to imitate Jesus Christ, then the incarnation shows that the focus of Christian mission has to be Christ in the context of this world. As Jesus Christ became part of the human race through his life and unveiled the intention of God, so has the church through her lifestyle to be part of the society and present the love of God.

This approach can be demonstrated by being friendly to all the people in their residential areas, helpful to the needy in the society, faithful and responsible in their working places, and generally by living an exemplary life that neighbours can view as worthy of imitation. Friendliness and charity to all, regardless of their religion, will break the ground for the sowing of the Word. In that way, the Christian community will teach the Gospel without preaching it and witness to it without vocally proclaiming it. Though indirect, I believe this to be an inspired effort towards evangelism.

Conclusion

Having considered the historical background of Zanzibar, the methods applied in the course of missionary outreach and challenges faced so far, I am convinced that the suggested strategies will work better in that context.

Living out the values of the Gospel in a Muslim environment, like that of Zanzibar, amounts to offering the Gospel in a non-confrontational and non-offensive way. As the suggested strategies happen to be non-confrontational, the chances of being effective are bigger because the society will no longer view Christianity as an enemy while at the same time the seeds of the Gospel are sown slowly. Although it might take time to see the yields, the fruits of such strategies are long-lasting.

MISSION IN A MULTI-RELIGIOUS SOCIETY: THE MISSION CONCEPT OF THE COMMUNION OF CHURCHES IN INDONESIA

Erick Johnson Barus

We will discuss some points of the concept of mission of the Communion of Churches in Indonesia (CCI) related to relationship building and cooperation with all religious people. These concepts became important as a step to develop mutual understanding between religious people in a multireligious society like Indonesia. Our mission is understood as living out the spirit of the love of Christ, so that we learn how we can live with other people and with love for each other.

Witnessing and proclaiming the Gospel to the whole creation[1]

Churches must proclaim the Gospel to the whole creation. Churches in Indonesia were born from the witnesses who started from Jerusalem, and then reached out to the end of the earth (*cf.* Acts 1:8). This call remains active till the end of the time (*cf.* Mt 28:20), so that the Gospel can be proclaimed to the whole creation (*cf.* Mk 16:15). Churches in Indonesia are churches on the journey which take part in this assignment.

Churches in Indonesia affirm that the Gospel is the Good News, solid and comprehensive for all creatures, for humankind and the environment. The whole Gospel needs to be proclaimed to all humankind because the Gospel is entirely related to human life, not only to the coming life in heaven but to the present life in this world; it does not only regard the soul or spirit, but also human wholeness and existence, both spiritual and political, social, economical, and cultural.

Churches in Indonesia affirm that the Gospel is for the whole world. They understand that the activity of witness is carried out by the church through all its aspects of life, and inspired by the Holy Spirit. This is done in the power of the presence of Christ who was crucified and rose in the Spirit into the world life and his church. (*cf.* Mk 1:7; 3:14; 16:15-16; Mt 28:16-20; Acts 1:8; 1Cor 1:17, 23). Therefore, the call and the responsibility for proclaiming the Gospel are received and borne by all church members. Each person who believes

[1] Dokumen Keesaan Gereja Persekutuan Gereja-gereja di Indonesia (DKG-PGI): Keputusan Sidang Raya XIV PGI Jakarta: BPK Gunung Mulia 2006, pp.51-54. *(Unified Documents of the Communion of Churches in Indonesia)*, Decision in General Assembly XIV of CCI.

becomes the carrier of the Good News that liberates, and becomes a witness in this world, particularly in Indonesia.

Because the Gospel that liberates and renews as well as unites also speaks of Christ's crucifixion, the activity of emptying oneself, of incarnation and his obedience (*cf.* Phil 2:7-8), these aspects must also be the basis of the witness carried out by the churches. In witnessing, they must consider their environment (ideology, politics, economics, social set-up, culture, and religion), use kind and respectful approaches with a tender heart and a humble mind and develop a constructive dialogue with all parties.

Churches that proclaim the Gospel, aiming at playing a cooperative role in a reformed society which is heading for a civil society, will give special attention to the victims of injustice and human rights abuse, as well as the poor and oppressed, to overcome their pressing problems. This was already started by the missionaries who came to Indonesia from abroad, and is continued by the local missionaries who follow this tradition and take part in the assignment to proclaim the Gospel to all creatures till the end of earth and till the end of time.

Churches in Indonesia understand that all religions are convinced that they have to proclaim their message to all people. In this aspect, the church is not different from the other religions. The message must be proclaimed in ways that are in accordance with a just and civilized humanity, and also in line with the religion itself. The Executive Board Meeting of the DGI[2] in Makassar (Ujung Pandang) in 1967 already gave the directions regarding the efforts to proclaim Gospel by stating that:

1) The church must proclaim the Gospel (*cf.* Mt 28:18-20; 1Cor 9:16);
2) The church must do this wisely (*cf.* Mt 10:16);
3) The church must face severe tribulation (*cf.* Mt 5:11).

The meaning of the Gospel proclaimed to all creation

The Seventh DGI General Assembly in 1971 reiterated that the church is to proclaim the Gospel of Jesus Christ. Further it was stated that the Gospel is the "good news concerning repentance and renewal available for humankind (*cf.* Mk 1:15) and also liberation, justice, truth, and prosperity which God gives (Lk 4:18-21), the power of God for salvation (Rom 1:16)."[3] To proclaim the Gospel to all creatures also includes the responsibility for the wholeness of God's creation. God mandates humans to manage and maintain all God's creation (*cf.* Gen 2:15). Therefore, churches in Indonesia affirm that the Gospel is the Good News which is solid and comprehensive. The Gospel is not the news of broken pieces, with one piece contradicting another, the vertical contradicting the

---

[2] DGI: Dewan Gereja-Gereja Indonesia, now PGI, *Persekutuan Gereja-gereja Indonesia* or CCI, Communion of Churches in Indonesia.

[3] *Ibid.*, pp.54-55.

horizontal. The Gospel covers the whole creation, not only heavenly matters but also the problems of the here and now.

The Christians themselves, either individually or as a church community, must continuously place themselves under the light of the Gospel so that they live their lives according to the Gospel of Christ (*cf.* Phil 1:27). They continuously need forgiveness, repentance, and renewal of their minds. Only in this way can they have the authority to proclaim the Gospel to the whole of creation. The Apostle Paul said that the message of the crucified Christ is a stumbling block for Jews and foolishness for the Greeks. (1Cor 1:23).

From 2004 – 2009, the current working period of the CCI, the issues of upholding just laws, respecting human rights, fighting corruption, collusion, and nepotism as well as poverty remained the main issues also in the nation's efforts to build a civil society. Consequently, the CCI used the sub-theme "Together with all national elements implementing a strong civil society and democracy in order to build truth, justice and maintain peace" to give attention to these issues in its proclamation of the Gospel of Jesus Christ. Consciously, this sub-theme of the CCI General Assembly XIV began with the word "together". What is meant here is that this assignment cannot be fulfilled by the churches alone, but needs the involvement of all levels of society including the government.

Methods of proclaiming the gospel to all creation[4]

In proclaiming the Gospel, each creature in each situation needs the most appropriate approach. This is exactly the Apostle Paul's attitude in proclaiming the Gospel: "To the Jews I became like a Jew, to win the Jews. To those under the law I became like one under the law (though I myself am not under the law), so as to win those under the law. To those not having the law I became like one not having the law (though I am not free from God's law but am under Christ's law), so as to win those not having the law. To the weak I became weak, to win the weak. I have become all things to all men so that by all possible means I might save some. I do all this for the sake of the Gospel, that I may share in its blessings." (1Cor 9:20-23) In a pluralistic society like Indonesia, we need to take into account aspects of culture, religion, language, tradition, level of modernization and education if we want to proclaim the Gospel to all creatures. To do this appropriately both in content and methods, we need to use all the plural gifts available in the churches.

All efforts to proclaim the Gospel through various methods and emphases must be placed according to the common call and assignment and may not contradict each other. Rather, they must always reveal the common loyalty towards the one God who called and assigned us to witness in and witness to Indonesia. Our efforts need to be further developed, for example by making use

[4] *Ibid.*, pp.55-58.

of the communication media. The assignment of witnessing and proclaiming the Gospel must be carried out showing integrity between words and action (Jn 13:15; 1Tim 4:12).

Every believer bears the responsibility to implement the call and mandate which has been given to the whole church. Therefore, each church member must be equipped to carry out the proclamation of the Gospel in the most appropriate way, with the gifts and opportunities given to him or her. In addition, churches can provide institutions to carry out the proclamation of the Gospel in a planned way. Therefore, it is necessary to provide general guidelines which govern the plurality of methods and approaches. For this it is necessary to have a common discussion from time to time regarding principal issues relating to the proclamation of the Gospel to all in Indonesia. Currently, the PGI sees the following important issues:

a) Freedom of religion and harmony need to be further developed. Religious freedom may not be victimized for the sake of harmony and harmony may not be victimized by religious freedom. This is guaranteed by Article 29 Paragraph 2 of the Indonesian constitution which states that "the state guarantees the freedom of each citizen to embrace (follow) his religion respectively and to pay his religious duty according to his religion and belief."

b) Proclamation and church unity serve as a testimony to the world. Therefore, proclamation is not boundless and may not contradict the efforts of church renewal and development, or the unity of the church which is the fellowship of believers.

c) Gospel proclamation and fellowship are closely interrelated. The fellowship is a form of proclaiming the Gospel and proclaiming the Gospel is the mandate of Jesus Christ for believers as a fellowship. The aim of the mission of the church is the communion with God together with all humankind and all creatures.

d) The proclamation of the Gospel to all creatures needs an in-depth understanding of society, nation and state, and the application of science and technology. Therefore, it is necessary to carry out studies and provide education and also common training.

e) Proclamation and service are different but related to one another. Both are expressions of the one call and assignment.

Relationship and cooperation with all religious people[5]

God created humankind in his own image (*cf.* Gen 1:26). God is the God of Israelites (*cf.* Ps 47: 9-10), but he does not love only Israel, but also Edom, Egypt etc. Jesus Christ instructed us to love one another as we love ourselves (*cf.* Mt 22:39). That is exactly the essence of the divine incarnation in Jesus Christ who became human for the sake of all others. Based on this, we weave relationships among us regardless of ethnicity, religion, race, or group.

As an integral part of Indonesian society, the churches gratefully acknowledge the religious plurality in Indonesia as God's blessing. This encourages us to continuously study and carry out witness and service in accordance with our context of plurality. To follow its call and assignment to witness to Christ in the midst of a plural society, the church should develop good relations and cooperation with all groups including religious people. Such cooperation may be developed in accordance with the *Pancasila*, the basic philosophy of our country, to take seriously our responsibility for the strengthening of a civil society of high morality. Lately, we feel concerned about the booming fundamentalism and sectarianism in nearly all religions. In order to overcome this, it is increasingly necessary to improve dialogue and cooperation among interfaith-groups of believers in the One God, seeking solutions in critical, wise, fair and transparent ways.

It is also necessary to develop and increase discussions and cooperation among religious people to overcome problems we face jointly, such as poverty, lack of justice and peace, secularism, consumerism, environmental degradation, abuse of human rights, corruption, collusion and nepotism. Together with other religious people we need to promote a culture of discipline. Essentially, religions are sources of motivation in developing discipline. Therefore, relationships and cooperation among religious people are seen as increasingly important to jointly develop and improve national discipline.

In developing the common future of the society, nation, and the Indonesian people, the relationship among Christians and other religious people needs to be built and promoted.

Developing mutual understanding between religious people in a pluralistic society

Basically religion is not restricted by space and time. Since humankind was born there has been the potential and instinct for religion, therefore in human history there has never been any community "without religion". This signals that there is nobody who has no religion; consequently, religious people should be able to coexist, and appreciate and honour each other, and cooperate well with one another. Historically, Judaism, Christianity and Islam are monotheistic

[5] *Ibid.*, pp.68-69.

world religions. In addition there are also other religions: Hinduism, Buddhism, Confucianism, Daoism, ethnic religions and other beliefs. The number of Jews is not so great, but Islam and Christianity are global religions with many followers which can become the basis for civilization. Together with Judaism, Islam and Christianity are understood to have come from the one same prophet, namely Abraham, so that in the history of religion, Islam, Christianity and Judaism are grouped together under the label 'Abrahamic religions.'[6]

Theologically speaking, the typical characteristics of Abrahamic religions are the belief in one God who is the Lord (monotheism), although the three religions have different concepts of monotheism. Therefore, monotheism can be regarded as one of the meeting points of Abrahamic religions. History shows us that the relationship of these religions was never easy and full of conflicts which are played out even today. While religious tensions were often triggered by various political, social and economic interests, conflicts were also rooted in the spirit of exclusive piety (the truth is only within *my* religion), in the inability to understand the other side, or in the absence of dialogue. Today, the growing problems of humanity make us more and more aware of the importance of increasing the involvement of religions when it comes to the search for common solutions. This is necessary because faith is not just be declared and realized in ritual forms, but rather claims concrete involvement in all the ethical problems of humankind. By paying attention to the plurality of societies nowadays, the polemic and hostility of Jewish, Christian and Muslim paradigms cannot be maintained anymore. It is time for Jews, Christians and Muslims to reformulate their worldviews to arrive at more universalist and pluralist concepts.[7]

Each religious community is influential in the life of humankind. Such influence should come in the form of finding productive 'encounters' and not seeking 'clashes' which are counterproductive. This can be achieved by building mutual understanding in the form of a willingness to open oneself to a dialogue for peace. Hans Küng, a theologian and observer of religious life said:

> "There is no peace among the nations without peace among religions; there is no peace among religions without dialogue between the religions; there is no

---

[6] Barus, Erick Johnson, Spiritualitas: Tantangan dan Harapan. Suatu Studi Tentang Makna Spiritualitas Menurut Al-Qur'an Sebagai Dasar Untuk Dialog dan Implikasinya Bagi Hubungan Islam Kristen *(Spirituality: Challenge and Hope. A Critical Study to the Meaning of Spirituality According to Al-Qur'an as a Base for Dialogue and Its Implication to Christian-Muslim Relations).* Dissertation, The South East Asia Graduate School of Theology, Yogyakarta, 2006, p.235.

[7] *Ibid.*, p.236.

dialogue between religions without willingness to understand the basics of religions".[8]

This observation signals that world peace can be realized through the participation of religions in developing mutual understanding (or a meeting point) in dialogue. Dialogue can help to understand the history of the emergence of religions, their teachings and mission, and their actual role in the life of humankind.

The emergence of a conflict is often one-sidedly ascribed to interfaith tension. But while conflicts are often rooted in political, economic, social or cultural interests, they can easily assume religious overtones, and this must receive the attention of religious believers. Religions need to pay attention to this phenomenon, because if a community is provoked to use religion as a means of conflict, it has not yet achieved a true understanding of other religions. Efforts are needed to understand other religions, to look for the meeting points, to develop mutual understanding and to achieve an attitude that will not allow religion to be used as an excuse for conflict. Religion as a call to faith demands an attitude of interfaith pluralism-inclusivism, and this sets the work agenda in interfaith relations. The significance of pluralism-inclusivism is reflected in an attitude of empathy, honesty and justice, in giving diversity and differences their necessary place while honouring and understanding each others' lives. We can study the spiritual wealth of other religions to enrich our faith (passing over and coming back), rather than seeking the deficiencies and weaknesses of the other religions or regarding them as untrue while holding our own religion as (the most) true. Therefore, pluralism is the common wealth, and an education towards an inclusive-pluralist attitude is understood to be more productive for humanity than an exclusivist attitude which is understood to bring counter-productive outcomes.

The PGI actively encourages participation in dialogue from the circles of the scholars of religions, from Judaism as well as from Islam and Christianity, and also from other religions. Willingness to open up is the basic condition for such dialogue, so that it can lead to a constructive understanding of the importance of religions of all traditions, and lead communities towards a universalist and pluralist perception.

Good deeds (Islam) and love (Christian) towards all humankind and the environment are the important driving forces in the plural-inclusive community's agenda for world peace. After all, the world belongs to the Lord who came to be human in this world. Therefore, an attitude of exclusivism and

[8] Hans Kung, Global Responsibility: In Search of A New World Ethic. New York: The Crossroad Publishing Company 1991, pp.72 - 138.

radicalism (or even terrorism and violence on behalf of religion) has no place in such interfaith relations.[9]

A peace symbol

في مصر يحب المسلم المسيحي و يحب المسيي المسلم0

انظر في سماء القاهرة ، ماذا ترى؟ ترى المئذ نة بجانب برج الكنيسة0

من المسلم؟ المسلم مصري0 من المسيحي؟ المسيحي مصري

من المسريون؟ المسريون مومنون بالحب0

"In Egypt Muslims love Christians and Christians love Muslims. Look at the sky in Cairo, what is there? We see the minaret adjacent to the church spire. Who are the Muslims? They are Egyptians. Who are the Christians? They are Egyptians. Who are the Egyptians? The Egyptians are faithful people who live with each other and love each other."[10]

Based on the above quote it can be seen that a spirituality which is developed on the basis of mutual love will have a good impact towards a harmonious and peaceful life wherever we are. In Asia / Indonesia, in particular, a model of harmony in the religious spirit like the Egyptian model can be established. We can simply replace the word "Egypt / Egyptians" with "Asia / Asian" or "Indonesia / Indonesian." In Asia / Indonesia Moslems love Christians and Christians love Moslems. Look at the sky in Asia / Jakarta, what is seen? We see the minaret and the church spire side by side. Who are the Muslims? They are Asian / Indonesian. Who are the Christians? They are Asian / Indonesian. Who is Asian / Indonesian? Asian / Indonesian people are faithful people who live loving each other.

Conclusion

To build or to develop mutual understanding between religious people is part of the mission in a multireligious society. We have to cooperate with each other. This cooperation can take many forms e.g. an interfaith alliance for the specific objectives, for example, the Interfaith Alliance for Drug Prevention, Interfaith Alliance for Gambling Control, Interfaith Alliance for the Eradication of Drugs, HIV/AIDS and Alcoholic Drinks, Interfaith Alliance against Crime,

---

9 S.H. Nasr, *The Heart of Islam: Pesan-pesan Universal Islam bagi Kemanusiaan.* trans., Bandung: Mizan 2003, p.135.

10 *Al-tariq ila al-lughati al-arabiati* (*Dar Comboni Lessons in Arabic*), Cairo: Dar Comboni 2002-2003, p.123.

Interfaith Alliance for Social Assistance, and Interfaith Alliance to Fight Corruption, Collusion and Nepotism.

Index

Notes on Contributors

Victor Aguilan is Professor of Christian Ethics and Church History, Divinity School Silliman University.

Ferdinand A. Anno is an ordained minister of the United Church of Christ in the Philippines. He undertook his theological studies at Silliman University (M.Div.), Edinburgh University (MTh) and the University of Leeds (Ph.D.). He is currently the Academic Dean and OIC President of Union Theological Seminary-Philippines.

Sören Asmus is a minister of the Evangelical Church in the Rhineland, currently in Duisburg. He holds an M.Phil. in Ecumenics from Trinity College Dublin / Irish School of Ecumenics. He teaches in Missiology and Science of Religion at the Kirchliche Hochschule Wuppertal / Bethel (Protestant University Wuppertal / Bethel) and the Evangelische Fachhochschule Bochum (Protestant University of applied Science Bochum).

Erick Johnson Barus is an ordained minister of the Karo Batak Protestant Church (GBKP) and serves as the head of its Koinonia Department. His research interests focus on witness and interfaith dialogue, especially concerning Islam.

Jutta Beldermann is the pastor of the Diaconic Community Nazareth and director of the Theological Training Centre of the Von Bodelschwingh Foundation Bethel.

Priscille Djomhoué is Professor of Greek and New Testament Studies, and Academic Dean of the Faculty of Protestant Theology and Religious Sciences at the Protestant University of Central Africa. She is also a member of the Symposium of Biblical Scholars, a member of the Joint Commission of Dialogue LWF / WARC, and of the Circle of Engaged African Women Theologians. Her research interests are exegesis (methodology), theology, poverty and development.

Andreas Heuser is Professor for Non-European Christianity (with a focus on Africa), University of Basel/Switzerland, and an ordained minister of the Evangelical Church in Hesse and Nassau. His research focuses on African Christianity, new religious movements and recent developments in Pentecostalism; he has done fieldwork in Zimbabwe, South Africa, Ghana and Germany on African Independent Churches, charismatic / Pentecostal Christianity and migrant churches.

Abednego Keshomshahara is an ordained minister of the Evangelical Lutheran Church in Tanzania, Northwestern Diocese. He finished his doctoral studies in Theology in 2008 in Germany. His research interests include the role of theology in socio-political and economic aspects of life. Currently he teaches at the Teachers College in Bukoba and coordinates the transformation of this college into a University College of Tumaini University.

Christel Kiel is an ordained minister of the Braunschweig Lutheran Church in Germany. Together with her husband, she served as a pastor for the Maasai in the North Eastern Diocese of the Evangelical Lutheran Church of Tanzania from 1986 to 1992. She received her theological doctorate from Humboldt University in Berlin in 1995 and taught theology at the Theological Lutheran Seminary in Mwika from 1995-1999. She lives now in retirement in Germany.

Reiner Knieling is Director of the "Centre for Congregational Renewal" (United Lutheran Churches of Germany) and Extraordinary Professor for Practical Theology at the Protestant University Wuppertal-Barmen.

Faustin Mahali is an ordained minister of the Evangelical Lutheran Church in Tanzania and Lecturer in Biblical Studies, New Testament at the Makumira University College / Tanzania. He also teaches Introduction to Research Methodology in the Faculty of Theology and the Faculty of Humanities and Social Sciences.

Jochen Motte is an ordained minister of the Evangelical Church in the Rhineland. He holds a theological doctorate from Kirchliche Hochschule Wuppertal (Wuppertal Protestant University) and is currently serving as Executive Secretary Justice, Peace and Integrity of Creation of the United Evangelical Mission.

Jean-Gottfried Mutombo is an ordained minister of the Church of Christ in Congo. Currently, he serves as a South-North coworker in the Office for Missionary Services of the Evangelical Church of Westphalia in Germany where he already worked as an exchange pastor from 2002-2008. In 2008, he received his doctorate in Old Testament from the University of Lausanne.

Fidon Mwombeki is currently the General Secretary of the United Evangelical Mission. He is an ordained minister of the Evangelical Lutheran Church of Tanzania. He received his M.Th. from Trinity Lutheran Seminary, Ohio, and his theological doctorate from Luther Seminary in Minnesota, and served as General Secretary of the Northwestern Diocese of the ELCT from 2000-2004.

Jerry Pillay, since 2010 President of the World Communion of Reformed Churches, is currently the General Secretary of the Uniting Presbyterian Church in Southern Africa (UPCSA). He has served as Senior Pastor in two different congregations over a period of 24 years. He was elected and served as Moderator of the UPCSA General Assembly from 2004-2006. He also lectured in Missiology, Church History and Contemporary Theology in the University of Durban-Westville, University of the Western Cape and the Cornerstone Bible College. He has a B.Th (Hon) and an M.Theol (cum laude) from the University of Durban Westville and a PhD from the University of Cape Town.

Wilhelm Richebächer is an ordained minister of the Evangelical Church of Kurhesse-Waldeck. From 1991-1998, he served as lecturer for Theology at the Makumira University College / Tanzania. He is now Executive Secretary for Mission and Ecumenical Affairs of his church and Associate Professor for Missiology and Religious Studies at the Philipps-Universität Marburg.

Roberta Rominger is the General Secretary of the United Reformed Church in the U.K. Ordained in the United Church of Christ, U.S.A., she came to the U.K. in 1985, serving as minister of churches in Woking and Newcastle-upon-Tyne and as Moderator of the Thames North Synod.

Chediel E. Sendoro is an ordained minister of the Evangelical Lutheran Church in Tanzania, Eastern and Coastal Diocese. He is the Deputy Secretary General for Theology, Mission and Evangelism in the Diocese and currently pursuing doctoral studies in Theology with Aabo Akademi of Finland.

Mangisi Simorangkir is currently a UEM co-worker for short term service as lecturer for Systematic Theology at Theological Seminary "Sundermann" of BNKP (Nias Christian Protestant Church) in Gunungsitoli, Nias/Indonesia.

Yak-hwee Tan received her Ph.D. in Religion, with an emphasis in New Testament from Vanderbilt University, Nashville. She is an ordained minister of the Presbyterian Church in Singapore and currently teaches at Taiwan Theological College and Seminary, Taipei, a position facilitated by the Council for World Mission. Her research interests are Johannine Literature, biblical theology, feminist criticism, ecological hermeneutics, and postcolonialism.

Anwar Tjen is an ordained minister of the Christian Protestant Church in Indonesia (GKPI). He studied theology in North Sumatra; biblical philology and exegesis at Union Theological Seminary in Virginia, Pontifical Biblical Institute in Rome, University of Cambridge (Ph.D.); and linguistics at the Australian National University, Canberra. As Bible Translation Consultant for the Indonesian Bible Society, he is currently in charge of some major Bible revision projects i.e. Indonesian Standard Version, Javanese Old Testament, Toba Batak Bible, and Simalungunese Bible.

Reinhard Veller holds a doctorate in theology from Erlangen-Nürnberg University. He served as Africa Secretary for Namibia, Botswana and Tanzania of the United Evangelical Mission (1984-97). He lectured in Old Testament,

Social Ethics and Systematic Theology at Makumira, Tanzania (1981-83) and United Theological College Harare (1997 – 2006). He is an ordained minister of the Ev. Church in Hesse and Nassau and retired in 2007.

Claudia Währisch-Oblau is an ordained minister of the Evangelical Church in the Rhineland and holds a doctorate in theology from Heidelberg University. She currently serves as Executive Secretary Evangelism of the United Evangelical Mission. Her research interests focus on global Pentecostalism and its theological challenges to Reformation Protestantism.

Kingsley Weerasinghe is an ordained minister of the Methodist Church Sri Lanka. He holds a B.Th. and a Masters Degree in Buddhist Studies and Pali and is currently working on his M.A. in Christian Theology. He serves as a parish pastor in Colombo and is the secretary of his District Synod.

REGNUM EDINBURGH 2010 SERIES
Series Listing

David A. Kerr, Kenneth R. Ross (eds.)
Edinburgh 2010
Mission Then and Now
2009 / 978-1-870345-73-6 / xiv + 343pp (paperback)
2009 / 978-1-870345-76-7 / xiv + 343pp (hardback)

No one can hope to fully understand the modern Christian missionary movement without engaging substantially with the World Missionary Conference, held at Edinburgh in 1910. As the centenary of the Conference approaches, the time is ripe to examine its meaning in light of the past century and the questions facing Christian witness today. This book is the first to systematically examine the eight Commissions which reported to Edinburgh 1910 and gave the conference much of its substance and enduring value. It will deepen and extend the reflection being stimulated by the upcoming centenary and will kindle the missionary imagination for 2010 and beyond.

Daryl M. Balia, Kirsteen Kim (eds.)
Edinburgh 2010
Witnessing to Christ Today
2010 / 978-1-870345-77-4 / xiv +301pp

This volume, the second in the Edinburgh 2010 series, includes reports of the nine main study groups working on different themes for the celebration of the centenary of the World Missionary Conference, Edinburgh 1910. Their collaborative work brings together perspectives that are as inclusive as possible of contemporary world Christianity and helps readers to grasp what it means in different contexts to be 'witnessing to Christ today'.

Claudia Währisch-Oblau, Fidon Mwombeki (eds.)
Mission Continues
Global Impulses for the 21st Century
2010 / 978-1-870345-82-8 / 271pp

In May 2009, 35 theologians from Asia, Africa and Europe met in Wuppertal, Germany, for a consultation on mission theology organized by the United Evangelical Mission: Communion of 35 Churches in Three Continents. The aim was to participate in the 100th anniversary of the Edinburgh conference through a study process and reflect on the challenges for mission in the 21st century. This book brings together these papers written by experienced practitioners from around the world.

Brian Woolnough and Wonsuk Ma (Eds)
Holistic Mission
God's plan for God's people 2010 / 978-1-870345-85-9

Holistic mission, or integral mission, implies God is concerned with the whole person, the whole community, body, mind and spirit. This book discusses the meaning of the holistic gospel, how it has developed, and implications for the the church. . It takes a global, eclectic approach, with 19 writers, all of whom have much experience in, and commitment to, holistic mission. It addresses critically and honestly one of the most exciting, and challenging, issues facing the church today. To be part of God's plan for God's people, the church must take holistic mission to the world.

Kirsteen Kim and Andrew Anderson (Eds)
Mission Today and Tomorrow
2011/978-1-870345-91-0

The centenary of the historic and influential World Missionary Conference held in Edinburgh 1910 presented a unique opportunity for the whole church worldwide to come together in celebration, reflection and recommitment to witnessing to Christ today. Edinburgh 2010 also engaged in serious study and reflection on the current state of world mission and the challenges facing all those who seek to witness Christ today. The results of this research was presented and debated within the context of Christian fellowship and worship at the conference in June 2010. This record of that conference is intended to give the background to that Call, to share the spirit of the conference, and to stimulate informed and focused participation in God's mission in Christ for the world's salvation.

Tormod Engelsviken, Erling Lundeby and Dagfinn Solheim (Eds)
The Church Going Glocal
Mission and Globalisation 2011/978-1-870345-93-4

This book provides thought-provoking and inspiring reading for all concerned with mission in the 21st century. I have been challenged by its contributors to re-think our Gospel ministries in our new local contexts marked by globalisation and migration. With its biblical foundation, its missiological reflection and interaction with contemporary society I warmly recommend this volume for study and pray that it will renew our passion for the Gospel and compassion for people.

REGNUM Studies in Global Christianity

(Previously GLOBAL THEOLOGICAL VOICES series)

Series Listing

David Emmanuuel Singh (ed.)

Jesus and the Cross

Reflections of Christians from Islamic Contexts

2008 / 978-1-870345-65-1 / x + 226pp

The Cross reminds us that the sins of the world are not borne through the exercise of power but through Jesus Christ's submission to the will of the Father. The papers in this volume are organised in three parts: scriptural, contextual and theological. The central question being addressed is: how do Christians living in contexts, where Islam is a majority or minority religion, experience, express or think of the Cross? This is, therefore, an exercise in listening. As the contexts from where these engagements arise are varied, the papers in drawing scriptural, contextual and theological reflections offer a cross-section of Christian thinking about Jesus and the Cross.

David Emmanuuel Singh (ed.)

Jesus and the Incarnation

Reflections of Christians from Islamic Contexts

2011/978-1-870345-90-3

In the dialogue of Christians with Muslims nothing is more fundamental than the Cross, the Incarnation and the Resurrection of Jesus. This book contains voices of Christians living in various 'Islamic contexts' and reflecting on the Incarnation of Jesus. The aim of these reflections is constructive and the hope is that the papers weaved around the notion of 'the Word' will not only promote dialogue among Christians on the roles of the Person and the Book, but, also, create a positive environment for their conversations with Muslim neighbours.

Sung-wook Hong

Naming God in Korea

The Case of Protestant Christianity

2008 / 978-1-870345-66-8 / xiv + 170pp

Since Christianity was introduced to Korea more than a century ago, one of the most controversial issue has been the Korean term for the Christian 'God'. This issue is not merely about naming the Christian God in Korean language, but it relates to the question of theological contextualization—the relationship between the gospel and culture—and the question of Korean Christian identity. This book examines the theological contextualization of the concept of 'God' in the contemporary Korean context and applies the translatability of Christianity to that context. It also demonstrates the nature of the gospel in relation to cultures, i.e., the universality of the gospel expressed in all human cultures.

Hubert van Beek (ed.)
Revisioning Christian Unity
The Global Christian Forum
2009 / 978-1-870345-74-3 / xx + 288pp

This book contains the records of the Global Christian Forum gathering held in Limuru near Nairobi, Kenya, on 6 – 9 November 2007 as well as the papers presented at that historic event. Also included are a summary of the Global Christian Forum process from its inception until the 2007 gathering and the reports of the evaluation of the process that was carried out in 2008.

Paul Hang-Sik Cho
Eschatology and Ecology
Experiences of the Korean Church
2010 / 978-1-870345-75-0/ 260pp (approx)

This book raises the question of why Korean people, and Korean Protestant Christians in particular, pay so little attention (in theory or practice) to ecological issues. The author argues that there is an important connection (or elective affinity) between this lack of attention and the other-worldly eschatology that is so dominant within Korean Protestant Christianity. Dispensational premillennialism, originally imported by American missionaries, resonated with traditional religious beliefs in Korea and soon came to dominate much of Korean Protestantism. This book argues that this, of all forms of millennialism, is the most damaging to ecological concerns.

Dietrich Werner, David Esterline, Namsoon Kang, Joshva Raja (eds.)
The Handbook of Theological Education in World Christianity
Theological Perspectives, Ecumenical Trends, Regional Surveys
2010 / 978-1-870345-80-4/ 759pp

This major reference work is the first ever comprehensive study of Theological Education in Christianity of its kind. With contributions from over 90 international scholars and church leaders, it aims to be easily accessible across denominational, cultural, educational, and geographic boundaries. The Handbook will aid international dialogue and networking among theological educators, institutions, and agencies. The major objectives of the text are (1) to provide introductory surveys on selected issues and themes in global theological education; (2) to provide regional surveys on key developments, achievements, and challenges in theological education; (3) to provide an overview of theological education for each of the major denominational / confessional traditions; and (4) to provide a reference section with an up-to-date list of the regional associations of theological institutions and other resources.

David Emmanuel Singh & Bernard C Farr (eds.)

Christianity and Education

Shaping of Christian Context in Thinking

2010 / 978-1-870345-81-1/ 244pp (approx)

Christianity and Education is a collection of papers published in *Transformation: An International Journal of Holistic Mission Studies* over a period of 15 years. It brings to life some of the papers that lay buried in shelves and in disparate volumes of *Transformation,* under a single volume for theological libraries, students and teachers. The articles here represent a spectrum of Christian thinking addressing issues of institutional development for theological education, theological studies in the context of global mission, contextually aware/informed education, and academies which deliver such education, methodologies and personal reflections.

J.Andrew Kirk

Civilisations in Conflict?

Islam, the West and Christian Faith 2011- 978-1-870345-71-2

Samuel Huntington's thesis, which argues that there appear to be aspects of Islam that could be on a collision course with the politics and values of Western societies, has provoked much controversy. The purpose of this study is to offer a particular response to Huntington's thesis by making a comparison between the origins of Islam and Christianity; the two religions that can be said to have shaped, in contrasting ways, the history of the Western world. The early history of each faith continues to have a profound impact on the way in which their respective followers have interpreted the relationship between faith and political life. The book draws significant, critical and creative conclusions from the analysis for contemporary intercultural understanding, and in particular for the debate about the justification of violence for political and religious ends.

REGNUM STUDIES IN MISSION
Series Listing

Kwame Bediako

Theology and Identity

The Impact of Culture upon Christian Thought
in the Second Century and in Modern Africa
1992 / 1-870345-10-X / xviii + 508pp

The author examines the question of Christian identity in the context of the Graeco–Roman culture of the early Roman Empire. He then addresses the modern African predicament of quests for identity and integration.

Christopher Sugden

Seeking the Asian Face of Jesus

The Practice and Theology of Christian Social Witness
in Indonesia and India 1974–1996
1997 / 1-870345-26-6 / xx + 496pp

This study focuses on contemporary holistic mission with the poor in India and Indonesia combined with the call to transformation of all life in Christ with micro-credit enterprise schemes. 'The literature on contextual theology now has a new standard to rise to' – Lamin Sanneh (Yale University, USA).

Hwa Yung

Mangoes or Bananas?

The Quest for an Authentic Asian Christian Theology
1997 / 1-870345-25-8 / xii + 274pp

Asian Christian thought remains largely captive to Greek dualism and Enlightenment rationalism because of the overwhelming dominance of Western culture. Authentic contextual Christian theologies will emerge within Asian Christianity with a dual recovery of confidence in culture and the gospel.

Keith E. Eitel

Paradigm Wars

The Southern Baptist International Mission Board Faces the Third Millennium
1999 / 1-870345-12-6 / x + 140pp

The International Mission Board of the Southern Baptist Convention is the largest denominational mission agency in North America. This volume chronicles the historic and contemporary forces that led to the IMB's recent extensive reorganization, providing the most comprehensive case study to date of a historic mission agency restructuring to continue its mission purpose into the twenty-first century more effectively.

Samuel Jayakumar

Dalit Consciousness and Christian Conversion

Historical Resources for a Contemporary Debate

1999 / 81-7214-497-0 / xxiv + 434pp

(Published jointly with ISPCK)

The main focus of this historical study is social change and transformation among the Dalit Christian communities in India. Historiography tests the evidence in the light of the conclusions of the modern Dalit liberation theologians.

Vinay Samuel and Christopher Sugden (eds.)

Mission as Transformation

A Theology of the Whole Gospel

1999 / 0870345133/ 522pp

This book brings together in one volume twenty five years of biblical reflection on mission practice with the poor from around the world. The approach of holistic mission, which integrates proclamation, evangelism, church planting and social transformation seamlessly as a whole, has been adopted since 1983 by most evangelical development agencies, most indigenous mission agencies and many Pentecostal churches. This volume helps anyone understand how evangelicals, struggling to unite evangelism and social action, found their way in the last twenty five years to the biblical view of mission in which God calls all human beings to love God and their neighbour; never creating a separation between the two.

Christopher Sugden

Gospel, Culture and Transformation

2000 / 1-870345-32-0 / viii + 152pp

A Reprint, with a New Introduction, of Part Two of Seeking the Asian Face of Jesus
Gospel, Culture and Transformation explores the practice of mission especially in relation to transforming cultures and communities. - 'Transformation is to enable God's vision of society to be actualised in all relationships: social, economic and spiritual, so that God's will may be reflected in human society and his love experienced by all communities, especially the poor.'

Bernhard Ott

Beyond Fragmentation: Integrating Mission and Theological Education

A Critical Assessment of some Recent Developments in Evangelical Theological Education

2001 / 1-870345-14-2 / xxviii + 382pp

Beyond Fragmentation is an enquiry into the development of Mission Studies in evangelical theological education in Germany and German-speaking Switzerland between 1960 and 1995. The author undertakes a detailed examination of the paradigm shifts which have taken place in recent years in both the theology of mission and the understanding of theological education.

Gideon Githiga

The Church as the Bulwark against Authoritarianism

Development of Church and State Relations in Kenya, with Particular Reference to the Years after Political Independence 1963-1992

2002 / 1-870345-38-x / xviii + 218pp

'All who care for love, peace and unity in Kenyan society will want to read this careful history by Bishop Githiga of how Kenyan Christians, drawing on the Bible, have sought to share the love of God, bring his peace and build up the unity of the nation, often in the face of great difficulties and opposition.' Canon Dr Chris Sugden, Oxford Centre for Mission Studies.

Myung Sung-Hoon, Hong Young-Gi (eds.)

Charis and Charisma

David Yonggi Cho and the Growth of Yoido Full Gospel Church

2003 / 1-870345-45-2 / xxii + 218pp

This book discusses the factors responsible for the growth of the world's largest church. It expounds the role of the Holy Spirit, the leadership, prayer, preaching, cell groups and creativity in promoting church growth. It focuses on God's grace (charis) and inspiring leadership (charisma) as the two essential factors and the book's purpose is to present a model for church growth worldwide.

Samuel Jayakumar

Mission Reader

Historical Models for Wholistic Mission in the Indian Context

2003 / 1-870345-42-8 / x + 250pp

(Published jointly with ISPCK)

This book is written from an evangelical point of view revalidating and reaffirming the Christian commitment to wholistic mission. The roots of the 'wholistic mission' combining 'evangelism and social concerns' are to be located in the history and tradition of Christian evangelism in the past; and the civilizing purpose of evangelism is compatible with modernity as an instrument in nation building.

Bob Robinson

Christians Meeting Hindus

An Analysis and Theological Critique of the Hindu-Christian Encounter in India

2004 / 1-870345-39-8 / xviii + 392pp

This book focuses on the Hindu-Christian encounter, especially the intentional meeting called dialogue, mainly during the last four decades of the twentieth century, and specifically in India itself.

Gene Early

Leadership Expectations

How Executive Expectations are Created and Used in a Non-Profit Setting

2005 / 1-870345-30-4 / xxiv + 276pp

The author creates an Expectation Enactment Analysis to study the role of the Chancellor of the University of the Nations-Kona, Hawaii. This study is grounded in the field of managerial work, jobs, and behaviour and draws on symbolic interactionism, role theory, role identity theory and enactment theory. The result is a conceptual framework for developing an understanding of managerial roles.

Tharcisse Gatwa

The Churches and Ethnic Ideology in the Rwandan Crises 1900-1994

2005 / 1-870345-24-X / approx 300pp

Since the early years of the twentieth century Christianity has become a new factor in Rwandan society. This book investigates the role Christian churches played in the formulation and development of the racial ideology that culminated in the 1994 genocide.

Julie Ma

Mission Possible

Biblical Strategies for Reaching the Lost

2005 / 1-870345-37-1 / xvi + 142pp

This is a missiology book for the church which liberates missiology from the specialists for the benefit of every believer. It also serves as a textbook that is simple and friendly, and yet solid in biblical interpretation. This book links the biblical teaching to the actual and contemporary missiological settings with examples, making the Bible come alive to the reader.

Allan Anderson, Edmond Tang (eds.)

Asian and Pentecostal

The Charismatic Face of Christianity in Asia

2005 / 1-870345-43-6 / xiv + 596pp

(Published jointly with APTS Press)

This book provides a thematic discussion and pioneering case studies on the history and development of Pentecostal and Charismatic churches in the countries of South Asia, South East Asia and East Asia.

I. Mark Beaumont

Christology in Dialogue with Muslims

A Critical Analysis of Christian Presentations of Christ for Muslims from the Ninth and Twentieth Centuries

2005 / 1-870345-46-0 / xxvi + 228pp

This book analyses Christian presentations of Christ for Muslims in the most creative periods of Christian-Muslim dialogue, the first half of the ninth century and the second half of the twentieth century. In these two periods, Christians made serious attempts to present their faith in Christ in terms that take into account Muslim perceptions of him, with a view to bridging the gap between Muslim and Christian convictions.

Thomas Czövek,

Three Seasons of Charismatic Leadership

A Literary-Critical and Theological Interpretation of the Narrative of Saul, David and Solomon

2006 / 978-1-870345484 / 272pp

This book investigates the charismatic leadership of Saul, David and Solomon. It suggests that charismatic leaders emerge in crisis situations in order to resolve the crisis by the charisma granted by God. Czovek argues that Saul proved himself as a charismatic leader as long as he acted resolutely and independently from his mentor Samuel. In the author's eyes, Saul's failure to establish himself as a charismatic leader is caused by his inability to step out from Samuel's shadow.

Jemima Atieno Oluoch

The Christian Political Theology of Dr. John Henry Okullu

2006 / 1-870345-51-7 / xx + 137pp

This book reconstructs the Christian political theology of Bishop John Henry Okullu, DD, through establishing what motivated him and the biblical basis for his socio-political activities. It also attempts to reconstruct the socio-political environment that nurtured Dr Okullu's prophetic ministry.

Richard Burgess

Nigeria's Christian Revolution

The Civil War Revival and Its Pentecostal Progeny (1967-2006)

2008 / 978-1-870345-63-7 / xxii + 347pp

This book describes the revival that occurred among the Igbo people of Eastern Nigeria and the new Pentecostal churches it generated, and documents the changes that have occurred as the movement has responded to global flows and local demands. As such, it explores the nature of revivalist and Pentecostal experience, but does so against the backdrop of local socio-political and economic developments, such as decolonisation and civil war, as well as broader processes, such as modernisation and globalisation.

David Emmanuel Singh & Bernard C Farr (eds.)
Christianity and Cultures
Shaping Christian Thinking in Context
2008 / 978-1-870345-69-9 / x + 260pp

This volume marks an important milestone, the 25th anniversary of the Oxford Centre for Mission Studies (OCMS). The papers here have been exclusively sourced from Transformation, a quarterly journal of OCMS, and seek to provide a tripartite view of Christianity's engagement with cultures by focusing on the question: how is Christian thinking being formed or reformed through its interaction with the varied contexts it encounters? The subject matters include different strands of theological-missiological thinking, socio-political engagements and forms of family relationships in interaction with the host cultures.

Tormod Engelsviken, Ernst Harbakk, Rolv Olsen, Thor Strandenæs (eds.)
Mission to the World
Communicating the Gospel in the 21st Century: Essays in Honour of Knud Jørgensen
2008 / 978-1-870345-64-4 / 472pp

Knud Jørgensen is Director of Areopagos and Associate Professor of Missiology at MF Norwegian School of Theology. This book reflects on the main areas of Jørgensen's commitment to mission. At the same time it focuses on the main frontier of mission, the world, the content of mission, the Gospel, the fact that the Gospel has to be communicated, and the context of contemporary mission in the 21st century.

Al Tizon
Transformation after Lausanne
Radical Evangelical Mission in Global-Local Perspective
2008 / 978-1-870345-68-2 / xx + 281pp

After Lausanne '74, a worldwide network of radical evangelical mission theologians and practitioners use the notion of "Mission as Transformation" to integrate evangelism and social concern together, thus lifting theological voices from the Two Thirds World to places of prominence. This book documents the definitive gatherings, theological tensions, and social forces within and without evangelicalism that led up to Mission as Transformation. And it does so through a global-local grid that points the way toward greater holistic mission in the 21st century.

Bambang Budijanto

Values and Participation

Development in Rural Indonesia

2009 / 978-1-870345-70-5 / x + 237pp

Socio-religious values and socio-economic development are inter-dependant, inter-related and are constantly changing in the context of macro political structures, economic policy, religious organizations and globalization; and micro influences such as local affinities, identity, politics, leadership and beliefs. The three Lopait communities in Central Java, Indonesia provide an excellent model of the rich and complex negotiations and interactions among all the above factors. The book argues that the comprehensive approach in understanding the socio-religious values of each local community is essential to accurately describing their respective identity which will help institutions and agencies, both governmental and non-governmental, to relate to these communities with dignity and respect.

Young-hoon Lee

The Holy Spirit Movement in Korea

Its Historical and Theological Development

2009 / 978-1-870345-67-5 / x + 174pp

This book traces the historical and theological development of the Holy Spirit Movement in Korea through six successive periods (from 1900 to the present time). These periods are characterized by repentance and revival (1900-20), persecution and suffering under Japanese occupation (1920-40), confusion and division (1940-60), explosive revival in which the Pentecostal movement played a major role in the rapid growth of Korean churches (1960-80), the movement reaching out to all denominations (1980-2000), and the new context demanding the Holy Spirit movement to open new horizons in its mission engagement (2000-). The volume also discusses the relationship between this movement and other religions such as shamanism, and looks forward to further engagement with issues of concern in wider society.

Alan R. Johnson

Leadership in a Slum

A Bangkok Case Study

2009 / 978-1-870345-71-2 xx + 238pp

This book looks at leadership in the social context of a slum in Bangkok from an angle different from traditional studies which measure well educated Thais on leadership scales derived in the West. Using both systematic data collection and participant observation, it develops a culturally preferred model as well as a set of models based in Thai concepts that reflect on-the-ground realities. This work challenges the dominance of the patron-client rubric for understanding all forms of Thai leadership and offers a view for understanding leadership rooted in local social systems, contrary to approaches that assume the universal applicability of leadership research findings across all cultural settings. It concludes by looking at the implications of the anthropological approach for those who are involved in leadership training in Thai settings and beyond.

Titre Ande

Leadership and Authority

Bula Matari and Life - Community Ecclesiology in Congo

2010 / 978-1-870345-72-9 xvii + 189pp

This book proposes that Christian theology in Africa can make significant developments if a critical understanding of the socio-political context in contemporary Africa is taken seriously. The Christian leadership in post-colonial Africa has cloned its understanding and use of authority on the Bula Matari model, which was issued from the brutality of colonialism and political absolutism in post-colonial Africa. This model has caused many problems in churches, including dysfunction, conflicts, divisions and a lack of prophetic ministry. Titre proposes a Life-Community ecclesiology for liberating authority, where leadership is a function, not a status, and 'apostolic succession' belongs to all the people of God.

Frank Kwesi Adams

Odwira and the Gospel

A Study of the Asante Odwira Festival and its Significance for Christianity in Ghana

2010 /978-1-870345-59-0

The study of the Odwira festival is the key to the understanding of Asante religious and political life in Ghana. The book explores the nature of the Odwira festival longitudinally - in pre-colonial, colonial and post-independence Ghana - and examines the Odwira ideology and its implications for understanding the Asante self-identity. The book also discusses how some elements of faith portrayed in the Odwira festival could provide a framework for Christianity to engage with Asante culture at a greater depth. Theological themes in Asante belief that have emerged from this study include the theology of sacrament, ecclesiology, eschatology, Christology and a complex concept of time. The author argues that Asante cultural identity lies at the heart of the process by which the Asante Christian faith is carried forward.

Bruce Carlton

Strategy Coordinator

Changing the Course of Southern Baptist Missions

2010 / 978-1-870345-78-1 xvii + 268pp

In 1976, the Southern Baptist Convention adopted its Bold New Thrusts in Foreign Missions with the overarching goal of sharing the gospel with every person in the world by the year 2000. The formation of Cooperative Services International (CSI) in 1985 and the assigning of the first non-residential missionary (NRM) in 1987 demonstrated the Foreign Mission Board's (now International Mission Board) commitment to take the gospel message to countries that restricted traditional missionary presence and to people groups identified as having little or no access to the gospel. Carlton traces the historical development along with an analysis of the key components of the paradigm and its significant impact on Southern Baptists' missiology.

Julie Ma & Wonsuk Ma

Mission in the Spirit:

Towards a Pentecostal/Charismatic Missiology

2010 / 978-1-870345-84-2 xx + 312pp

The book explores the unique contribution of Pentecostal/Charismatic mission from the beginning of the twentieth century. The first part considers the theological basis of Pentecostal/Charismatic mission thinking and practice. Special attention is paid to the Old Testament, which has been regularly overlooked by the modern Pentecostal/Charismatic movements. The second part discusses major mission topics with contributions and challenges unique to Pentecostal/Charismatic mission. The book concludes with a reflection on the future of this powerful missionary movement. As the authors served as Korean missionaries in Asia, often their missionary experiences in Asia are reflected in their discussions.

S. Hun Kim & Wonsuk Ma (eds.)

Korean Diaspora and Christian Mission

2011-978-1-870345-89-7

As a 'divine conspiracy' for Missio Dei, the global phenomenon of people on the move has shown itself to be invaluable. In 2004 two significant documents concerning Diaspora were introduced, one by the Filipino International Network and the other by the Lausanne Committee for World Evangelization. These have created awareness of the importance of people on the move for Christian mission. Since then, Korean Diaspora has conducted similar research among Korean missions, resulting in this book. It is unique as the first volume researching Korean missions in Diasporic contexts, appraising and evaluating these missions with practical illustrations, and drawing on a wide diversity of researchers.

GENERAL REGNUM TITLES

Vinay Samuel, Chris Sugden (eds.)
The Church in Response to Human Need
1987 / 1870345045 / xii+268pp

Philip Sampson, Vinay Samuel, Chris Sugden (eds.)
Faith and Modernity
Essays in modernity and post-modernity
1994 / 1870345177 / 352pp

Klaus Fiedler
The Story of Faith Missions
1994 / 0745926878 / 428pp

Douglas Peterson
Not by Might nor by Power
A Pentecostal Theology of Social Concern in Latin America
1996 / 1870345207 / xvi+260pp

David Gitari
In Season and Out of Season
Sermons to a Nation
1996 / 1870345118 / 155pp

David. W. Virtue
A Vision of Hope
The Story of Samuel Habib
1996 / 1870345169 / xiv+137pp

Everett A Wilson
Strategy of the Spirit
J.Philip Hogan and the Growth of the Assemblies of God Worldwide, 1960 - 1990
1997 /1870345231/214

Murray Dempster, Byron Klaus, Douglas Petersen (eds.)
The Globalization of Pentecostalism
A Religion Made to Travel
1999 / 1870345290 / xvii+406pp

Peter Johnson, Chris Sugden (eds.)
Markets, Fair Trade and the Kingdom of God
Essays to Celebrate Traidcraft's 21st Birthday
2001 / 1870345193 / xii+155pp

Robert Hillman, Coral Chamberlain, Linda Harding
Healing & Wholeness
Reflections on the Healing Ministry
2002 / 978-1- 870345-35- 4 / xvii+283pp

David Bussau, Russell Mask
Christian Microenterprise Development
An Introduction
2003 / 1870345282 / xiii+142pp

David Singh
Sainthood and Revelatory Discourse
An Examination of the Basis for the Authority of Bayan in Mahdawi Islam
2003 / 8172147285 / xxiv+485pp

For the up-to-date listing of the Regnum books see www.ocms.ac.uk/regnum

regnum

Regnum Books International

Regnum is an Imprint of The Oxford Centre for Mission Studies
St. Philip and St. James Church
Woodstock Road
Oxford, OX2 6HR
Web: www.ocms.ac.uk/regnum